STASHES

PJ Colando

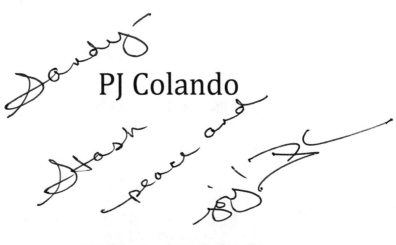

STASHES

PATTIS PRESS

Pattis Press

Copyright © 2014 by PJ Colando

Library of Congress Cataloging-in-Publication Data
Colando, PJ
STASHES: a novel/ PJ Colando
ISBN - 978-1-6319208-9-9

COVER ART ©2014 by CLIFF CRAMP

To Larry Colando
'the best man alive'

One: Born to Run

The refrain of Springsteen's "Born to Run" jangled on Jackie's iPhone as she peeled potatoes at her polished aluminum sink. She frowned at her reflection, tucked a curl behind an ear, and swore, *"Porca puttana!"*

Daydream interrupted by ringtone. She paused to wonder what her mother might think of Italian, cursing, and ringtones? Mrs. Clayton, now deceased, would have known about interruptions because that's a mother's life – and daydreams because that's a woman's.

Jackie knew a little Italian because she was a singer and an Internet trawler bored with a daily life conscribed, conscripted, and safe. Her new phone brought portable intrigue: 'Words with Friends' and calls to fling gossip around town. Plus, she no longer had to fear deleting Steve's business data on the desktop computer.

But this wasn't one of her friends calling – they knew not to interrupt her supper chores because they had the same. The song signaled Brandon, only kid and light of her life, he of the never-ending energy since his first day on earth, calling to check in.

Jackie loved the song, her son, and the fact that he called her frequently, but not necessarily in that order and not at this time. In her reverie, she had been in Rome, skirt hiked to step into the Trevi Fountain, its cool-toned water swirling her ankles. She wiped one hand on her apron and reached into its pocket for her phone.

"Hi, honey, I love you!" Jackie said, trying to not sound as perturbed as she felt. Farm ways don't allow for unwelcome. "How's everything?"

"Mom, it's all turning to shit!" Brandon's stage whisper sounded like a shriek. "We're gonna lose our home. I'm scared to tell Dad. You gotta help me, Mom."

A request for help was expected – history did repeat itself – but her daydream whispered provocatively, *Come back to Rome!*

Jackie didn't speak. If there'd been a cat about, she'd have blamed it for stealing her tongue. The Breeden's dog, Sparty, tail wagging to the beat of dairying, was in the barn with Steve.

"Mom. Mom. I wanna see your face. Why won't you use FaceTime?"

"Brandon, honey, you know that your rural Michigan farmwife mom can't always look like the Avon lady when you call. Hold on, will you? I'm fixing your dad's supper. I have a knife in my hand."

"OK. I'll call back in five," Brandon said.

Jackie set the phone down on the new granite counter, gingerly because of the price of both. She dropped the knife into the sink and elbowed the faucet to a tepid blend of water to rinse and wipe it on a fresh dishtowel, then did the same with her hands. She beamed at the lengthy one-piece potato peel in the sink. It was a game that she played to break the tedium of having peeled more potatoes than McDonald's.

Then Jackie strode to the fridge for iced tea, poured a tall glass, and took a gulp to further unlace her nerves. The kids' house loss was going to be most unsettling to Steve, her steady-eddy, church deacon, dairy farming man. Was she going to have to go-between again?

She put the cool glass against a pulse point, willing panic to leave the premises. She topped off the series of actions with a count to ten, something that she tried to drill into Brandon, but it never took. Instead, he called Mom or Dad.

When Brandon called back, Jackie was a traveler returned from Rome, rested and ready for what was to come. She was Problem-Solving Mom, garbed in an apron as cape.

"Now, what do you mean that you're going to lose your house, Brandon? Haven't you been making payments on time? It's Amy's bank! Can't she handle this since she's the vice president?"

She could see Brandon without FaceTime. His head was sunk into his jersey-clad chest as he lounged on his football-colored couch, but she just couldn't stop the Judge Judy lecture. "Your dad and I taught you better! How did this happen? Why haven't you told us before? Your dad is going to be so embarrassed in this community."

"Mom, I lost my job at the GM plant."

Suddenly Jackie was in a déjà vu moment, awash with sadness, and she felt like she was inside the cold glass of tea, gasping for breath. Steve had made a similar call from a payphone at New Lothrop Tavern. Was Michigan becoming hell?

"Mom, did you hear or are you gonna make me say it again, like when you always made me tell Dad about the dumb stuff I did in school? I don't want to stutter like Phil."

"Did Phillip lose his job, too?" Jackie said.

"So you heard me," Brandon said. "And yes, he did. There's 3700 of us let go today."

"Where are you, Son?"

"Sitting in my shiny red truck, looking at our house. It looks good, real good from here. Like some kind of hero lives inside, not a loser like me."

"Now Brandon, you know I don't ever allow you to say that word. Neither does your dad."

"But, why does losing your job mean you'll lose your house? At the same time?"

Jackie began to pace about the house, her left hand flailing at the air; the right wishing it could turn the situation into something to applaud, like during Brandon's active sports years, rather than gripping a phone filled with disaster. Wishing she could wipe away this set of circumstances like toothpaste splats on a bathroom mirror. She felt useless and weary.

"We're behind on the mortgage, truck, car and credit card bills. We even have bills left from our honeymoon in Jamaica. It's more of a cliff than we thought. I just got home from the bank. It don't matter that Amy works there, Mom, and she's the Vice President. It seems to be more of a handicap than a help. Her boss was as stern as Coach when a play fell apart. Said that he'd already contacted the paper to run the foreclosure notice on Monday."

"You said you're in your truck. Where's Amy, Brandon? Did she take off somewhere?"

"She stayed behind to grovel. She doesn't want the notice to run." Brandon sighed, then continued, "Dad'll hate it worse. Mom, please don't make me tell Dad."

"I'll tell him light, tell him about the job first, get his empathy working to forestall the volcanic eruption. We'll take this one step at a time. Maybe have you and Amy over for Sunday supper. Sound good?"

"Thanks, Mom. I'll call you later."

Jackie pressed 'END' and dropped the phone back in its apron pocket so she could use both hands to tally the months. Yes, it had been 21 months since Steve lost his job at GM.

She scuffed around the golden oak floors, trying to visualize herself skating on a frozen pond or something similarly carefree - or to re-purpose her meander as floor polishing to gussy up the place. Nothing doing. Even Italy had withdrawn to its place on the globe beside Steve's chair, tiny and farther away than ever.

Jackie spun the globe hard with each pass she made through the first floor rooms: kitchen, family room, living room, dining room, a lap that took 42 seconds if she wedged herself between the coffee table and plaid couch, and 48 if she didn't. She did not enter the small study where the computer lay with its Internet enticements.

She found herself in the bathroom, pressing harder than necessary to clear the mirror. Just before she scrunched the paper towel for trash, she polished her tiny diamond with a corner wet with Windex. It winked at her, like her husband often did, and she felt better.

She took time to glance in the mirror, telling herself that she was just affirming its cleanliness. She wasn't bad looking, but she wasn't good-looking either. Her mother had labeled her face pleasant, like her manner.

Green eyes that flashed "go ahead" to the schemes and dreams of others, matching her role as cheerleader. Grey mingled with her brown hair as an uninvited partner, yet her hair still flounced and shone from daily shampooing. How could she not keep her personal appearance as fastidious as her house?

Yet she knew that her long-sleeved shirt had seen better days and had a ketchup plop hidden by her apron.

Jackie resumed supper's chores, believing in the absolution of routine. She baked a cake from a box, smacking the egg on the bowl to unleash its contents. As the mixer whirred, she practiced vocal scales, allowing the final note to loft to the ceiling as she watched the kitchen clock. Twenty seconds. Not bad for an asthmatic.

The deep breathes helped. Later, as she put the cake in the oven, the click of the door closing reassured Jackie that while appliances could complete dinner without her, her life remained half-baked.

As she cleaned the counters, an egg white string oozed to the floor before she got the shells to the garbage. She wished that Sparty was an inside dog, so that he could lick the mess up rather than her stooping down. Wished he could clean up Brandon's mess, too.

Maybe I should wish I were a dog, living rent-free and unfettered by time, Jackie thought as she creaked down.

After she hoisted herself up, she rinsed and wrung the sponge as if it was Brandon's neck, then scuffed about some more. She considered whether to prop up the few remaining mums and mulch the flowerbeds in front, maybe carve a pumpkin for the porch. Though its sentinel might soften the confrontation looming with Amy and Brandon - and she could take the jack o'lantern to work - she didn't trust a knife in her hands with this case of nerves. Her stomach felt like the late days of pregnancy when Brandon was in there kicking.

Dark was descending earlier each day, and the wind swirled to force winter's gloom on autumn. More leaves dumped outside the kitchen window, so Jackie abandoned ambition and sat in the family room.

Ding-a-ling! She jerked out of the chair to stand, forgetting that her new phone was in her lap, in her apron. Her knees didn't forgive her quick when she fished the phone out to answer.

"Hi, Bonnie. How are you?" Jackie said with perk. Bonnie's voice was revival.

"No, I hadn't thought what I would make for the Bazaar? What are you making?"

She let Bonnie prattle on, tossing in a murmur here and there like she always did. Bonnie was Pastor Rankin's secretary, and Jackie was his do-gooder-in-chief. Both were professional listeners, the diaries of the parishioners in their heads, and tonight felt like Bonnie's turn. Church people do not have problems - they had prayer requests – and Pastor Rankin appreciated that the women arbitrated both.

But Jackie wasn't in the mood for sharing. As the pot roast aroma began to permeate the family room, Jackie found a way to beg off Bonnie's one-sided conversation just before she heard Steve stomp out of his boots and hang up his coat. Her sixth sense had rewarded her once again.

"Hi, honey. How's the big, wide world of the milk man?"

"Wholesome, honey, wholesome," Steve said as he strode in and blew a perfunctory kiss. Jackie loved to watch his barrel-chested body fill the doorframes of their old farmhouse. She did not love the cap imprint on his dark hair – and neither did he. One hand combed his hair while the other slung the Detroit Tigers cap on a peg. His caps lined their mudroom walls like Brandon's trophies in the rec room downstairs.

Steve's dark eyes percolated under creased brows as his head swiveled to the table, not ready-set as usual, then back to look at Jackie's face: "What's up, dear wife?"

"Sit here beside me in your chair, Steve. Oh, look at the time! Will you get the cake out of the oven and set it on the counter for me first?"

"Where?" Steve asked.

"Anywhere. Granite is safe to set things on, remember? That's why we made the investment with your first profit check."

Jackie tried not to be surly, not again, not tonight. Why could it be important *where* the hot cake pan sat? *When* was most important. She grimaced at the parallel to Amy and Brandon's inability or unwillingness to prioritize.

"You look uneasy, Jackie. Should I open a beer to wash the news down?" her husband said.

"Perhaps so. And one for me, too."

After moving the cake from the oven to the counter beside it, Steve ambled into the family room, armed with two beers, watching the weather report on Jackie's face. Farmers are good at weather, whether their wives like it or not. He set the bottles on coasters that were permanent side table accessories, along with the TV Guide, channel changer, and pencils in various stages of sharp.

Jackie watched him arrange himself carefully in the chair, watched his feet swing to the ottoman, and felt his silence protract until she lifted her beer.

"Brandon lost his job at the plant." Jackie kept her gaze bolted to the bottle, just as the bottle seemed bolted in her grip. The pot roast smell hovered, stimulating her appetite, and still she couldn't lift the bottle to her lips, couldn't look at Steve. He loved stew, but the true stew of their lives had already been set on their plates: their football hero, with the conniver wife who eschewed kids, was no longer a steady-working American male, but a statistic of the failures of a once-great economy.

Steve finished his beer, simple and straight forward fast, and then stood to help Jackie out of the club chair, grabbing her bottle as he nudged her into the kitchen. "I'll set the table, dear. Supper smells mighty fine."

Jackie washed her hands again; calling over her shoulder, "Don't forget to wash your hands, Steve."

"I didn't shovel any shit today, Jackie. GM did. On Brandon's head."

Right-angled at the table, they thanked the Lord in rapid rote prayer, heads almost touching as they bowed. Though the kitchen's counter top extended like a '50s diner with stools, Jackie insisted on the sanctity of a table. She made sure they ate with cloth placemats and napkins, reluctant to alter her mother's traditions. The cherry wood table was heirloom, with carved legs that deserved to be seen. It had served generations of family meals, held by the super glue of memories to the same spot, despite their recent kitchen remodel.

Jackie watched as Steve picked out the carrots, as he had for thirty-some years, but shaving and cutting carrots were part of her supper ritual, another of the motions that propelled her through the afternoon. Quiet and earnest as Steve's cows, they commenced to chew, eye contact reserved for when they got past ravenous. The mix of foods was familiar and undemanding; it allowed their brains to click in sync with their teeth. They often ate like this to avoid gossip and politics, not peaceable topics when you're worn down by chores.

"Want ice cream with the cake or do you want me to open a container of icing?"

Steve met Jackie's eyes…they seldom ate dessert on weeknights. The nightly shift of milking was coming up.

"Ice cream'll do. What's up, Jackie?"

She sliced the cake, placed hunks on two festive plates, and topped it with butter pecan. She stalled more by fussing over whether to offer a spoon or a fork, befuddled to not fetch the 4-H rule easily from memory. If the mind was supposed to be the first thing to go, it was too late because of her knees, but Jackie was alarmed. 4-H had been one true thread of her life. If this fact was gone, what else?

Then it occurred to her that it might be best to share the final guillotine stroke while she was standing at the utensil drawer, with the kitchen island between them: "The kids are going to lose their house." She didn't look at Steve as she handed him a spoon.

"Holy crap," Steve grumped. "Isn't that a fine mess! I guess they'll have to move in here, won't they? I'll have to tolerate that icy statue girl up close and personal." He shoved a spoonful of ice cream in his mouth to punctuate the statement, maybe as an anti-profanity measure.

"On a positive note, you can help Brandon through this tough period. Oprah talked about empathy today, and I think you've got that in spades." Jackie aimed for the positive, and then winced. Not only did Steve not like it that she watched Oprah or Ellen, though they weren't the soap operas others endlessly discussed; he also didn't like to be reminded of his unceremonious dismissal from GM.

"If we ever get a word in edgewise. Holy crap. How did this happen?" Steve took another big bite of ice cream, but dessert wasn't cooling him down.

Two: For the Road

Steve carried his dishes to the sink and sighed as he set them down. He turned to Jackie: "Remember when we re-wound videotapes? That's what I wish: that I could re-spool today, maybe even erase it."

"Honey," Jackie said, her fingers at his elbow, "you and I drew closer together because of bad stuff we lived through, beginning with the Vietnam War when we dated. We can do this. We specialize in it. The national economy is at war, and we are the victims, but we'll all bounce back."

She squeezed Steve's shoulder before he headed back to grab the beer bottles and the pot roast platter, something he'd never done before. He usually headed out directly to milk the cows after supper.

He was halfway back to the sink when he stopped and grinned, "We can't erase the present or past, but we can re-invent the future. We always said we'd explore the USA when we retired, Jackie. Let's use some pension money to buy a Winnebago. We can let the kids move in here while we move out onto the great open American highways. We'll be like Charles Kuralt!"

Excited at the prospect of fulfilling dual purposes, their dreams swelled the kitchen beyond its walls, so that they fell almost like those of Jericho, willing them into the world.

Jackie was tired of traveling via Internet voyeurism. Steve was just tired. He said it seemed like he was huffing and puffing earnestly, diligent 50 years at 15 hours a day. He deserved respite. He longed to let his fingers walk across a map like the old Yellow Pages ad or to palm a globe rather than cow teats. He was sure that his son would enjoy fondling teats, no matter whose.

That's when Jackie thought, but didn't say, *Holy crap! What a job recommendation!* He was her beloved, talented, and capable married son.

Then the cows interrupted in a cacophony of agony from full teats: *Come squeeze me, darling!*

Chores never got done so fast, not even when they had hiked it to Brandon's college games. Thank goodness they only had six cows. Milked by machine in practiced hands, it only took a half-hour.

In the spirit of their new whirl, Steve danced Jackie around the kitchen island before they donned coats and hustled out the door to go Friday night shopping at Travel Land over on Route 40.

Maps of the USA had long been stashed in the lowest drawer of the desk, awaiting their turn in life. Steve swore he heard them singing, "America the Beautiful", and as he and Jackie drove off their property, they took up the refrain.

Later neither of them recalled who said what or when or how the ideas wound out so fully formed, though they agreed that it resonated like heaven's angels singing, not the hell's bells it all became.

The opening chime of the Mac was firmly attached to their shared memories because they did loads of research over the next several days; they didn't just leap willy-nilly. That was Brandon's game.

They felt jubilant, like kids, not like forbearing, encumbered adults. They were in possibility realm again, their longed-for and well-earned place.

Their truck headlights were among the few on the dark country road. As Jackie and Steve arrived at Travel Land, the sky was lit like noon, and they were suddenly very awake.

American flags whipped the perimeter of the RV lot, waving like the flag squad with a band. Vehicles lined up like football players along the perimeter of a field, ready to scrimmage America. Bright as Michigan State's stadium, the lot's affinity was instant. Some of the vehicle doors were open - sort of a *'send me in, Coach'* welcome - and others had their headlights on in the *'come hither'* look of a big-eyed actress. RVs came in all lengths, widths, and interior plans, a cornucopia of vehicular living, according to the salesman. *Christmas on steroids.*

As Jackie stepped into the first vehicle, right into the kitchen, down the hall was a full-length mirror. She fluffed her darkish ringlets, and then noticed that her apron was still on. *Must be God wants me to inhabit this home,* she thought as she crammed the apron in her purse.

Steve caught her lapse, smirked, and then admonished: "Don't go moving furniture, Jackie. Most of it's fixed to the floor."

Jackie elbowed his side before he stepped directly into the armchair-like driver's seat of the RV. He could have his cockpit and she'd have hers – *my, this kitchen is dreamy!*

The salesman posed casual, but Jackie could see his brain counting cash. Steve obviously could, too, and dipped his chin to signal an exit.

Steve glanced at his watch – it was near time for the nightly news, their ritual before bed. They left with a dozen brochures, saying that they needed to prospect some more before they made a decision. The salesman's face went as blank as their home TV screen when the 10:00 news was over; as if he was run by Steve's remote, too, Jackie thought.

Despite its dual dump of her good men from its work line-up, Jackie felt lifelong GM loyalty kick in. While Winnebago was the name on their lips, maybe they should pull pension money to buy a GMC, to invest in their future with Steve's past. Maybe if they wrote a note to that effect, the company would hire Brandon back.

When she floated that fairytale aloud, Steve grimaced. "Jackie, this is not public school, where notes from parents amend disgrace. Besides the GMC hasn't been made since 1978, when we were newlyweds."

Then he swerved so strong into rant that she worried that they might leave the road. Thank goodness they'd lived here all their lives, so that everything was familiar, where everything could be counted on: even the roadside fencing seemed like clasped hands to hold their truck in place. And, for its part, Steve's truck had every turn memorized.

Steve wasn't talking religion, yet Jackie couldn't shake an image that the steering wheel was his lectern. She knew not to interrupt, though she longed to comment...that while he'd probably helped assemble several million GM vehicles, all of his laser-straight plowing had been atop a Ford. And, look at which company was on top? But this was not the time to confuse him with the facts.

Steve paused and they looked at each other in simultaneous recollection of Brandon's prized red Ford F-150 truck and Amy's black Benz: family member duplicity in the GM breakdown.

Steve resolved to buy American, and Winnebago fit. Jackie heartily agreed, like the good wife she was. Steve declared a financial check with the bank as the next step, and she agreed with that, too. They'd circled purchases like this many times, slow and methodical as a bird built a nest.

"I just can't wrap my mind around the kids losing their house," Steve said. "I thought we raised a saver like us and, with Amy working at the bank, you'd think it would be all copacetic."

"Have you ever noticed that, while Brandon always wears Michigan State football jerseys and jeans, new boots peek from his pants every time he visits, sometimes with exotic leathers and designs? He doesn't wear cheap Levis either. Amy seems to wear all of the make-up at the Wal-Mart in layered rotation? Like she replaced the NBC peacock. Notice how her cell phone, almost another body part, seems to have a new cover each week; that Brandon's TVs get larger or their rooms get smaller, I don't know which? Amy's suitcase-sized purses match her boots, and she may have more boots than Brandon. Those kids could shoe an army in an small European country from their closet."

"Speaking of cell phones, do you realize the monthly bill will mount higher than our barn?" Steve said. "The tether will be inelastic. Strangulation by kinfolk, crisis-laden calls constantly dogging our trip."

"You can't have it both ways, Steve," Jackie said, lifting a curl behind her ear. "We've always encouraged Brandon to check in. Amy seems to have taken to it, like back when I was included in the wedding planning."

She had worn beige, like a proper groom's mother, embellished with a bulbous corsage, in Amy's absent mom's stead. She wondered whatever happened to that woman?

"I'm just doing what I do, thinking of details, Jackie," Steve asserted. "And some of the details are drat."

"Where did 'drat' come from? You sound like a cartoon villain," she said with a chuckle, hoping to get him to lighten up.

"When did you say the kids were coming over to talk? Sunday? I didn't want to add cussing to my sin list. I don't think it's sinful to want to kill a bogus daughter-in-law, but my son? I refuse to laugh about this, Jackie."

"Steve, I'm just trying..." Jackie began.

"You've been trying, since the day I met you," Steve cut in. He grinned before he threw a peck at her cheek.

Jackie moved a little closer on the truck seat, just as they pulled in their lane. Before Steve could open his door, she gave him a kiss, a full-on, lip smacking, shoulder-hugging caress.

The bickering began with breakfast, after they'd slept on their dreams: Steve focused on the power of the sleek-as-a-yacht RV motors, while Jackie reveled in the layouts and plush upholstery colors. The bedcovers weren't tumbled and twisted, and their pillows lay close in the middle as evidence of their travel pact.

But reality bites, as they say. Years of farming had carved its methodology into their DNA - and they were family. They couldn't sashay off and leave Brandon in a lurch, Jackie thought as she descended the stairs. A little voice added *like he did to us.* Her highness, the Crayola-eyed queen, wouldn't protect him.

My goodness, my floors are clean; her inner voice easily shifted topics. Suddenly, Jackie was alarmed at the thought of Amy taking over the household. Steve's parents' home with its richly grained wood floors. Her new granite counters that she was just learning to take proper care of. Her flowerbeds and garden would become their own compost. Though Amy could have raked the beds and drilled out the weeds with her nails, Jackie couldn't picture her at household chores of any type. Amy might take her Crayolas to the walls like Brandon had done years ago.

Jackie glanced at the grandfather clock, as she held tight to the oak banister. She'd slept later this morning because excitement forestalled sleep until the clock chimed midnight. Steve should be in from the milk barn, seated at the table, reading the morning paper or completing a crossword puzzle by now. She ambled toward the kitchen, but startled awake before she got there. She blinked her eyes, expecting a change of scene like the click of a toy View Master.

"I'm glad I didn't plan to vacuum the carpet today," she said when she saw the family room rug layered with maps. Her husband looked like Brandon five minutes into Christmas, with piles of wrapping paper flung aside to display all the new loot. *Was it truly 20 years ago when he got the Lionel train set?* Steve could have been playing with that toy for all the attention he gave Jackie.

"Who knew that our maple trees could teleport their leaves into our living room?" she quipped to the Star Trek fan. That got Steve's attention, and he grinned.

She loved his ear-to-ear grin, loved the man. His summer tan was faded, yet he was a six-foot wonder to her. Brown hair, flared at the ends when he needed a trim, to which he seldom surrendered. Not because of price - the barber in town only charged $20.00 – but because of time. The hair flipped out behind his ears as extensions of his smile, he said.

Squinting at the legend of the map he held, Steve must have already applied his farmer legacy of tallying crop yield to the mileage math of a transcontinental trip, because he said, "Honey, this is only going to work if you share in the driving. Do you know how many miles it is to Yellowstone Park? And gas prices are going up. Today's paper says the national average is $2.69."

"Do you have to get rational already?" Jackie sighed. "I haven't even gotten a decent breakfast in me, and you go finding what's wrong with our dream."

"Jackie, what's wrong is that Brandon and Amy are near homeless and haven't even agreed to our solution."

Jackie put her hands on her hips. "I'm sure they will. They have to," she said, "especially when you present the plan right." Then she turned and continued her route, "But let's talk after I have coffee. Want some?"

Jackie didn't wait for his reply because she knew he'd already had his two cups, or else the cows would be mooing. Loudly. She walked to the coffee maker, its shiny red light alert as a lighthouse on Lake Huron. Steve was scribbling details on one of his many yellow pads, one of his hobbies, Jackie often said.

A slurp or two later Jackie slipped upstairs for bed-making chores, trying to forget the melees that awaited. Her brain was streaming a Kuralt-like travelogue while she smoothed the bedding, and then showered and dressed for the day. Each layer of clothing made her more complete, then...

Holy crap! She thought of Amy and Brandon sleeping in her bed – *yikes, Amy is like Goldilocks! I can hardly bear it,* she thought and grinned at her pun. Humor was helpful in the middle of one of Steve's harangues, so she tucked that quip in her mental stash.

Winter was coming to central Michigan, and they'd have plenty of time indoors to cycle around the travel topic.

But Brandon and Amy need a place to live, no matter what. If we don't travel, they could sleep in his old room. Jackie liked that scenario better, with Amy in the guest room, sleeping under Grandma Bree's Sun Bonnet Sue quilt.

Well, tomorrow's supper summit would be interesting, as her friend, Fran would euphemistically say.

Jackie finished coffee and inner sanctum chores, and then suited up for the autumn ritual of raking leaves. The wind rustled them alive, a flame of color like an Indian bonfire; they were flirting, luring her out of the second story window. *Today,* she mused, *I will rake them into one pile and jump in the middle. I want to squander time today.*

Her shoe soles thumped the steps as she descended the staircase, and Steve's head perked up, his face as eager as his dog's when they headed to town. "Jackie, what's your favorite place in the USA?"

"'Bout time you asked me. Let me think while I rake, okay."

"Bring me all of the colored highlighters from the desk," Steve yelled, though his voice was tempered with request, not command.

"You shouldn't even be down on the floor, Steve. What would your doctor say? Probably cancel your knee surgery pre-authorization for blasphemy. What are we going to do about that on the road, by the way?"

"Jackie, I feel like this trip has rejuvenated me, so clam up about my knees."

Jackie let that remark pass as she fetched the pens. Jackie was all about patience – and getting things done. You could lead a horse to water, but you couldn't make him drink, especially if the horse was named Steve.

Thinking of the phrase made her thirsty, then hungry, and she recalled that she'd not eaten breakfast, a certain sign that she was gyrating out of routine. Too much news, good and bad, she thought. Too much to assimilate without eggs.

"You always ask me, but you mean *do it*, just like a Nike Wifey," she said as she handed him the pens. "Please don't mark on the maps until I get to tell you my places. Okay?" She waited until he lifted his head. With eye contact she continued, "There's not enough white-out to make changes on a map, and I don't want to go to AAA again."

"Fair enough. I'll just list them on a yellow tablet. Can you bring me another one?"

"I'll bring you two, but you've got to let me have breakfast first. Diabetic comas aren't pretty, they tell me."

Perhaps it was the crack of the egg on the side of the cast iron skillet that brought her back to the fact that their handsome football hero, 4-H star, rock 'n roll loving son had lost his job. The Sesame Street jingle: "One of these things is not like the others; one of these things doesn't belong" came to mind.

She put a piece of chocolate cake on the plate with her bacon and eggs, balanced another cake slice on a plate on her wrist - like Sally, the waitress at the Koffee Kup - because she had to grab the tablets. Walking slowly Jackie arrived in the front room, where Steve took the tablets, then with a happy eyebrow boogie, the cake plate.

Jackie sidled onto the club chair ottoman, just outside the perimeter of the maps, and said as gently as she could, "Honey, do you think you could call Brandon, to talk, you know, about what happened, what he knows, how he feels?"

Steve plunked the tablets down, probably harder than intended, and stuffed the cake into his mouth in rapid bites. Jackie recognized stalling – food was the safety plane – so she was respectful and ate breakfast, wishing she'd made wheat toast. She'd offer him her cake if he agreed to talk to Brandon. Positive reinforcement. Jackie believed in it as much as she believed in God.

"Honestly, Jackie, I thought of it, but I guess I was so hungry for the play of our dream – our turn – that I covered it up, sorta like the maps I spread on our floor." He swept his arm back to show the mound, like this was an infomercial for the road trip. "Why don't you call him, Hon? You've always been the one to handle the feelings of the family. This is all too much deja voodoo for me."

"But Oprah says there's value in empathy, and that makes it your department. You're his father. Also, have you thought of anyone you could call to get his job back?"

The tablet in Steve's hand dumped to the floor: "I burned up my mind thinking of how I could save the job for myself, and it did no good, so how could I do that for Brandon? I'll call him though. Just to check in before Sunday supper, okay? We'll see where the conversation goes."

"Don't mention our plans." He was lucky Jackie had plates in hand or she'd have shaken a finger at him like a poker. He was also lucky her mouth wasn't full, so she could say what needed to be said. "I don't want Amy to have a clue, so she can lead off with her prideful naysaying. We need to hear if they have any plans because Amy is sure to have one. Amy's always sure."

Three: Hijacked

Hello, Reader. My name is Amy, and I have hijacked the book – had to because Fran, who massaged it into being, is Jackie's best friend. The tale would be biased and not the truth and nothing but the truth, so help me. I've never been accused of being shy or without point of view. I have a keen sense of self-protection, so I feel compelled to control the message. Don't ask how I got in – just sit back and read. You'll enjoy my part.

Sunday ritual set up the discussion, the meeting of the minds of Jackie, Steve, Brandon, and me. My bank's bald president was not invited nor was Sparty, my in-laws' dog. The bank president was in my doghouse, but Sparty couldn't be – he owned the farmhouse garage.

Later the Breedens would call it the 'Supper Summit', though my private term was 'The Hoedown Showdown'. Trying to alliterate Machiavelli didn't fool me, and I like rhyme. I studied English as well as Economics on an academic scholarship at Michigan State that wasn't quite a full ride. That's where and how I stole Brandon from the cheer squad: I was his tutor. He wasn't The Prince. I was.

I showed up in a dress so yellow, I looked like a yolk, Brandon said, seeming a bit embarrassed. I cuffed him and told him that I was trying to be a good egg, get the yoke?

Did he wince? Not in front of his parents. He shrunk in front of them, hid behind 'A Me', now that he'd lost the job that his dad had worked connections to get him. After he screwed the pooch of a pro football career. He should have known better than to jump from our balcony to the pool on our honeymoon – no, I did not push him. He thought he was a god because his mom and dad pushed him into thinking just like them.

Brandon's B.S. in geography was all that. B.S., I mean. There weren't more than five job interviews to fail after torn ligaments wrenched him out of a pro football career, but fail, he did, and his dad intervened. Within a week, Bran made $25.00/hr. working assembly line at GM, 50% more than the average factory worker and as much as me, the local bank VP.

That October Sunday I was physically as well as psychologically taller than Brandon, because I wore new Jimmy Choo boots. Their name was Major and, as they say, if you have to ask the price, you can't afford them. Ann Taylor, Macys, and Zappos online informed my ambitions to outclass this tiny town. I outranked everyone in the room, because I had a full time management job.

I was also the only blonde.

I could see that my new frock set Jackie's teeth on edge. I notice teeth because I have braces, the invisible version, a promise to myself when I had money.

Perhaps it was because the dress was Easterish, and it was six weeks past Labor Day. Michigan people have fashion rules that didn't exist in California. New clothes don't need a season or a reason, I say. I liked to look sharp as my mind. Another promise made and kept to self.

My mind is mostly where I converse when I'm in Jackie and Steve's home. Maybe I'm schizophrenic, like my mother, but I think not. I have my wits about me. I try to blend into the family scene: be pretty, be patient, be seated. Do the dishes, help Jackie when I can; bow to Steve as the master of the homestead. Brandon's a cheap imitation, not what I thought.

"You look pretty, Amy. It's nice to see you in a dress," Jackie said with a sweet smile.

"Thanks, I got it on sale."

I beamed at my newly worn thriftiness. The women at the bank consider me stuck up, but I maintain distance. They are assistants, and I am management. Ha, I hear their inane coffee klatch conversations on break, all nail polish colors and Kohl's. I stash info like rich men stash money.

"It's a nice dress for going to church," Jackie said.

I recognized another religious ploy and shifted the topic to supper's preparation: "What can I do to help?"

"Well, there's not much to do. Kroger's had small turkeys on sale, pushing Thanksgiving upon us, so that's what's in the oven. I guess you could help mash the potatoes. We're going to make them with Mrs. Molden's recipe." Jackie tucked a curl behind her ear to punctuate   her   proposal.

"Oh, the ones with the cream cheese. Bran loves 'em!"

With that I moved into the farmwoman's place, in the kitchen. I saw Brandon and Steve drop onto the couch in the family room, a pillow's distance apart. Crowd noise soon alternated with commentator drone to signal more TV sports.

Jackie's kitchen always befuddled me: a spacious square with an island in the middle, reminding me of town where two-story buildings - windows mostly shuttered with plywood to resemble unfinished wood cabinet doors - surrounded a stocky courthouse. Jackie's bounty of drawers, shelves, and appliances were a respectable homemaker's template: a utensil for every food project stashed until called up for duty, bedded in flower garden paper changed annually in Spring-cleaning.

Jackie even has a walk-in closet, though it's called a food pantry. It's as big and well stocked as the one I have for clothing. All of the abundantly stuffed storage spaces are cloaked in cherry wood - planed from trees on the farm property, I'm told.

Our kitchen's got lots of stuff, too, and I am sorry to be losing its prestigious bling. The stove alone could finance a small car – if we could wrest it to sell before the foreclosure.

Sustenance, food is central to farm life. It shows love. I'd lived on cold pizza most of my life, never been in a grocery until I moved here. Though fields and fields of corn cover the land, fresh vegetables scare me. I avoid the Kroger rainforest bins; the automatic mist that blesses the produce to keep it alive longer for the ravenous always startles me. Michigan has more fat people than I'd ever seen. In California body fat seemed forbidden, so Mom, my brother, and I fit in.

I was grateful for the familiar chore of making Molden potatoes, but am I the only one who considered the image of moldy potatoes gross? Or perhaps the old lady is moldy? Is the casserole molting or molten? Here's the recipe:

Mrs. Molden's Potato Casserole
Blend thoroughly with mixer:
- 2 c. mashed potatoes (can use instant)
- 8 oz. cream cheese, softened
- 1 small onion, finely chopped
- 2 eggs, whisked before adding
- ½ t. salt and ½ t. pepper

Spoon into greased 9 in. baking dish. Sprinkle 3 ½ oz. can French Fried onions on top. Bake 35 minutes @ 300 degrees.

I was also grateful that Jackie didn't want to chat. It appeared that she was straining to listen to the man talk, so I strained along. Their backs heaved intermittently with serious contemplation, but their heads were inert. Their necks never swiveled away from the TV to address each other personally. I knew this was not a sign of impoverished interaction; it was just men watching football.

"Did you see it coming?" I heard Steve say. I couldn't wait to hear Brandon's response because, of course, he didn't see our bankruptcy coming. He'd lived his entire life by someone else's playbook, a script of Xs and Os, jiving to a rhythm that few could match. He's accustomed to worship and adoration. He ceded thought and arrangements to me. I'd seen to that quickly. What little initiative he'd shown, I smashed like these potatoes.

He took it so easily that I imagine I wasn't the first. It has become my project to determine which of his parents lamed Brandon most. Otherwise, life in mid-

Michigan dairy land would be udderly boring. *Ha! I crack myself up.*

The serenity that sucked me into the central Michigan vortex is repelling me. I am ready to spit it out.

The man I loved spoke: "Well, Dad, I didn't hang in the bars after shift with the other guys much, so I wasn't tuned in to the plant gossip. I didn't like the union cranks. On breaks, the guys loved to tease me about being a college boy, a former football hero who couldn't catch a job, or having shiny apple cheeks 'cause of 4-H. I didn't take to teasing."

"Amy's more fun anyways." I smiled at his compliment as I scooped the potatoes into a casserole, listening as he continued.

"I like to take off my boots and put my feet up, not hang 'em down from a bar stool. And I rule World of Warcraft! I been playin' a guy in China and one in Taiwan, and I'm doing better than our bond traders."

Steve turned to gape at Brandon, perhaps surprised by the tangential take on world affairs, but I smiled again. I was used to Brandon's mental limits. Hell, that's how I snagged him.

"Wish I could help you, but I don't have pull at the plant anymore," Steve said, and turned back to the TV set.

The two men, who resembled each other in every way except initiative, lapsed into silence. There wasn't much else to listen to except the roar of the crowd.

I wonder if Brandon misses it? Central Michigan is quiet and unperturbed. I long for the ocean, the relentless soundtrack for all Californians, even a Costa Mesa street kid. The Pacific Ocean roars.

With the snap of the oven door, my share of food prep was done. I moved to setting the table with the china and silverware pointed out in the glass-front cupboard. I figured out the drawer for cloth napkins and placed their folded edge like a wave ready to crash onto the plate, burying the silver treasure. Then I circled the table and righted everything. I knew that Jackie was particular about the table setting.

The silverware meant something was up and I knew what, but I focused on alignment. I was aware that I was supposed to call the meal supper, but *supperware?* It sounded fearsomely like Tupperware, and who wanted any part of that? Burping lids. Really? I had burping Brandon.

With that thought, I finished the table setting, and, without notifying the hostess, I sat between the men after giving both a shoulder squeeze. Our butts touched. They both loved it.

Jackie hadn't noticed my escape, and so when I rose with the men to her, "wash up for supper, guys", I flashed a benign grin. She didn't swerve. I told you about habit; she hadn't even missed me in the kitchen.

My hands were clean, so I waited until the others settled into their usual places at the table, then sat down with silent prayers already begun: all earnest and 'thy will be done', though my version was for my will to be done. As soon as I determined what that was. To tell the truth the foreclosure had blindsided me, too. Probably most of all, to tell even more truth.

Our heads lifted in unison. For likely the first and last time at the table tonight, the group was in accord. The serving plates and dishes began to circulate among hands, each serving him/herself just right. Weight Watchers had no place at a farm table.

Jackie is a forthright talker and I am her equal, while the two men carefully dance around the edges of the conversation most times, but Jackie started soft that night.

"We're sorry, kids. Seems like the national economy is tanking deep in our own community."

"How many places do you owe, Brandon?" Steve lithely avoided the sum of our debt. My red warning flag must have been flying. Perhaps Steve's fisherman brother, David, taught him semaphores; David's daughter, Tessa, is my semi-friend within the family.

"We have two mortgages on our place, credit cards, and two vehicle loans, that's all," I interjected because I had the facts. "We haven't got any student loans to be paid like most of our friends." I also have the pride.

Jackie snuck a look at Steve. I knew she had high expectations for her college boy, who was favored with a football scholarship. But what could be a better life than being married to me? He has every tech toy on the planet. And he craves my well-practiced sex; I know how to cradle that injured shoulder.

"Why didn't you bring your concerns to us earlier? Don't you know we always help?" Steve looked levelly at his son, his mirror without wrinkles.

"I just figured it would all work out, Dad. Amy said it would." He looked at me like an obedient pup.

Brandon gave me credit. I smiled and squeezed his knee. He was plowing new fields with his parents. I was proud of him.

"How long've you got before the bank forecloses?"

I asserted myself quickly. The bank was my employer; my authority was my own. "I've been able to negotiate 90 days before the proceedings. I've already been looking at some second story spaces above the dead businesses downtown for us to live. There's incredible potential with high ceilings, brick walls, even old wood floors that Bran can refinish," I paused to smile, then added, to be politically correct, "so it would look as good as this place. Since they've been empty awhile, owners are eager to deal. We've been watching the renovation shows on HGTV. I just love how the show hosts call it *space*." I looked at Steve with my final word, to align with the avowed Star Trek fan.

Finally Brandon spoke, facing his dad squarely at last. "Dad, we just got used to things always working out. Like they always have. We didn't ever add things up; we just sort of kept buying stuff. You know, like you have here."

Jackie dared not drop her head into her hands. Nor did Steve, not now that Brandon had pushed that button. It was true, his parents were models for acquisition; we'd just had more toys available to us, more lavishly presented as the latest and greatest wants translated into needs.

Brandon's reasoning often seemed stuck in third grade, but he'd hit the nail on the head. Credit cards, conceived in his folk's newlywed years, had iced the consumer cake. By bank invitation, no one had to decide between 'have it now' or someday in the future.

Advanced by virtual shops – my special vice - buying is no longer a visceral experience, not like working the land, but Jackie and Steve don't get it. Brandon and I are pros to their amateur status. Jackie and Steve are still burdened by consequences. Sure glad that they didn't pass that on to Bran.

Jackie spoke brightly: "Your dad and I went shopping last night. We thought we'd buy a motor home to travel the U.S. and let you two live here."

Brandon's head shifted back a little, but he didn't have time to look at me before I blurted, "No thanks, Jackie and Steve."

I'd never accepted their invitation to call them Mom and Dad, and now I was glad. These people were addled spendthrifts masquerading as upright farmfolk like everybody else. I saw their kind every day at the bank. I wish I could charge extra interest to fools.

Jackie flushed stop sign red. Steve folded his hands in front of his now-empty plate. He looked his son in the eye while he extended his arms to us both. "Well, it's an idea to consider. Why don't you two stroll with me while your mother clears the table and sets a dessert. Time for night milking."

Steve was always quick to change the scene when Jackie's heart's desire was thwarted, for her mouth often rose to defend her heart in rebel yell. I should be in witness protection for the times I've taken heat. "Grab your coats, and let's go."

The mudroom door was an easy portal to the small farm lot. Outside we stepped onto a tight rectangle of concrete that corresponded to a small roof that hung out like an overbite and was just as useless. Our trio walked the brief swatch of sidewalk that led to the gravel lane. If it had been daylight we would have stopped beside six-year-old Brandon's hand and footprint, establishing that the Breeden family had its own Hollywood star. "A man's theater here in Michigan, farming the land as God surely intended," someone would say. That always sounded like so much cow manure to me.

Jackie always says that Steve breathes easier outside. I see that his clothes seem to fit him better in motion. Not much more than a glorified garage is needed for micro dairying, and my in-laws have three buildings built in a triangle, nature's strongest shape. The spacing is minimalist. It eases an older man's daily tramp to the milking chores, rain or shine or snow because cows always gotta be milked two times daily 365. What a leash!

Leaves crunched against the sidewalk, then the grass, then gravel, with differing pitches to punctuate our steps across the lot. The sounds echoed among the buildings and in my head. I chewed an inner lip, keeping time with my feet's cadence, with my silent thoughts.

I matched the men stride for stride, though they sauntered while I worked it in heeled boots. When we turned the corner of the garage, and I saw the skylighted bulk of building behind it, heard the dog barking his head off at the sound of footsteps, I whirled to face Steve: "Okay. We'd love to live here. You can even leave Sparty with us!"

Sparty stopped barking and the cows quit their mooing, impatient plaints for evening milking. Brandon and Steve's mental recalibration, as they pondered my reversal, was palpable, yet neither uttered a word. Not even a cricket solo broke the silence as we all walked back to the house.

My pronouncement was the near-final word of the night. Just inside the back door I easily parlayed my work commitments into early exit because Jackie and Steve had them, too. Steve glanced at his sturdy Timex and headed for the barn, though Jackie hooked his elbow to make him wave his good-bye. Dessert was forsaken for the night – with thanks. I have an egotistical figure to maintain.

I was also in a hurry to get out of the dress and knew that Brandon would assist.

Brandon was alone as the abruptly unemployed, yet he was the one most in a hurry. He started his plush truck before I got my seatbelt buckled. "So what's the plan, Queen Amy?" Brandon knows to address me as royalty when my Hapsburg jaw is set.

I stared at my hands, thumbs twiddling round and round, my reliable thinking posture. Brandon is as loveable as Sparty at times – and just as foolish, for he never thinks of the future. For that he has me. If he'd had a tail, it would've drummed the custom leather seats.

"Your dad has built a solid small business selling organic milk. Pardon the pun, but we are going to milk more profit out of the business with another product, green cookies."

"Beer can be green when ya pretend to be Irish on St. Patty's Day; but I remember Dr. Seuss' <u>Green Eggs and Ham</u>, and green cookies would be as gross as that!"

"Sweet thing, consider chocolate chip cookies made with pot butter. Environmentally sustainable products are in right now and the weed is green, so connect some dots."

"Pot butter? What's that? How do you know about that stuff, Ms. Well-suited Banker?"

"My brother's going to Chico State in California, remember. Everybody there smokes and cooks with weed. He sent cookies and a recipe in my birthday package."

"What? You mean, those cookies were… I'll be."

"Yes, you will be, my friend. You will be wealthy: 'Everybody must get stoned.'"

Brandon turned on the radio, like he always did when I started to sing. "I always wondered why my folks considered Dylan an iconic singer. He was prehistoric when they were married. Come to think of it, though I love you, your voice crackles and pops like a grainy old Dylan record."

I let him get away with that crack. I love the lunk. He's a big, warm puppy dog, my well-leashed pet.

Four: Bygone ERA

"Well, what did you say to turn her pretty blonde head to your point of view, Mr. Genius?" Jackie said as soon as Brandon's red truck spun the gravel of the U-shaped drive. She crooked his elbow in hers to get this conversation in before he strode off to dairying.

"I wonder why Brandon is dusting the shine off his beloved machine?" Steve said as men do. That seemed inconsequential in the face of multiple crises, but as the wife and the mother, Jackie remained as mum as her flowers.

Brandon's truck got tiny fast as it sped down the road, and she wished the crises could too. She waited for Steve's answer to either of the questions.

When Steve turned toward her, he beamed, hands in pockets. "The glory of our spread must've bedazzled her. It seemed to turn at the corner of the garage. The buildings just painted last summer and, well, our little golden triangle gleamed under the day glow of our security light. Amy must've gotten high inhaling 'Mellow Yellow' paint fumes. Jackie, we're gonna go on the road, and the kids are gonna live here," he said as he headed to fetch coat, cap, and boots.

Jackie followed him inside and watched as he shrugged quickly into his chore duds, then high-and-low fived before he sped out the door: "Doncha just love win-win!"

After a brief watch of Steve's familiar gait as he headed back to the dairy barn, Jackie set about washing the supper dishes, foregoing the dishwasher because she thought best with hands engaged. She gazed blankly out the window above the double sink. The security light made an eerie presence of the farm buildings, atmospheric for the upcoming Halloween holiday. The haunting call of a loon – mated for life like she and Steve – was the voice of the wood stand north of the barns' golden triangle. Jackie wished that the facts of their life would reframe into a Thomas Kinkaid.

Her brain whirled like a weed whacker, blending her concerns for Amy and Bran, her hopes for herself and Steve, with foibles and memories tumbled in. Her grimace reflected in the window caused her to shift her gaze to the calendar mounted on the cupboard perpendicular to the window. Its vibrant pumpkin stack photo reminded her of a classroom bulletin board - and that the next day was Monday.

Jackie was still an employee in the local school cafeteria, dishing up meals in which ketchup counted as a vegetable. At their wedding reception, she'd famously quipped to Steve, "I can only be good in one room at a time." Jackie hoped that karma hadn't relegated her life to a kitchen because of it. Pots and pans and grating and peeling; now there wasn't even an outdoors break to mow the large lawn, which used to make her Florida tan.

Steve had claimed that chore when he was let go from GM – the big green riding lawnmower became part of the man's realm without a whimper – ceded like a farm wife should. The chore hand-off might have afforded more time for reading a book or two, something from Oprah's list, but, like sand in an hourglass, other tasks sieved into her daily life.

The school job was as stale as the bread sometimes toasted for tuna salad sandwiches, but the district's health insurance was the prize. Steve had worked for years in the auto industry and his retirement benefits remained in limbo, government bailout or not. They were several years away from Medicare, so they needed her job - yet daily Jackie contemplated giving it a shove - along with the trays that swept past her station in the cafeteria line. The kids no longer responded to her smiles and encouragements. They stabbed their phones, thumbs so fast you can hardly see movement, and then burrowed in, not even chatting with a person next to them in the line, let alone the lady who'd sliced off the crusts, like Brandon had always expected.

Jackie even tried to learn slang in her efforts to rekindle the camaraderie of Brandon's team sports decade, but apparently her 'hip' was only a plump body part. If she spoke, the kids just eye-rolled while they nudged the trays along, loyal to the code of youth that adults didn't know anything.

At their home, laughter had flowed easily back in the day - belly laughs. Jackie made chocolate icing s'mores, always had gummy worms and Bazooka Gum and, because the farm supplied Orville Redenbacher, popped corn in minutes, whether it was *Lion King* or *Transformers* to watch. Later Steve served beer, clad in cooler cup disguise, rather than pop.

Steve invested in the latest electronics, rocking and rolling the kids that filled their basement rec room. Shoes bigger than her shoeboxes were strewn about as Jackie taught the boys to dance for the Winter Formal and Prom. The walls had a few pool cue pocks where the pool table, emblazoned with Michigan State's seal, held court. Jackie and Steve knew Brandon was going to college there before he got the scholarship.

Jackie and Steve were mildly aware that they were celebrities by association because everyone in town and on campus gave them credit for Brandon's birth and talent. Everyone – young and old and in-between – wanted to hang out with Jackie and Steve.

All gone, like the wild animals subdued with the success of Cirque d'Soleil. Jackie especially missed the elephants when she attended one in the tent at Wal-Mart - though not the one in the room now that Brandon had lost his job, home, and integrity. Jackie didn't want a ringside seat for this event. Let PT Barnum load it on his circus train and haul it from her life.

No, there wasn't much mirth to augment the worth of those holy health benefits. Lord help her, Jackie hated each workday. Saturday lunch with Fran and Sunday church with Pastor Rankin were high water marks, leavened by Bonnie's "Let's fix this" chats or a haircut at Maybelline's. But even these were routine. Too many days Jackie wore a big white apron, garbed like the Pillsbury Dough Boy, with a giggle as silly as his.

Mutual bad knees had shaken the foundation of the '70s set of dreams that she shared with Steve, along with china and silverware. It made it hard for her to pray for more, for better, this worse cycle of life. Days dragged, like a kid-nagged scab that wouldn't heal.

So, Jackie surrounded herself with occasional bling, to thrive in the twinkly newness: new kitchen counter, new cell phone, new earrings. Intermittently moving forward and feeling better, or what passed for both in life's cha-cha-cha.

Just as she wiped her hands, her phone rang. Jackie untied the apron and wriggled it off before she fetched the phone from its pocket. "Hi, Fran. I was just thinking about work."

"Are you in a good mood or should I call you back?" Fran said.

"Now's a good time. Supper meeting's over and done."

"How'd it go?" Fran got to the point. It would all eventually come out – and better now, so that Jackie could get some rest, to be fresh and pert for peeling potatoes in her school cafeteria tomorrow.

"Better than expected," Jackie said. "Amy's actually eager to move in here. More eager than me at the moment and that makes me nervous."

"Think positive, Jackie. Perhaps she's following your good farm wife example at last and going along to get along, doing what Brandon wants and needs. After all, you and I agreed long ago that the kids' marriage would work just fine because they were both in love with the same person…only we thought that person was Amy. Maybe we were wrong."

"Well, right or wrong, the kids have taken to the plan, and Steve and I can buy the Winnebago to travel the US. I envision my Steve as Steve McQueen in the famous movie motorcycle scene – gone, goodbye, good riddance."

"Jackie, I like you, but you're no Sheryl Crow. See you tomorrow," Fran said in lieu of good-bye to her friend.

Singing made Jackie think of Amy, she of the crackly voice. Jackie wondered if that crackle began because Amy choked on the wedding vows, and renewed her intent to keep on loving Brandon best and most, more than Amy ever could or would. She certainly had more practice, more investment. Maybe Amy would change when she became a mom.

It was so hard, sometimes, to love the heresy of a young woman, not cut of the country cloth, as Jackie's mother would say. Every pore of Amy's face was smothered in make-up, probably even when she slept. With lashes lifting over her eyes like the leggy dancers on TV, you feared that those tentacles could reach out and strangle you if you didn't agree. You wanted to warn her against making wrinkles as she worked a furrow between her brows and sulked her way to success. *Success in a bank that didn't even have seperate bathrooms for female employees before you were born, chickadee* – because there were no female employees yet.

Jackie wished that she had the courage to tell Amy that she'd been an Equal Rights protester – but then she'd have to let on to Steve, who'd been in Vietnam at the time. She'd abandoned the fight when Michigan passed the Equal Rights Amendment and turned to the task of supporting a soldier abroad with care packages and letters scented with Blue Grass perfume.

When Steve came home at the end of the war, Jackie shifted to maintaining that sense of equal rights with him. It was not always easy. Relational landmines delayed having a child, now a grown-up married to a forthright, bold young woman who was the unappreciative benefactor of Jackie's feminist efforts. Jackie grieved sometimes, for her younger self, the one who never got to act on a dream, who never got to be entitled to a past, present, or future of her own. *I live the good old-fashioned way: I earn.*

Five: Amy's Potted Plans

By Monday evening, I had web-searched, verified, savvied, and sourced enough bits to whirl anyone's head. I couldn't believe I was going to be a farmer, but I was, simple as that. I guessed I'd have to buy black jeans, though not brown. I didn't want to look like a turd. I refused to emulate Jackie, Steve, and Brandon in blue.

Just before I placed a meat lovers' pizza on its cardboard platter in front of Brandon, I called to invite the model farm couple - my in-laws - for a Saturday feast featuring Brandon's barbequed ribs and homemade ice cream. The electric ice cream maker I'd just ordered online was being Fed-Exed 2nd day air.

It was a coming out party; my twist-your-arm social graces had tied up the demure daughter-in-law and stuffed her into a closet. Mow-you-down Super Woman had suited up – and homemade ice cream would suit the simple farm folk.

"Not my folks again. I grew up with them. I don't want to see 'em every week. You'd think that we didn't have any other friends," Brandon protested, not looking beyond the game screen. He sounded like a whiny child, not bold like you'd expect from his size. I plowed past his pout with conviction.

"What friends? Besides, entertaining costs money." I pulled his face to mine with both hands, "Focus with me, Brandon." I batted my long eyelashes, slurped the pizza sauce smear from his cheek, and then wiggled my tongue between my lips.

"They have an agenda and we have an agenda, and there's quite a lot to get done," I continued as I went to the counter to retrieve a tabbed file from my briefcase. When I returned, I sat with a leg swung over his, almost knocking the game controller to the floor. I kissed the cheek I'd licked earlier.

"Here, read the pot cookie recipe, and then I'll show you the prices for little cellophane bags and ribbon for packaging our green cookies." I didn't yet know who'd prepare the cute packages. I knew that Brandon's big fingers couldn't finesse it, and I wasn't into tiny tasks; I was into big plans.

Brandon paused his game to take the recipe card as commanded, then looked me in the eye: "Amy, how are we going to get away with this?"

He made direct eye contact since he lost his job, so I knew he was serious.

"Brandon. I've already gotten away with it, with you. You think that your friends and neighbors are going to be more clever than my big, wonderful man?" I said as I wrapped him in a hug. I had to work it since he'd gained weight; the chest that was threatening to become belly.

Brandon held steady, receptive for the information to come. I shifted my weight, motioned him to shove over, so I could settle in beside him.

We seldom shared the IKEA couch because its entire surface seemed to disappear with the bulk of my former football player. I was the quarterback now. Soon I'd have him in my pocket.

"We are going to grow a sativa strain of marijuana. Your folks' third building is perfect as a grow barn: it has a windowless wall exterior and is tucked behind the other buildings. All are painted the same color, so folks' eyes read them as one building. Inside the walls are painted white, white, white, which, as you know, reflects light, so we'll maximize the grow lights. Importantly, it has access to power lines, and the cops don't drive by on any regular basis."

Brandon's thinking was so visible, I anticipated and answered his next question: "Pot's been legal here a year. There are dozens of strains to choose from, but I haven't sourced them all out yet, so don't ask me how much it'll cost. My brother said he'd call to talk it over rather than email once his midterms are over."

"Besides, it doesn't matter because I'm gonna sell your iPad to your folks for our start-up costs."

"Why my iPad, not yours? I've got my games history stored in it." Brandon's jaw clenched like a bear's.

"Because mine has all of my pot research on it, and you know as well as I know that anything can be recovered from a hard drive at anytime by dedicated government hackers. Besides you've got thumbs, Bran."

"Yeah, I got diesel gaming thumbs – oh," he switched gears at my glare, "you meant data storage thumbs. I thought they were only for your work stuff, spreadsheets and all," Brandon's forehead relaxed, his ears lowered, and his shoulders slumped into the couch. I often witnessed this sequence of body actions, showing that processing my speeches gave him whiplash.

"Your data is just game scores. Less likely to draw jail time. Anyways, read the cookie recipe."

Brandon took the 8-½ X 11 sheet I'd just scooped out of the printer tray and began to read aloud, so third grade.

Cripple Chip Cookies (Pot Cookies)
Ingredients:
½ c. pot butter
1 1/3 c. flour
½ t. salt
½ t. baking soda
½ c. brown sugar
¼ c. granulated sugar
1 egg
12 oz. package of chocolate morsel chips

Directions:
Pre-heat oven to 375 degrees. Combine the baking soda, salt and flour. Mix in a large bowl (by hand) the butter, sugars, and egg. Slowly add the flour mixture to the batter mixture and mix well. Stir in the chocolate chips.

Shape the dough into 1-inch balls and place them 2 inches apart on a greased cookie sheet (use the emptied butter wrapper to achieve this easily). Bake for 10-12 minutes or until light brown. Let cool for 3-4 minutes then grub!

"Mmmnn, like my mom's Toll House Cookies - I'm getting hungry already. Pot butter is what it is?"

"Yup. You mix ¾ oz. of marijuana into 5 sticks of melted butter – obviously that makes enough for lots of batches of cookies, enough to package one with each bottle of milk delivered on your dad's route – with an order form for more. And, what's great, too, is that you don't do time if busted with less than an ounce on you."

I could almost smell our future. "Everybody loves milk and cookies", I mimed the Cookie Monster's phrase. Brandon and I had grown up with Sesame Street. Who would have guessed that chocolate chip cookies were more deeply embedded in culture because of a bulky blue creature that didn't even have a nose? We were much like the Cookie Monster at this point, because we didn't have a nose for the scent of pot, either baked or smoked, and had no idea of the complications inherent in the perfect scheme.

I got ready for work the next morning, amazed that Brandon could sleep soundly through the noise of my morning routine, including hair dryer and electric toothbrush. His early shift work prep had always connived its noise into my wee hours of sleep, driving my dream world away. Today my dreams were alive and well, getting more fulfilled with each step.

For breakfast I settled for PB&J toast rather than a Starbucks confection or Krispy Kremes. I'd forced Brandon's concession to sell his iPad to his folks, so I had to add some parity. However, I wasn't going to let go of a double-pump latte on the way into the bank. Balancing a briefcase, Benz keys, and a grande cup accentuated my status, my mystique. No McDonald's coffee for me – yet.

The drive to the bank was smooth as my baby Benz could achieve, unfazed by the constant fall of leaves across its hood. Their contrast to its deep metallic black was artful, expressive. Even Mother Nature looked wealthy swept along with a Benz.

It was Tuesday, the second day of the workweek, so there'd be less wasted time on the trivialities of weekend gossip, one of the workplace rites of Monday. I set my paraphernalia on my desk, a formidable slab of glass atop metal struts, pleased once again that I'd been able to coerce its purchase. The desk strengthened my presence to industrial.

I wasn't hiding one of my *advantages* in the cave of a dark walnut desk, no matter how proud the locals were of the purportedly rare wood. Even when covered in my chestnut brown leather slacks, my legs were of interest to men and envy to women.

The phone rang almost as soon as my booty touched the black leather swivel chair. I slid my elbows into place on its padded arms, ready to fend off whatever, as soon as the receiver reached my ear.

"Dad invited me over to start learning the micro dairy business this week."

"Hi to you, too. So, your dad's call was your alarm clock this morning." I moved the pencil holder to precise placement on the leather desk mat. My name and title plate was awry, so I squared it. Damn the cleaning service!

I selected the tallest pencil and began to doodle on the bank note pad. Bran's conversation often went in circles, and the motion helped me to trace its path, to make sense of his ramblings. He never talked to anyone but me this way. He said I loosened his creative mind. I'd say unhinged, but that would be disrespectful.

Despite my fingers' motion, my mind wandered and I only registered bits of what he said: "Dad said to wear...I'm going over there as soon as I can... He's waiting the route deliveries on me, but wants to leave by 4:00 this afternoon... Then there's the second, night milking – who knew cows worked two shifts a day?"

"Good, hon," I was already thinking that where there's milk, there's butter, so I added it to my tone, "I'm proud and thrilled for you. Weren't you the one who got your dad started with cows?" I smiled with the triumph of my insight and connection.

"Amy, I raised steers in 4-H," Brandon said as I whirled away to turn on the computer. "Cows and steers are not the same."

There was reason to hang up, so I did.

Six: Brandon Boy

Talk with Amy was good; she listened to me like Mom did, to center my mind. I opened the black leather sales binder that she'd gifted from the bank and laid it on the steering wheel as my desk. The lined paper tablet inside was primed for micro dairy information.

I was, too – I loved listening to my dad. I felt like his best little boy again, what he used to call me 'til I was ten. After my growth spurt, I was his best big boy, then his big star man until I got hurt on my honeymoon, spoiling our Minnesota Vikings ambitions. I could have been Brett Favre.

Suddenly a fifth grade poem chanted in my head: "I never saw a purple cow and I never hope to see one; but I can tell you anyhow, I'd rather see one than be one."

Why did such nonsense stay in my mind when I couldn't even remember Amy's or my parents' birthdays? Hell, I tried not to remember mine in most years. It just made me feel glum, and I preferred feeling great.

Which is why I'm hunkered in my truck before I drive over to meet Dad, getting my game face on to become a dairyman. I'm confident in the bucket seat of my F-150, high off the earth in its Super Crew cab.

All windows are clear, not a bug speck now that summer is over. I feel like a part of a diorama, like I saw at the Gettysburg Museum, a stop on the class bus trip to our nation's capitol. I gaze at the winter sun struggling to blast out of clouds brewing over the north woods. Wind's not blowing yet, so I got the moon roof open, arm slung across the back of the seat, seated casual in new jeans and boots. My leather jacket, smooth against leather seats, reminds me of the Michigan cherry jam I slather across peanut butter when I make my own sandwiches just like Mom did. Wish I had me one now.

The dashboard outside temperature gauge tells me that it's 50 degrees. Sirius radio plays any kind of music or comedy I want. I finished being proud to be an

American with Lee Greenwood; next was kick-ass American with Toby Keith.

I'm white, my truck is red, and I was feeling blue until I sang along with them guys. Toby makes more money than Favre, I'd bet. And neither of 'em's got my truck.

My F-150 has a six-and-a-half foot box behind, clad in plastic liner to assure she doesn't get marked by what I toss hard. She even has a trailer sway control with a trailer brake controller because it's fully tricked-out and loaded, the primo model made by Ford. I wonder what I could attach and take with me – maybe the old assistant coach, Victor's mobile home. Wouldn't that be a Halloween hoot!

I laugh at my reflection in the custom side mirrors. I crack myself up – which works because I only see myself these days. I didn't fall in with many plant guys, and town guys kind of drew back with the latest plant lay-off, as if it were a disease one could catch with contact.

I learned that what Lou Holtz said is true, too true, "Never tell your problems to any...20% don't care and the other 80% are glad you have them". He also said, "The man who complains about the way the ball bounces is likely the one who dropped it," and maybe that's me, like Amy says.

My football hero heyday is long gone. I trashed it myself, some say, when I thought I could fly like Superman into the pool. The thick resort logo towel didn't cushion my slam into the pool coping anymore than it held me aloft. My super hero days drowned before I even got to sign the pro contract. Instead of training camp, I got to spend the summer in physical therapy.

My linemen and receivers moved to other states. They don't call, and neither does the cheer squad nor the guys in my frat. The coaching staff has new players to mold into champions. Only Coach Uhrig here in town is a constant.

After every tutoring session, semester after semester in college, Amy used to sum up my progress, laugh, and tell me that Day-Glo glory wasn't something to bank on, so's I ought to put more effort into learning. Now that she's a banker – with a job - I can't disagree.

I never did, so how would I start? Since I lost the job, I just stay in my truck or my online games. I'm whipped, but not into shape. I quit my gym membership as soon as the bankruptcy posted - to save face as well as save money. I'm not good at failure, and here it is, in my lap.

When I wash my truck every Saturday, I can see my reflection in the 20-inch premium six spoke wheels, almost as good as the mirrors. It's all good. I keep a soft cloth and a long-handled car duster under the seat, so's I can fluff and buff my baby after a road trip. Don't need to put as many miles on her now that I'm not driving to Flint. That's what the 36-gallon gas tank was for.

Wonder who Phil is driving with now that I'm gone? Bet he misses Sirius radio, any station you want 24/7.

The electronic six-speed automatic transmission made driving easy, but expensive with the 5.0 V-8. Never tested it, but I believe it's a fact that I could outrun any county mountie if I'd done anything untoward. I may have to do that soon; credit cards are maxed, and the engine doesn't run on air. Amy gave me the money lecture last night. She wondered how I go through a half-tank of gas a week, when I've got nowhere to go.

I finger comb my hair, scratching to re-focus my mind on business, like when I learned the playbook for Coach. I check my look in the side and rearview mirrors, shrug my shoulders, re-group.

Stray, yet pertinent thoughts keep interrupting me: why didn't Mom and Dad just offer to pay off our house? Gallivanting off in a Winnebago would be the same price, I am sure, and then I wouldn't have to milk some damn cows. Somehow I didn't think gray cloddy

boots up to my knees would look as jaunty as Johnny
Depp bein' Captain Jack Sparrow.

And, while Superman wore blue pants, they were
not stone washed jeans. My superhero dreams are sunk.

Seven: Amy's Dinner Plans

Soon it was Saturday, and we two Breeden couples were *dining*: a different moniker for the evening meal had moved to Michigan with me. Dining was civilized, not country. Cuisinart had fresh-churned the ice cream from Breeden Dairy cream. We had topping choices, sort of a make your own sundae a la carte: Michigan cherry jam, Hersey's chocolate syrup, and Chambord Liquor to pour over fresh strawberries, stickered as fresh from California. I left them in the carton, so Jackie and Steve could see that special.

'Two Breeden couples' – ha! We were co-mingling, but not breedening. That sounded too much like a sex den with my in-laws, more than mildly disgusting and against the law. If Bran and I had been breeding, Jackie would have been cheering – on that I could bank.

Speaking of Jackie, I was the solo chicka as I busied myself in the kitchen, rejecting her help, with little time for chitchat and hugs, let alone farm-based banalities and weather. I didn't want Jackie to see me sweat: opening the blue boxes of Mac and Cheese to cook, then fold in Brussels Sprouts roasted in olive oil on the stovetop. Exotica gently stirred into the pot.

Through our window in the kitchen/family room wall, so very local diner, I watched Jackie settle uncertainly on the leather couch Sparty style, scooting around to establish berth. She wasn't used to sitting during meal prep, not even at church suppers, events to which Brandon and I had been ceremoniously paraded. I could see her body tense amidst the predominance of glass and metal in our home-soon-to-not-be-our-home. There were few plastic pose photos and no Wal-Mart flower arrangements.

Brandon and Steve, of course, were instantly at ease, now slouched into our side-by-side La-Z-Boys with the barbequing chore completed. I will not express what came to mind. Farm folk are proud of their work ethic, so the La-Z-Boy is only allowed in local homes because it is a Michigan brand, I'm fairly certain.

I hated those butt-ugly chairs, so heathen to my mid-century style. All man cave in corduroy tan. I used to think that corduroy was Ivy League; another media-swiped notion up-ended and removed from the attic of my childhood's lustful, good life daydreams.

Thank goodness I won the battle of how to paint the walls: our interior was more USC than Michigan State, with maroon accents on soft taupe, not forest green and white. Huge boldly colored canvases, hung unframed, caused visitors to murmur about a museum, instead of a home, which I took as complimentary. Golden sunshine-painted kitchen walls showcased the ebony cabinetry. The appliances were busy, so the bee metaphor worked. We had every modern-themed chandelier that the area stores carried, rheostated to control the mood.

When called to dinner, Jackie lagged behind the hungry lugs – she actually called them that – a half-smile covered with her hand. Her coy manner irritated me, but I counted to ten for my agenda, my purpose, my yen. On paper, this was no longer my house, and we needed to move into hers, so I re-focused on the political, not the personal. A life skill that I can count on – switching gears to sustain focus on the prime objective.

The tabletop was arranged like modern art with a casserole and platter on vibrantly colored hot pads, bookending flowers fresh from Trader Joe's. It may have been obvious that the quartet of cookware had never been used, not even once. I knew that she judged, but these wedding gifts were my trophies, and I was as proud of them as she was of Brandon's football junk: they craved display. The white tablecloth retained its fold lines as a grid for product – I mean food – placement.

The tableau was spartan. Hey, since Michigan State football was our common bond, I was working the metaphors to keep me on track. I typically remained pretty, polite, and seated when with this family, but tonight I had to be proficient at sales.

I had no idea what pot butter looked like at this point, but I knew that butter was how you spread goodwill. I focused on our commonality, not potential criminality. Yes, I had considered that: while medical marijuana was legal in Michigan, it was not nationally. But that was the fine print of my presentation, not to be pointed out.

"Looks like green footballs in Mac and Cheese. What're you mixing with ribs, Girlie?" Steve pronounced while Jackie continued to subrugate judgment with her do-gooder grin.

Steve was perennially dubious about my cooking. Why hadn't I copied Jackie's recipes like Jackie had copied his mother's, he'd once ventured to ask. My cooking adventures were infrequent as well as inadvertent, so why waste time and ink? I suppose it was one of the marriage rites, but I had not grown up on a farm or in Michigan, irritants that surfaced constantly. Shoot me and give up your chances for offspring, Steve.

When I stared a hole in him, Steve clamped his jaw shut as if with orthodontic wire. The man was predictable, steady-Eddy. An inessential jab always fell out in my presence. I don't wonder what a shrink would say about passive-aggressive lips, but what would a counselor say about Steve's reversal to clam-up?

I studied Psychology in college; but with my family background, I didn't have to study much. And, after one semester's contemplation, I didn't want to study more.

"It's a blend of special cheeses for Brandon's favorite, Mac and Cheese. I aim to please my man," I said with a wink at Jackie, all girlfriend style. "The little footballs are Brussel Sprouts, and – I held my hand up Girl Scout style - before you go grousing, they are not food from France."

"We know that Brussels is in Belgium, dear," Jackie said with a look at Steve. He remained mum.

Did I mention that the floral centerpiece was potted mums? Not subliminal.

I forged ahead, allowing everyone to jockey for seat position, standing beside the chair nearest our kitchen. I'd learned this much from regular family suppers at Bran's parents' house: it was the hostess chair. I liked being the hostess because, as you may have surmised, I like being in control. I am an Alpha. I always got an A.

Thank goodness, Brandon didn't belch. Yet. He does that when he's embarrassed, a frat house stunt gone awry. I knew how to soothe Brandon's soul, though I never paved the way with honey like Jackie did his father's, and I'd never finessed people with home cooking before. Not when the bank paid for dining out, and Brandon liked leftovers.

I surprised everyone by offering prayer. I'd printed the Lord's Prayer and recited it from the copy in my apron pocket. Yes, an apron, so very farm wife. I'd officially become a mid-Michigan cliché. The apron was a found object like the dishware, packed carefully in our cupboards, placed there by our bridal party, I suppose.

I idly wondered what happened to those people. One of them was Tessa Breeden, my actual cousin-in-law. I ought to check in with that tortured Rapunzel-trapped teen. There were four people in her family, so there were four kinds of crazy in their house, making it a great place to visit, but I'd only been there once. Apparently they were under quarantine from interaction with Jackie, Steve, and Bran.

Yeah, Psychology mixed with Math. I excelled in college and have carried the skills forward.

Everyone observed the social rule by amply serving him or herself, as if they'd farm labored all day.

Brandon's barbeque stint had been out-of-doors, where winter was gathering its will to deep freeze us thoroughly. His nose had reddened like Rudolph's. It wasn't cold enough for ski masks yet, though gloves had been pulled from the closet. I knew that warming a freezing body burned calories, my only welcome of winter.

Sociality stalled as steady chewing, punctuated by murmurs of "Mmn-n" lofted to the vaulted ceiling. I felt a new feeling: hostess bliss, soon to be parlayed into financial exploit, which I loved better than other members of the party.

I looked around and everyone looked pleasant, so I cut to the chase. While the group gnawed at ribs, I directed my iPad sales pitch to tech-phobic Steve, the entrée being the bold-faced statistic of "More people access the web via mobile devices than from personal computers", including "It has a larger screen than a phone, so the information is easier to see", and ended with "I've already downloaded map and mileage calculators for your travels, standard features of AAA."

Words that Steve understood: AAA, the Automobile Club of America, author of his many maps. Fast-talking sales professional that I was, he kept up. Jackie just kept murmuring "mmn-n", eyeing Steve, her facts vs. fiction barometer.

Brandon huddled with his plate, inhaling a triple portion of ribs, Mac and Cheese, while sidestepping the sprouts as well as our conversation. He was still steamed about his iPad. He'd get over it, and maybe his eyeballs would ease back into their sockets without all that computer eyestrain. *Keep murmuring, "Yum", babe, and you'll get special dessert tonight.*

My audience was sated, primed. I offered coffee with a Cool Whip dessert. With the first genteel bite, I turned heads with the plan of the evening.

"I can engineer an equity line of credit on your farm house. It's long paid-for, total equity, and you two are solid and capable citizens, well known countywide. Interest rates have backed off slightly to 4.6%, and there are no closing costs, no points. The loan term would be 15 years, so it's feasible."

I watched their faces closely. Did their potential mortality unnerve them? Lenders were bent on re-payment. But Jackie and Steve remained impassive and pleasant. I realized that I didn't know how old they were.

Then Steve put down his ribs, sucked at his fingers, and wiped his mouth to ask, "I'm confused. Are we discussing money or sports with those points?"

I don't think I breathed during that entire interlude. There was no threat in his manner, so I proceeded with replenished breath.

"Points are bank fees, but there won't be any, so it's moot. We're discussing money *for* you, not *from* you. I figured about $50,000 for an RV..." Jackie's quick look at Steve told me I was right, "and ran some numbers with a computer model the bank has. I think that a monthly sum from Steve's pension could be auto-deposited into your bank account to cover an RV payment. A tidy in-out package, just like a burger joint - where you can use the ATM card I will issue."

I winced at my analogy because the local burger joint is what I'd thought our kitchen resembled with its pass-through window. But basic foods mediated swallowing novel ideas. I'd watched Steve do it when he fed Sparty worm pills. I'd used the ploy often with farming community bank customers: lunch at the Koffee Kup was cheap per the deal.

Though I'd employed the food gambit, I hoped that Bran wouldn't reboot his appetite. He didn't need to pack on more pounds; we had to move soon. I needed him strong, not inert.

I kid you not: the room went electric. Steve spoke first, "Thanks, Amy. You must be clairvoyant. We went to Travel Land and have a stash of brochures at the house. We hadn't even gotten to financing yet. We haven't had a bank payment since I begged off active farming some years back. Fifteen years is good; I'm heartened that you didn't encumber us with debt after we died. Wouldn't want to burden the grandchildren, would we, Jackie?"

I did not cringe. I did not combat. I did not tell Steve that the owner of Travel Land had already broadcast their looky-looing when he came in to bank the week's proceeds. I was humble. I was pretty, polite, and seated.

I most certainly didn't stumble into discussion about having children or not. This was not a debate. The spotlight was on them, not me; I would not let it re-route today.

Jackie didn't prattle about grandchildren. Her eyes shone like Las Vegas neon. Like deuces, she said, in a casino she wanted to visit on their road trip. She began to burble about beaches, mountains, and discovering herself. I'd never seen her like this, so I spectated like I'd done at Brandon's games. She was childlike, and I almost loved her.

With her last bite, she boogied out of her chair, hefted her plate, and reached for the platter to clear the table, singing something about 'Glory Days'.

I watched Brandon's face crumble, taunted by the words. We'd heard the refrain often on Jackie's lips, but had not drawn inference before. I wanted to hug Bran close, and resolved to fight for him more. He hadn't dealt well with being a forced dairy farmer, and his pay package hadn't been discussed yet in this grand plan. I wished he could be enthused about it, about anything, to join his mother and father's Conga line. But, as I'd often heard Steve say, "If wishes were horses, poor men would ride."

I wished mighty. I wished hard. I maybe even prayed. We needed this plan to work. I needed Brandon whole and hearty once again, like the football hero I'd tutored in college.

Jackie needed to dance, I thought, so I lingered at the table. She needed to look ahead and not behind, especially since the shape of hers was broadening. I hoped that I wasn't doomed to that farmwife fate - and that someday I would have my turn to dance in Las Vegas.

As Jackie and Steve strolled out the door, I heard Steve say, "Well, I'll be darned," as he nuzzled her.

I couldn't hear more because I couldn't go outside to wave them away in farm folk tradition. It was too cold - and I had to intercept Brandon, who was wearing a face of funk as he dragged himself, fork-by-fork, glass-by-glass, from the table to the dishwasher.

But he'd shrugged into his coat and grabbed the steel bristled brush to clean the grill before I could fetch him, fold him into a hug, and bring him on board with sex or reason. That boy was going to pout for a while. He was gonna stew. That boy needed a salary, a self-esteem booster, and/or a kick in the butt.

He needed a life befitting the one-and-only Brandon Breeden. Make the banners, buy the pom-poms, and hire a marching band. My babe was going to rise and shine.

But I had to feed Jackie and Steve slowly, bit-by-bit, bite-by-bite to get the diverse interests aligned... I hadn't figured out the salary angle yet. Hell, I didn't even know the income stream of the micro dairy or expenses, except for poor Brandon's indentured servanthood. I was sure that pot paid, but wasn't sure how much or how fast.

The creditors were already calling me on my smart phone, annoying and indiscreet. I'd taken to leaving the phone on vibrate mode and had missed poor lonesome Brandon a few times. His messages were whiney laments; often about what time would we eat supper. I never returned those babyish calls, didn't want to reinforce the negative. Let him eat pizza or chew his nails. I had too much on my plate.

I opened the dishwasher. I'd heard Brandon punch it on before he stalked outside. I re-arranged everything, and then I added soap. I wished that we could stow all our problems in the dishwasher, cleanse them, and make them right. I washed our long-stemmed crystal wine goblets by hand, slowly like it was the last task I would do on earth, begging their forgiveness for serving cheap Michigan wine.

After I dried and put them away, I looked in all our cupboards, purposefully opening doors in sequence around the wide space, relishing the abundant sparseness, wishing that the cupboards of my life were as bare and unburdened as them. Please, magic dishwasher, wash away our debt.

Then I slammed each cupboard door closed. I was getting too wishy-washy to suit myself. I got out my iPad to plan.

Eight: Magic Carpet Ride

In their ride home, Jackie and Steve talked more about the Winnebago venture. The ATM card that Amy burbled about seemed like another credit card, and Steve was leery of that. They'd just received Master Card.

But to be able to withdraw cash from their bank account for expenses while on the road seemed like…'A magic carpet ride', the song actually playing when he turned on the radio. They loved that song. Surely it was affirmation from God, never mind the drug theme of the song. Hadn't someone famous called religion the opiate of the masses?

Amy had given them her formulations on paper. Jackie retrieved these from her purse when they arrived home and accompanied Steve out for the night milking, since she had no kitchen cleanup chores for a change. She wrote the figures on his big chalkboard, and they talked while the cows delivered the goods. Steve shared that the monthly payment was about one fourth the current income stream of the dairy, so that a pension withdrawal wasn't necessary. Jackie was excited, though she worried about the health insurance. They were at an age where their social life included weekly doctor visits.

Neither of them considered that Brandon would want a salary. Farm work needed doing, not compensation. It was the Lord's work. They all did what needed doing, day and night, year-round. Cows didn't vacation, so how could they – until now. This was a God-blessed opportunity, copacetic and four square; they had earned this trip!

Nine: Amy Gets Coached

I serviced Brandon thoroughly, as local folks say. I went to work on his mental as well as his physical balls, a seamless twenty-four hour loop of responsibility. I could see my effect on his stride as he bounced to the barn, within a day.

In the afterglow, I followed up on the idea that came as I lay back: I could service the loan with a couple of keystrokes. I could even do it remotely, which I couldn't do with Brandon. So I wiggled out from under him as soon as I heard him snore.

I picked my way through our flung away clothing, co-mingled with Brandon's eclectic piles, and found my laptop. I beamed as it booted; how cool that I could accomplish this naked. My perversely stolid bank president would come unhinged, if he knew. No way would he find out: he was not exactly computer capable. Besides, I'd cover better with this loan than I had with our home loan. He was too old a dog to learn new tricks. Especially hacker-type tricks. Sparty could do better than him.

Tap-tap. I upped the size of the Home Equity Line of Credit (HELOC) application to $75,000.00. Brandon deserved a salary of $2,000.00/month. Click.

I went to work on Monday, impertinent as ever, capped and complete. I hadn't let on to my bank president that the $50,000.00 credit line was to finance a get-away vehicle for Jackie and Steve, so it was neither appropriate to share that I'd increased the amount of that HELOC nor that Brandon and I would be running a milk-and-cookie business. I'd taken care of my man and might even toss a dab of dough to the creditors, if they were nice. If they agreed to quit calling my smart phone. It was just too disruptive.

I didn't let on that I'd given the business a name: Milkweed Goods, a pun on nature's weed that meandered along every country fencerow for miles, attracting the beauty of butterflies. Never mind that milkweed was poisonous to some species. Nothing could muck up my plans.

When the bank prez yelled for one of the clerks to fetch his morning coffee and croissant from the Koffee Kup, I volunteered. I needed to walk. The secrets swirling in my head wanted to explode.

"Amy, want me to top off your cup? Again."

I checked the glass carafe that suspended near my jaw. It was orange-handled, so I nodded. "As long as you're pouring decaf, go ahead."

"What about your in-laws?" Sally, the Koffee Kup waitress, said. "Everyone is eating up their new plans for breakfast, lunch, and supper. Opinions all over the map: some say they're crazy, some leave it at foolish. Who'd leave a successful small farm business and a public school job to traipse around the country in a tin can no bigger than Charley's Chips?"

"Have you traveled anywhere, Sally?" I asked to deflect response. I was well schooled as a country banker.

"I been to the Mall of America." I swear Sally stuck out her chin with this assertion. As if that were the best destination on earth. *Is she competing with their proposed trip?* "And, we drove a ways to step our toes in Canada. Didn't see anything different when I looked north, east, south, and west. Same as here, only colder."

"Who'd you go with?"

"My boyfriend, John Ellis. He bought me a white furry coat with real rabbit fur all around the hood. It tickled my face when I looked sideways."

"I've seen you wear the coat," I said kindly.

"Yeah, I still got it, but John's gone. Driving truck for the mines in the Dakotas. He tried to get me to come up there. Said McDonalds paid $18.00 an hour. Can you imagine it?"

"Hi, Amy Breeden, wife of my favorite football player ever." I looked up at the boisterous voice of Coach Uhrig.

"What, no football game to watch on one of the hundreds of Dish channels?" I teased.

"I came with purpose. I'm worried about Brandon," he said, nodding to Sally as she returned with a fresh mug of high-test, which everyone knew Coach ran on. He said it was good for the liver.

"Well, that's a switch," I replied. "Seems most everyone else is worried about his dad. Think he's lost it."

"Brandon's the one that's lost. Kid's got his head up his ass and backwards. He's driving round and round the county roads, washing the road grime off at dusk, then going at it again the next day."

I stared at Coach. "How can you know this, since you are supposed to be working on weekdays?"

"My son, Phil, used to ride share with him over to the plant and back. He has tried to get him out, especially with you playing that Roller Derby every other night."

"Roller Derby?"

"Do I hear an echo? Be a good sport and confess, Amy."

"That's your turf, Coach. Do tell," I said, daring him to continue with a thrust of my jaw. I wondered what he'd do to keep his male upper hand…and it was sort of endearing to hear someone put Brandon foremost. Like Brandon still had a flag to fly, a constituency.

"Football on roller skates. Best female sport going, except for mud wrestling and Hooter waitresses balancing beer on trays," Coach said. "Apparently 'Bad Ass Amy' is the star player of the Bay City Rollers. Best in the league and practicing three nights a week in addition to having a match. Your Benz has been seen skating all over Michigan."

I stared Coach down, gritting my braces-straightened teeth, the ones I suddenly realized I was risking along with my marriage and job, "This may be true, but you better not tell your wife, Maybelline, or the whole county will hear."

Coach just sipped at his cup, so I continued, "Jackie and Steve might pull off their dream trip. Coach, you and I have to make a pact to help Brandon succeed all we can. He could be a big man again."

"Buy me a piece of pie to go with this coffee, and you've got a deal."

I smiled as I got Sally's attention. Coach took care of himself, too, but his esprit d'corps was earned at a lot lower price than mine.

Ten: Lucky

Seven had been Jackie's lucky number since she was seven years old and found a four-leaf clover twined with a three-leaf in Grandma Clayton's front yard. It was the first thing she showed Fran, safe in the pages of Rebecca of Sunnybrook Farm, when they became friends in second grade. Steven, her husband's given name, was spelled similar to the number, she often remarked, so destiny had cast their union.

She knew that seven was Biblical, too, so she was all the more convinced of God-incidence on Wednesday, October 7th, when she overheard a storeroom conversation between Ginny, the kitchen supervisor, and Principal Fran.

"Budget needs cutting, Ginny. Government subsidies of milk and basics have been cut, effective January 1."

"I don't see how we can do it, Principal Fran. We're close to the bone already."

"Well, think on it and call me next week. Something's gotta let up or be given up."

"I'm on it -'cuz I can't let it be me. I got four kids and bills to pay."

Jackie hurried back to scrubbing the big pots used to boil potatoes for the German potato salad she made from her mother's recipe. The wash water had grown cold and gray as the sky outside the window – winter was rushing itself upon them, as it seemed to do every year. She tumbled an idea like the dice in the cup envisioned in her hand in Las Vegas. The road trip was going to happen.

Her van couldn't get her home fast enough, and she rousted Steve from his afternoon nap. She got him on the Internet to research basic school employment law with a promise of cold beer. Google opened a world of information, but reading-and-comprehending the information took brains that were not soused. The information was more germane than a visual tour of the Louvre, finding a recipe for kale, or learning the name of the bird in the tree outside the kitchen window. Besides, Steve had gone through unemployment before. Jackie hadn't bothered her curly head about such details. Unemployment didn't happen to a wife.

Steve got out his yellow pads and sharpened his pencils as if to prepare for a final exam. Jackie tried to view the screen over his head, paced, and then went to fix supper. He was used to budgeting; she just followed his lead.

Jackie bought lined yellow paper pads by the ream at Wal-Mart because Steve was fond of chicken scratches with doodles on the side, which often looked like a casserole for a church basement supper. He was also fond of changing his mind, ripping the paper off and scrunching the paper to toss. He didn't keep the trashcan nearby – heck, sometimes he even moved it to increase the sport.

When Jackie tiptoed in the study to announce supper, the area looked like it was covered in yellow snowballs. "Steve, don't quit your day job; you'll never make the paper basketball team," she said.

Jackie scooped up a scrunched paper ball - and hit the trash so easily that Steve retrieved the trashcan from the downstairs bath to set up a quick game. With a wood floor seam as free throw line, they tossed away, not caring that the casserole was getting colder. Their road trip was getting warmer, and that was a higher goal.

Steve served up a better meal than Jackie did that night, at least as food for thought. The news was better than the butter on biscuits avoided on doctor's insistence.

"Jackie, looks like you can draw about $350.00/month unemployment for twenty-six weeks, like what steadied us before I got the dairy business going…"

Jackie interjected, "Seems kind of funny that I'm hoping to lose the job that Fran helped me get."

"I know, it's not usually the way we rock-and-roll. But, Jackie, I feel like I've earned being on the dole. It's our turn to receive, to have and partake."

"My gosh, I'm going to be trailer trash!" Jackie said with eyes that invited Steve's eyebrows to dance. Their free-spirited association swelled past supper; they were feeding on their dreams. So Jackie covered the casserole and stashed it in the fridge, to be warmed for another day. There was always another day. There was always appetite in human life.

When she returned to the table, Jackie scooted her chair beside Steve so that she could read his tablet figures. She followed his pencil point to the circled HELOC payment: $385.06, which had the same numbers as her monthly unemployment check, though differently ordered and not a seven in sight. There'd be expenses for food, gas, and incidentals, but they figured that they had the biscuits and the butter, so the jelly would be found. Pastor Rankin constantly assured his congregation that the Lord provided. If the lilies of the field need not worry, neither did they. The money afforded travel from Michigan winter into early summer splendor - not splendor in dollars and cents, but in nature to be adored, principles esteemed by all farmers and their wives.

Steve recalled a newspaper article in the morning paper and retrieved it from the avalanche of scrunched paper in the trash. Written in the dire verbiage of a hard-scrapping reporter trying to make his name by scaring local yokels, it related that Michigan had historical double-digit unemployment, among the highest in a troubled nation. The reporter hinted that unemployment benefits were in jeopardy. Jackie looked at Steve, who said, "Best take them while they're hot."

And we're not. Winter could be brutal in mid-Michigan. At the very least, it was boring. Jackie wearied of air freshener that barely concealed the stale air of rooms that must have felt as cooped-up as she did – and winter hadn't even formally appeared on the calendar.

Even as she thought it, Jackie could feel her nose tickle. She reached into the pocket of her apron to retrieve a slightly used tissue, wondering why she hadn't tossed it in the trash to win the free throw game. When her fingers brushed against her phone, an impulse overcame her sneeze.

With only a nod to Steve, she made an appointment with Fran for the next day. This wasn't an untoward move among longtime friends, especially ones who'd learned iPhone settings together, including its calendar.

Jackie wore a dress to the meeting. Fran's eyes narrowed, as she instantly knew something was up. She'd seen that dress in flashes before-and-after the choir robe was on. It was the dress of Christmas, Mother's Day, and Easter.

"I've been watching the news and hearing a little school gossip lately," Jackie began.

Fran smiled benignly, hands folded in her lap. She'd heard a little community talk herself. Jackie was one of her most reliable sources. Anything could be whispered pseudo-sneeze into a choir robe sleeve when searching for a Kleenex – tidbits, tidy tidbits to inform, to run a school like a factory assembly line.

"I was wondering if the nation's financial crisis had impacted our school system yet?" Jackie asked lightly.

"Not impacted in specific, but the superintendent has alerted us to seek ways to trim expenses."

Fran watched Jackie labor to keep herself settled, subtle-voiced, the opposite of the suggestive, arm-twisting verbalization that Maybelline adopted with beauty shop clientele. "I was wondering if staff was on the chopping block, to use kitchen metaphor. I was wondering if someone were to volunteer for a lay-off..."

While Jackie paused to clear her throat, Fran had what she called a locksmith moment: her mind opened like a safe in a spurt of cognition, because she read Jackie's intent to mutual advantage. This talent was terrific ammunition against wayward teens, helicopter parents, and teachers in salary negotiations.

"Jackie," Fran began and then leaned forward as co-conspirator, "people who are fired receive unemployment benefits. These include cash for awhile, as well as health insurance benefits for eighteen months under COBRA. The district also pays out for unused sick days. Are those helpful details?"

Jackie swept her arms wide as she popped up with a smile. Fran was reminded of Mickey and his Mouseketeers that they'd watched together after school, only a year before it went off the air. Jackie practically jumped over the desk to hug Fran; she of the bad knees who'd made Fran order thickly cushioned pads for the path she had to walk in the school kitchen. She didn't even wait for specifics, just asked when she could sign the paperwork, then fished her phone from her purse, to call Steve.

Jackie had just helped Fran solve an economic situation and, though Fran didn't know all of it yet, she'd solved several of Jackie's. Reciprocal relationships were best. Fran's secretary's hassles were just beginning – and she would pay Fran back with heavy grousing as she pulled the forms from the district HR department in haste.

Eighteen months of COBRA insurance reinforced twenty-six weeks of cash...that could be extended with Fran's signature. It was enough time to explore and circumnavigate the globe, so Fran wasn't surprised when Jackie perked back into the office and said, "Yes!"

Jackie signed the paperwork on Friday, and she and Steve were back to Winnebago shopping, kicking big-ass tires, that night. It was not a spontaneous buy – purchases with that many zeros took time; Steve and Jackie took twenty-four hours per zero. Their favorite Winnebago had a complete cozy kitchen, Ultra Queen mattress, automatic transmission, pushbutton stabilizers, and was clad in pine forest green and white – Spartan colors, of course. *Go, Spartans! Go Us: buy, then bye-bye!*

Eleven: Are You Ready for Some Football?

Brandon and Steve got through a week of dairying and delivering without accident or incident, thriving as they always did, in convivial silence with occasional grunts and pantomime, gifted athletes of space management. The shiny aluminum vats filled and flowed with product, and flicking switches and watching gauges was about as manual as the labor got – except for the hard scrubbing and cleansing required by the law of the license.

Not so repetitive as the assembly line, perhaps this work would be okay, Brandon remarked to his mom. Jackie smiled. She'd already witnessed, in head turns and other gestures that Brandon thought more nobly of his dad and being a dairyman, especially when they got out to their customers, his extended family of kin who remembered his football prowess and forgot his screwball pranks.

Jackie wondered if Brandon would have the milk delivery truck re-painted red and fit with premium wheels when he took over the business. He'd also probably have that Blue Tooth thing installed so that he could call his dad at every turn in the road.

Maybe he was a child of his time. All youth seemed to be perennially plugged in, if allowed, messaging as total existence with twitter on the show side.

But Jackie wondered about Brandon's sense of self. He'd always been golden, so well physically balanced, and still was, but he appeared to be 'with phone' 24/7 - like some women Jackie had known who craved being 'with child'. Brandon listened intently to anyone, anything, anywhere – who knew, perhaps he called China to talk to another gamer. It was as if without that prop, his head would fall off. Perhaps he missed a helmet, protection, a barrier between himself and reality. Perhaps it enhanced his ego, to appear larger than life, like he once had, in full uniform.

When the iPhone wasn't near his ear, it was between his thumbs, gaming now that his iPad was gone. At least he didn't twiddle his thumbs in empty space like Amy did. Jackie, and most of her generation, disdained both actions – they weren't producing anything. God blessed people with opposable thumbs to hold onto life and to earn their keep. The Garden of Eden was gone.

Perhaps without the phone, Brandon wasn't certain he was alive. Football had been a career not readily replaced, not even with a college degree. Fran often remarked, though it had yet to seconded, that Brandon was all esteem and expectations - with no earn.

On Saturday the kids came over to watch the Michigan State-Michigan game, televised via satellite. Jackie didn't like football now that Brandon was no longer playing, but this was an important rivalry - *like Amy and I have, and she's soon going to be mistress of my house.* Jackie's realization panicked her, so the invitation multi-tasked, befitting a woman. The Sunday supper ritual had failed to transform the kids into churchgoers, so a Saturday routine might suffice. Her intent was to try to familiarize Amy with the contents of the kitchen and the cleaning supplies.

Jackie decided to make popcorn snacks since the cash renter had just dropped off another 20-lb. bag of prime popping corn, skimmed from his contract with Orville R. Though their pantry had three bags full, she'd smiled graciously and allowed the man to haul his gift in. It was fluffy edibles, so easy to grab and gulp.

Huge bowlfuls were gone by half time.

"Amy, you'd do an old woman a favor if you'd go to the pantry to pull out one of the heavy bags of popcorn," Jackie said moments before halftime. She craved watching the marching band in the few moments before the commentator babble began. She didn't want to miss a glimpse of spangle or bugle shine nor the cadence of the drums. She'd strutted and twirled back in high school, sending the baton as high as the store fronts on Main for the 4th of July parade.

Amy popped up from the fringed floor pillows, managing to not tangle her toes in the process. She slipped into her Uggs and went to the pantry, posing as dutiful daughter-in-law.

She paused just inside the pantry, reaching for the doorjambs to steady herself as she processed what she saw: four large bags of popcorn - in huge clear plastic barrier bags. She didn't know these delectable items existed. They were the size and weight of the cast-off turkey package she'd wanted to retrieve from the trash of the Summit Supper. She smiled as she massaged the heavy weight plastic between her index finger and thumb, and then measured them with her forearm, which she knew to be ten inches long. Her research indicated that the thicker plastic bags would be perfect for keeping the bugs out and the smell in for storing their weed. Oh my, oh my, indeed. Her plans just seemed to get more fluid all the time.

The couch scrunched as Steve shifted his weight and said, "Jackie, don't you go putting silly corn syrup over my popcorn."

Before Jackie could counter, an idea popped in Amy's head, complete with a cartoon light bulb. She leaned out from the pantry to share: "My mom made popcorn balls for trick-or-treaters before crazies ruined the holiday by putting razors in apples."

She watched Jackie's face bloom as Jackie declared that she'd done the same thing for Brandon and his friends. Pitch perfect, Amy thought, and I can't even sing! *But I can lie like a dog.*

Sorry, Sparty. Where was that dog anyway? Not allowed to watch the big game. Maybe he scarfed up too much popcorn and got banished to the barn.

Amy lugged a bag from the pantry and tugged it open. Energized despite the tough hauling, she began to hum as Jackie entered the kitchen, sounding like an old record that had endured a few parties.

Buttering up relationship, Amy helped to deliver the popcorn to the men in big bowls and worked alongside

Jackie with the corn syrup and candy thermometer. She wasn't much of a football fan either.

She complimented the granite counter tops, how they were perfect for candy making like at the mall's Rocky Mountain Store. She babbled about this and that, trying to gain conversational foothold with a woman she'd not wanted to know before. Who knew that plastic bags would be a commonality? *Maybe we'll even discuss Tupperware.*

When the game ended in an overtime win for Michigan State, the ladies had rows of popcorn balls for Halloween, lined up on the granite counter like miniature horizontal snowmen. *I rolled my own; I am on a roll,* each woman thought, though with different meanings assigned.

Amy and Jackie had made treats for the little ghosts and goblins, both in wonder that she'd not felt twitchy or witchy in the proximity. They had dipped their hands in the same bowls, touching at times. They had even chatted about mall shopping, which neither of them did, and cracked a few blonde jokes at Amy's behest. It wasn't a blast, but it was passable.

And, Amy considered adding *pot*corn balls to form a menu of edible snacks to partner with delivered milk.

After Michigan State defeated Michigan, Jackie was *into* football again, acting as if she'd invented the sport, referencing Brandon's glory days for one and all. At work she became an outlandish cheerleader, boldly inserting herself into conversation with the kids that slid past her counter in tandem with their trays. They were fans, but only of their high school team; they saw Brandon's jersey framed high above the basketball goal in the gym, but claimed allegiance to current heroes. He was history.

Even school staff members began to roll their eyes at Jackie's overly animated game renditions. Fran had a private conversation with Jackie - the operative word was overbearing – and she stashed her gusto in fluffy mashed potatoes and creamier gravies.

The couple began to invite friends and church folk to watch the games on their Dish TV, to not be too fully entwined with Bran and Amy, Jackie wanting to leave well enough alone. Everyone knew that the Breeden home had the largest big screen TV and a Surround Sound system; knew from their kids who'd gathered there in Brandon's hey day if not invited there themselves.

Jackie delighted in making snacks. She shuddered at the whack of the tackles, like they resounded inside her, so she needed the intermittent pop into the kitchen, like a grade schooler needed recess. Too much reality and reminder of her body's aches, especially the knees, though most of their guests – read male guests - loved the smacking as well as the snacking. The players were so *in your face*, the men identified. They secretly placed one of their daily life antagonists into the body of a felled player on the field. *Take that, boss!*

At every choir practice Fran reminded Jackie not to yell herself hoarse because she had a Sunday duty; Pastor Rankin counted on their songs to persuade church attendees to throw lots of cash as the collection plates passed, to enact God's glory days.

The next few Michigan State football games seesawed between win and loss, hope ripened by a surprise smash of Purdue on October 24. Jackie dressed in team colors almost daily; easily accomplished because of the fan wear amassed when Brandon was on campus. Green suited her, the Spartan version a bit deeper than her emerald eyes for a swell effect, Steve said.

For Halloween she dressed as a player, wearing one of Brandon's football jerseys with popcorn-filled Baggies as shoulder pads, cheerily handing out popcorn balls to the few who came down their lane to trick-or-treat. Their wiggles and fidgets for candy and possible recognition buoyed Jackie because *her* team had lost to Minnesota that day.

Still she was glum on Sunday, November 1, as she sang in full voice. She barely heard a word of Pastor Rankin's sermon, which was about forgiveness.

Colored pins sprouted on the map on the laundry room wall as fast as weeds in a flowerbed, as Jackie and Steve marked places of interest, but neither made any perceptible effort to finalize their travel plans. Amy and Brandon's move-in was imminent, but Jackie's mind was not yet in that game. She'd never been good at details; that was Steve's role, but he was not steering their road trip, either. Football was immediate gratification, delayed difficult discussions, and kept their eyes on a different clock than the countdown to Amy and Brandon being ousted from their home.

Jackie now knew what Steve had long known: during football season there was always good news, and this season was superbly better than other sectors of their lives. Within a week Michigan State got a bid to go to the Alamo Bowl, to be played in San Antonio. *Sunny San Antone.*

A flurry of phone calls brought the bowl bid celebration to Michigan State Mecca, the Breeden house. Folks brought beer and pizzas and snacks of every crunch, color, and texture; chatter and music rocked the house. Oldies, but goodies, just like Jackie, Steve, and their friends.

Everyone was having the best time of their lives, or so they believed in the moment, but Jackie was thinking more: soon they'd be on the road, missing their friends big time. This night needed a special memory, some flair beyond the usual for this small town crowd. But what?

Jackie found herself in the pantry, scrounging among the ample supply of snacks that she'd grabbed off Kroger shelves; there was nothing here that wasn't on the table and kitchen counter. Except... She was suddenly snagging the Zip-lock bag from the back of the topmost shelf, pulling out the medical marijuana she'd secured to ease the pain of Steve's knees. She hadn't mentioned her own knee pain to the special doctor with the pot dispensary two counties over, knowing that a stand-by-your-man approach would play better to get a letter of recommendation that masqueraded as a prescription to obey the law. That was the best way to get things done and, besides, she was a public school employee. Steve was a deacon of their church, more shielded as God's direct servant, and in greater knee and back pain due to assembly line, dairy farming, and soldiering tours of duty.

Their crowd got enthused when Jackie began to make her signature brownies. Now the celebration got sweet! None knew the secret ingredient; it was Jackie's party experiment.

Her nose reacted at the uncommon scent, but because Steve spent all day in a barn, some of it shoveling cow manure, his mudroom clothing negated any telltale odor for their guests. Still, she baked cinnamon buns for anyone who might be on the couch, chairs, and floor for early breakfast, just in case.

As the brownies disappeared, ideas proliferated, and the path of the road trip altered with schemes and dreams accelerating in a giant Tilt-a-Whirl – or maybe it was the room that was tilting. The Winnebago road trip was headed toward San Antonio to see the Alamo Bowl where the Michigan State Spartans would tackle the Red Raiders of Texas Tech, the team colors' combo of green and red worthy of skipping the post-Christmas sales head their travels that way.

The game was to be played on the evening of January 2, 2010. In synch with New Year's resolutions, stagnant farm life would be transformed when Jackie and Steve scored tickets in the alumni lottery @ $55.00 each. It didn't matter where they sat in the stands; they would be on the road trip! *Drop kick me, Jesus, through the goalposts of life!*

Twelve: Heaven Sent

The next morning, after the party stragglers left, Jackie went out to visit the new Winnebago parked behind their small barn garage. It was a crisp November morning, alive with marvel despite the mild headache that she was dosing with coffee and Advil. Saturday had its own rhythm, so there was time for her somewhat eccentric-in-winter scurry in green housecoat and scuffs – and space, too, because the nearest neighbors were miles away. She walked the perimeter of the vehicle as she sipped her coffee and, by the time she'd circled back to the entry, her headache was gone. She smiled and opened the door to climb into the sanctuary of escape.

She set down her coffee cup and ran her hands over the abbreviated kitchen counter, feeling impending adjustment to the smaller Formica expanse. She'd gotten used to cutting directly on the granite in the refurbished kitchen, hard like the Colorado Rockies that she'd soon see, *where it was likely from. Sure hope Amy appreciates what she's been given.*

She stepped toward the bedroom with its queen-sized bed clothed in Spartan green and checked her look in the bathroom mirror, readily accomplished without moving a foot from the passageway. Her mouth opened, awed: this was not the same person in the bathroom mirror in her house a few moments ago. Had she discovered the fountain of youth?

Jackie ran back into their home, soon to be unsubtly sublet to Brandon and Amy, her knees barely creaking as she sped up the stairs to the bathroom, the same bathroom that she'd used for thirty-four years, the same mirror she'd looked into as she splayed dark curls laced with gray over her cowlick earlier - and Jackie saw, truly saw, the crone that she had become.

After church the next morning Jackie wondered anew how everyone seemed to know the details of their purchase, while Steve was practically handing out cigars. Community closeness had a bright side and a dark side, and sometimes Jackie couldn't discern remarkable difference.

Such as now. The pastor caressed Jackie's back in his 'I'm going to convince you' gesture, herding her to his side. Steve was already enfolded on the other.

"Would you two have a moment to join me for coffee?"

Jackie looked at Steve too late to kibitz before he nodded his head. They followed the pastor to his office.

Pastor Rankin was a man of hubris and joy. He readily clapped people on the back, just as he clapped for them in plain view, a consummate appreciator. The coffee was perked and ready. Jackie hoped it wasn't burned, for she hated that flavor and smell. His secretary, Bonnie made the daily coffee, because Pastor was known to always botch it, unlike his sermons. Steve surprised her by agreeing to a cup. The pastor knew Jackie liked hers black.

"I hear you've lost a job, Jackie, and that the school district's loss is your travel gain. You'll be celebrating Christmas here, then New Year's on the road to San Antone."

"Wow, you've got it all wrapped up in holiday paper, Pastor," Jackie said. "Are you gonna tie a bow on it with prayer?"

"The Lord's work is woven with many angels' voices, my friend. And sometimes the voice is an alto."

Ah, Principal Fran had pushed their road trip plans into the realm of the closely-knit farming community, where it had likely been abundantly embellished by Maybelline, then salt-and-peppered by Sally at the Koffee Kup. But, coming from their Pastor, the revelation seemed more mystic than gossip. Jackie felt her skin tighten and loosen in all the right places, for a lighter version of herself. Pastor Rankin sat down at his broad oak desk laden with Post-it notes, motioning piously for the couple to sit on his blue silk loveseat. The congregation knew that Widow Braghorn donated all the furniture except for the Pastor's ergonomic desk chair.

As usual, Steve was silent, sipping coffee as subterfuge, a man who habitually held his cards close to his vest, er, farm coveralls. He waited, in his way, for the Pastor's cards to be on the table. Pastor Rankin was known to keep one up his sleeve.

"I was wondering if you might do the congregation a favor." Jackie's and Steve's silent smiles were a half version of his gleeful look. *Wait for it...*

"Widow Braghorn is feeling unfulfilled because her husband longed to be put to rest in Colorado, blown in the winds off the Rockies. Big Bob Braghorn was a cowboy before he returned here to his father's farm, married her, and natural gas was discovered on the property. Until now she has disregarded his wishes, keeping his ashes in the coffee bin, waiting to bury him with her in her casket. She'd thought it was a good idea because she switched from coffee to tea when Big died and it, well, the empty blue pottery container had a nice lid that sealed tight and all."

"But she's afraid she's gonna open the wrong container some morning when she's not quite awake and brew up her dear departed." Steve glowered at me, in a face that telegraphed his discomfort. *Too much information!* "I was wondering if you'd take his ashes to Colorado for her?"

Steve almost spurted out coffee when he blurted "What?"

"The widow will donate money to re-furbish all the stained glass windows of the church if this good deed can be accomplished," Pastor Rankin continued, smiling with eyebrows arched, much like the church's windows that were about to be re-furbished, directing their wills to a yes. "Shall we pray together?"

While their heads were bowed, Jackie nudged her elbow into Steve's side, their signal of two nudges to mean *yes* long established from dealing with Brandon and his antics.

And so it came to pass, that the road trip became a quest of higher calling beyond their personal mission. Further, they garnered the additional blessing of tax benefits, which Pastor Rankin said was 14 cents/mile for charitable service *or* 24 cents/mile when moving. Most certainly, Jackie and Steve were moving Big's ashes to a proper resting state, so they took their write-off pick.

Gas at $3.00/gallon, when the Winnebago was projected to get 6-10 miles to the gallon, seemed affordable with this purpose. Prayers they hadn't even uttered had been answered. Where there's a will, God has a way. Amen.

Thirteen: Amy's Re-Arrangements

Amy here. Thank goodness I am in my big office chair behind my big desk in my big bank office – because I am feeling small. Not a familiar or desired feeling, if any feeling was. Huffing and puffing and floundering aren't familiar territory for me.

I whisked a pencil from the stash on my massive office desk and hovered its eraser above the columns of numbers, on the pretense that I could sweep it like a magic wand across the spreadsheet on my computer screen. *Budgeting was for shit!* Now I understood my boss' public mourn for paper documents. Erasers worked on paper.

Paper could be crumpled and crushed into a tight ball, then tossed in the trash, creating visceral release when amnesia wasn't a problem-solving option. My mind clouded to match what looked like turbulent weather outside, and I slammed the pencil to the desk like thunder. When my eyes hit the calendar on the wall, I vented my rage on it, ripping October's page off, smooshing and stomping it before depositing it in the trash, wishing fervently that it would morph into hundred dollar bills, newly minted and ready to pay off our debt.

It was November, with the ticking clock lurking like Captain Hook's alligator in the deep water we were under. I knew how to swim, but not this hard, this fast, and in this many directions. Which hole in the dike should I plug first? Brandon and I had to give up our house in sixty days exact. I did not like it. I did not like it one bit. But, wait, as the infomercials said, there's more.

I'd so carefully projected that Brandon and I would be able keep my Benz and his feisty red F-150 – but our vehicle bling dreams were dying on the page of black and white numbers bleeding red. I sat back in my chair, crooked my arms akimbo, looked at the screen and then away fast. As my eyes shifted down to my keyboard, I flashed on blood dripping to splash my finger tips; then realized the vision was my red polished nails. Crazed visions from possible mental illness - which I feared as much as poverty - flash flooded again.

There's so much water in here, I might as well tear up, I thought abjectly. *But, I will not cry. I will not.*

I bit my knuckles, and then tumbled my thumbs, rolling those red fingernails into a Ferris Wheel mirage, to avoid looking at the glum winter scene outside. When my eyes drifted back to the window, the tiny tears that had trembled inside my lower lids had vanished. I smiled weakly: the big white flakes scattering against barren black trees weren't all bad. They obliterated any sign of red: no cardinals, dirt-hazed red vehicles or pedestrians bundled in red coats or boots. Along with concealing other colors that only spring would reveal and not soon enough to suit. Spring brought hope. I spurned hope. It seemed to walk on helpless legs. Wishes were for victims and sissies; I made plans.

As the snow followed the whimsy of the winds, refusing to settle anywhere just yet, I took it as a good omen. I hoped – *shit, self betrayed* - that the snow didn't become piles because I had not yet searched out my winter boots or gloves with hats that matched. Hats smashed hair, and gloves hid polish. There was no spirit in flat hair and naked nails – ugh!

Uggs! I despised *weather*. I longed instantly to talk with my brother, Andy, in California. He'd called when his midterms were over, reopening the wound of distance. Text messaging didn't warm my spirit like Andy's voice did; days, weeks, or months that had slipped away due to personal busy-ness evaporated. Our bond was primal: we'd kept each other intact through a childhood dominated by Mother's schizophrenia.

I slammed my mind's door, as I always did, to glance off the topic of Mother, to not let her creep in. Just as I looked forward to Andy's intermittent phoning, I feared the inevitable call informing me that my homeless mother had been found dead. When would it come – and from where; the last fact I knew was that she was in Santa Monica, California, where sunshine and welfare were always in season.

The arc of my arm as I pulled out my cell swept my mind clear with the efficiency of my Mercedes' wiper blades. I didn't feel like a misguided flake anymore. It was Brandon on speed dial, not my idyllic brother, because he could partner to enact the solution I had in mind.

"Hon, did your mom and dad buy their RV yet?"

"Yeah, it's tucked behind the garage." Sparty the dog wagging his tail when Bran talked like this.

"That was fast. You sure? I just finalized the Home Equity Line Of Credit."

"Dad and I delivered the milk in it this morning. It's just an oversized van. Mom is comfortable from the inside out; her test drive's only glitch was when Dad had to wrench the wheel over to guide it down the middle of the street in town. Some long-armed, naked tree branches raked the top of the rig, made a big racket, Dad said."

"Hmmm-m. I wonder how they are going to get around and explore at Disneyland, Vegas, or wherever. They don't just plan to highball it on the interstates, do they?"

"Dad's talking about a Segway." Jackie's phrase, almost uttered in pride, flashed a neon scroll line across my nails: *The only difference between men and boys was the price of their toys.*

"Bran! Your parents can barely handle a bicycle on a gravel road!"

"So, what's better – walkin?"

"Your truck is one of Detroit's finest and would be able to haul an RV."

"Amy, don't go there. I love my truck. No way!"

"I know, but your parents are going to leave a van and a truck behind when they go on their trip. My lease'll end soon and, if your parents took over the payments on your truck, we could drive their vehicles and focus on paying off our credit cards. The start-up numbers on the supplies to grow weed are huge, especially the high wattage grow bulbs. Halide bulbs are $2000.00 a pop. I'll show you the spreadsheet tonight, Bran honey."

I hung up so I wouldn't hear the whining. Hadn't he learned in sports to suck it up?

I was relieved that everything was rolling along as planned. I felt as productive as the auto plant assembly line that Brandon used to brag about. Jackie and Steve intrigued me when they indicated that no pension withdrawal was necessary for the Winnebago payments as they signed up for the Home Equity Line Of Credit (HELOC). The Fifth Wheel cost was less than the full size Winnebago... It wasn't my math to do, so I didn't.

I smiled through Steve's declaration that the micro-dairy income would cover all financial needs, including a salary for Brandon, pleased at the consideration. The amount was low, sort of like an allowance, but I maintained my daughter-in-law persona of *pretty, polite, and seated*, with no comment.

I was a step ahead. The Ford F-150 payment would fit somewhere in the budget; it had to because I'd switched the auto payment from Breeden to Breeden account. I kept myself on mute: pretty, polite, and seated - in the power chair.

The HELOC was already secretly set at $75,000.00, so Milkweed Goods was going to happen. I could not, would not reveal my business plans. Brandon didn't feel insulted now with his salaried position, and he would feel elated with the money that Milkweed Goods made. I reveled in my projections – along with a hope that Brandon might be a grown-up man at last rather than the perennially incubated version of his dad. *I mean, a plan not a hope.*

I knew I could yell, push, and gouge all I wanted in just a few hours, when I was suited up as Bad-Ass Amy, jamming for the Bay City Rollers, a premier roller derby team. My cousin-in-law, Tricky Tessa, had enticed me to the team. Tessa was a tiny-shorts version of Medusa, even in a ladybug-like helmet. We sizzled together – *sometimes more than I sizzle with Bran.*

Bay City was some 80 miles away. I'd drive very carefully in the mounting snow. I have considered the bruises to body, as well as reputation, if a bank VP was discovered under the crash helmet and multiple body part pads of a Roller Derby babe. The risks make play more delicious, I have to admit.

I enjoy the bully of the sport with its violent bursts of energy and crowd rage echoing about the arena, my outlet for unfinancial feelings. There will be blood on my fingers tonight. Real blood; facts not metaphors. Econ trumped English once more, like it had back in college when I decided my major was money. Money talked louder than text.

Fourteen: Truckin'

Steve heard Jackie's swift inhale, simultaneous to his jaw drop, at Amy's logic for trading trucks. He realized that, in his road-trip-addled hurly burly, he'd forgotten details like their van and truck left in the garage. Now a pull-behind would be their home-away-from-home. They hadn't even departed, and plans had already re-routed.

When he and Jackie returned to the lot to explore vehicle options, the Travel Land salesman didn't argue at the exchange, not with so many unsold vehicles in his inventory. Thank goodness it hadn't rained or snowed, so there was no weather scum to remove. *Thank goodness no one checked the top for possible tree branch scratches.*

Steve had been uncomfortable with the unseemly customer bait and switch, but the art and grace of the deal was settled just like most things in a small community: with a handshake and a strong belief in the parity of God's will.

Thanks goodness the salesman went to the same church.

There was no mention of truck payments. Used to cash, Steve didn't even consider this fact, nor did Brandon, he with the money-grows-on-trees mindset.

Not until Steve and Brandon drove the truck for the Winnebago Fifth Wheel mount did Brandon's payments get mentioned. Steve's ashen face in his rearview mirror said it all. Now there might be pension withdrawals because he knew he did not have extra money stashed under the mattress – nor did it grow on trees. Money had to be made – as in earned, not plucked or printed.

He considered purchasing a lottery ticket for a minute, but just one. He remembered that the new RV cost $15,000.00 less than the full HELOC amount. Everything was copacetic, on track. *Ha-ha, on truck.*

Steve tempered his fervor for the bold, shiny truck for Brandon's sake and promised to take great care of the vehicle. He invited Brandon to share in a primo wax job that could be accomplished during a workday since the machines did most of the dairying. They both considered this a proper send-off for its road trip.

It took about five leisurely hours, with a six-pack – just to relax their arms and wet their whistle, of course – for the men to wash and wax the beloved vehicle.

Jackie stopped her chores now and then to watch her men, not knowing whether to cheer or cry. While she had complained that the truck color was arrest-me-red, she was delighted to trade the $50,000 vehicle behind their garage for a $35,000 Winnebago Fifth Wheel with a cute name like Sunnybrook, just like a favorite book of her childhood. Besides being less of a drag on expenses, the vehicle literature promised it was less of a drag to pull. Out West there were mountains.

Steve began selecting the musical sound track for the trip, while watching Brandon for signs of remorse or regret as they got together to milk, bottle, and deliver. There were none, but Bran only grunted at the play list suggested. Online games were his passion, so Steve feigned interest, trying to feel connected. Football was a long-standing shared enthusiasm, so he relied on that, using sports analogies as he taught the micro dairy business to his son. Steve smiled when Brandon said he sounded like Coach.

And Amy remained apart, aloof and self-contained behind her enormous desk. She smiled because she was a part – though no one appreciated as fully as she – of a higher plan. She was considering everyone's interests, especially A Me.

Fifteen: Thanks Giving

The Thanksgiving holiday arrived, that uniquely American extravaganza of food consumption. The Breeden couples were becoming four peas in a pod, two of them into pot, though together they knew it not.

The two men were either unwilling or unwitting, which was typical in everyone's experience. On this fine day, the smell of secrets permeated the household as strongly as the turkey and fixings. Invitation of a widow, a principal, and a pastor added spices to the feast.

Jackie didn't care if the grouping invited congregation gossip about her intent to pair any guests as odd couple or otherwise. She knew who her friends were and who *they* were not. She'd hated *they*, that nameless, amorphous mass of rancor and recrimination, since she was a teen. This pet peeve was one of the primary bonds between her, Pastor Rankin, and Principal Fran in the small farm community, though the secretaries didn't share the sentiment. They delved into the feast of human foibles with gusto.

Another bond was the love of vocabulary used well. Nature deserved delicious description. The trio's shared gambit was applying old adages and uncommon verbs to the twists and turns of small town behaviors. Without judgment, for that was God's domain.

The Widow was a new presence in Jackie's sphere, so she vowed to mind her tongue, as well as her manners, and to not be cowed by misperception. That lady even wore pearls with her pajamas, *they* said.

While Jackie had pet peeves, she had some definite preferences, too. For example, she loved to use her mother's china, silver, and linens. She retrieved the pale lavender tablecloth from the cupboard, mashed under other cloths, napkins, and placemats because it hadn't covered the table in years, a sort of figurative time-out. Lavender was her dear mother's favorite color and plant. Jackie layered her yard with it.

Jackie noted that a few worn spots punctuated the

tablecloth's thinness as she lovingly smoothed it into place. Since it had traveled across the Alleghenies in a Conestoga wagon, she reckoned the cloth had earned those worn spots, fortunate to survive Indian arrows, creek stone washing, and Brandon's carelessness with ketchup.

Jackie continued to layer the table, covering the worn patches and stains with lace-edged placements. Her mother's china pattern gleamed in its framing, and the silver shone with the patina of hundreds of hours spent polishing. To the place settings, she added candlelight in single silver sticks, though Steve always nerved up at the potential of flame. When he attempted protest on his pass through the room to lay the newspaper crossword puzzle by the club chairs, she shushed him, stating her need to romance her home like he was romancing the road trip ahead. Between the candles she placed an arrangement of mums from the plants that flanked the doors outside. As she stepped back to look, her mind flashed on the tomb of the Unknown in Washington, D.C., and she murmured a quick prayer of thanks for Steve's return from Vietnam.

It was only a month until she shed her homemaker aprons, so this was Jackie's festive last supper. Because of its fragility, the lavender tablecloth retained its wrinkles and folds today. *Like me.* There'd been no farmwife chores like re-arranging vehicles from field to field for some time, but thousands of clothes had been washed and hung on a line. It was time to be done with homemaker monotony – though I will launder my mother's cloth with care before it's laid on top of the stash in the cupboard. *Should I put a lock on it or trust Amy and Brandon with my treasures?*

Fussing on this scale was infrequent, special. She and Steve would be gone indefinitely, so she'd decided to savor each homemaking ritual in this last month. Today's feast seemed reverent, church in a box of china. Say amen and pass the biscuits.

Seven is Biblical, Jackie mused as she scanned her

seated guests, and here we are. She reached for Steve's hand, glowing when he clasped hers on cue before the group bowed their heads.

Steve had barely said "Amen" before Jackie bobbed up to say, "Let's sanctify our trip by showing our guests our maps."

"Please, Mrs. Breeden," Pastor Rankin said. Jackie blinked at Amy, who blinked just as fast in Morse Code-like manner: *Oh, no, more prayer* - when Pastor Rankin raised his arms to heaven to dramatize his protest. "We'd love to see your trip maps, but can your husband carve the turkey first?"

"Yes, Jackie, let's savor the turkey and all its fixings. If you bring out my maps now, we men folk might use them as extra napkins." Steve grinned as he included himself in the teasing.

"Or we'd get *my* iPad screen greasy, don't you mean, Dad?" Brandon interjected. "Didn't you use my iPad that Amy made me sell you?"

Steve looked at Brandon briefly, and then turned back to the table topic. That boy was holding a lot of hurt.

"Today is Thanks-for-giving-to-us Day.*"* Steve declared with the set jaw that defied disagreement. And, no one was going to call him wrong because he had a carving knife in one hand and a pitchfork-like utensil in the other.

"Steve, you remind me of Grant Wood's painting," Fran said. "I used to pretend I was studying it while I was sitting study hall."

"Me, too!" Jackie said.

"Where was Dad? In detention?" Brandon interjected.

Steve kept his head down, into his task. He was not a dangerous man, with or without his knife. Unflappable as ever, despite Brandon's tweaking.

"Don't bother your dad," said Pastor Rankin. "Don't want him to carve up his only tie, do you?"

Now Steve smirked. He had to, because it was God's

truth that it was his only tie. He hadn't turned it around like a ball cap on a rapper, to avoid splattering it while carving. Jackie gaped in surprise because it was a ritual.

Everyone was surprised when, after the turkey was ceremoniously carved and plated, he held the tie out in front of him and sawed it off. Six mouths dropped open in unison.

"What an emphatic signal that you are cutting your ties," Pastor Rankin said, and everyone howled.

Silence settled the gathering as each garnered a heaping plate of feast and put their forks and knives to use. Dishes were passed fluidly whenever there was empty space on a plate, in response to a mere raise of an eyebrow. Eating was an act of graceful synchronicity that day. There was peace for twenty minutes: a meal as meditation.

Pastor pushed back from the table, unsnapped his collar, and gave voice to the shared perspective: "Now we know how the turkey felt several hours ago, folks, stuffed and well basted. Only we get a nap, less permanent than the turkey's sleep status."

Everyone chuckled. The Pastor's jocular lines and easy conversational tempo, though sometimes irreverent, could add spark or sobriety, as needed, on any occasion. He was blessed with an uncommon ability to gain a sense of a group, of a whole room, knowing when to lift or lower the tone. He was a great guest.

Pastor Rankin looked as if he'd like to loosen his belt. Instead, he moved his hands up to snap his collar back in place, and then open his arms in an air hug.

"You may have wondered why I requested this little assemblage," Pastor said as Steve opened his mouth, "but, as you recall, we have a blessing to perform today."

He nodded toward the widow who went to fetch the over-large purse that she'd carefully propped in one of the club chairs, almost as if it were going to watch TV. *Had she stashed the ashes in her purse?*

"First, I want to give blessing to Jackie and Steve's road trip and to Amy and Brandon's move-in to work the dairy. You do have me on the top of the home delivery list, don't you, Brandon?"

Brandon bobbed his head before he said: "Check. Can we hurry this to watch football?"

Thankfully no one remarked, or noticed when Brandon winced. Amy must've kicked his shin with her pointy-toed boot.

The Widow Braghorn appeared at Pastor's elbow, but held the blue container behind her back. Jackie looked around the table. She wasn't the only one squeamish at a stash of ashes so near the table. The meal was over, but everyone knew that the leftovers were the best. Wouldn't want to contaminate the next days' snacks.

As always, Jackie and Fran were quickly sympatico. Steve was on a similar trajectory. He suggested that the ceremony be performed in front of the TV, though his agenda differed: he wanted to move on to football, like Brandon.

The transfer of Big Braghorn's canister to Jackie and Steve's RV, coupled with prayers for safe travel and the dairy business, was simple and spiced with humor, as per the Pastor's sumptuously human style.

It was also brief. Pastor Rankin touted Franklin Delano Roosevelt's famous public speaking advice: "be sincere, be brief, and be seated."

Amy sneezed – or chuckled. No one was certain. Steve hugged the square blue vessel with "Coffee & Tea" scripted on one side, as if to assure that the ashes wouldn't spew. Widow Braghorn's tape job to affix the top looked as unsophisticated as a kindergartener's might. Pastor Rankin made the cross sign over the canister, and everyone relaxed.

Jackie ended the ceremony by extending her hand. Steve gladly gave up the canister to one more familiar, yet hoped Jackie wouldn't absent-mindedly stash the canister in the pantry. He made a mental note to check in the morning – or maybe volunteer to make the coffee.

Guest farewells began as the TV-hyped Detroit Lions game. Pastor was known to drink a few during sports, assuring that he'd snore through at least part of the game, no matter how exciting the play. Amy and Brandon did not want to witness and neither did the Widow. Besides, the Widow said, now that Big was gone, she wasn't much a fan of anything, except reading God's Word. Pastor Rankin blessed her for that as well as the check that she handed him.

Fran wasn't a football fan, but lingered to assist in the kitchen. She seated herself on the plaid couch after Jackie said, "No help necessary; go hunker and holler!"

Jackie had pledged allegiance to Michigan State solely, so she'd clean up alone, lovingly cleaning the china and silverware and soaking the stained linens before dumping them in the wash. Hands busy/mind freed, she was mulling over the Widow's whispered confession that her husband had been neither big nor horny "for at least forty years," an empty man full only of himself, so that the small canister suited him just fine.

I would never say that about Steve, my stable, equable man. He reminds me of my dad, a cross-generational comfort.

Jackie loaded the dishwasher with great care, mostly pots, pans, and glassware, noting that the number of dirty dessert plates – someone had skipped pumpkin pie? - matched the weeks until their departure. She relished compulsive little counting games like that. She'd noted that Amy did, too, when they'd made popcorn balls together. Though an odd commonality; *at least we have more in common than wresting control over Brandon.*

Jackie fetched Sparty from the barn, tail wagging in time with her quick strides through the snow, into the kitchen to lick a plate laden with table scraps. Never mind that it was her mother's china and that Sparty's vet would fret at feeding the dog table scraps. Sparty's tail wags disclosed that he loved the furnace warmth and the food.

His tail reminded Jackie of the pendulum swing of her Grandfather clock, with its pride of place in the den. She merely imagined a ticking sound, she knew, because the clock's pendulum moved soundlessly, steadily, inevitable as their impending trip, with its tandem turn over of their home and business.

She'd accomplished the clean up by halftime, wishing there were bands, like at collegiate games, to reward her efforts. Tupperware containers of leftovers stacked the fridge shelves. She was trying out the new wares she'd purchased for the road trip, in this year's festive colors. Pastor Rankin took a few leftovers with him when he left at that juncture, begging off to work on his sermon. Jackie hoped she got the containers back in time, but what could one say to one's Pastor?

Fran exited with him, but declined turkey leftovers. As Jackie watched the swing of their walks and brief chat before climbing in their separate cars, she pondered the feasibility of a principal dating a pastor. She'd leave that topic in the Lord's hands, though she considered a nudge to Fran. The two friends needed to pow-wow about the road trip anyway.

When Jackie returned from hugging her guests out the door, Steve was pulling at the turkey carcass. He'd been doing so throughout the game, sometimes joined by Pastor Rankin, both savoring every edible bite. It was a typical male version of helping clean up, like *jackals ravaging a carcass on the savannah*, Jackie imagined. The image she'd seen on the Nature channel wasn't consistent with central Michigan manners. She had a mind to say something.

Jackie saved herself from the precipice of spite; she felt grumpiness' shift into sleepiness and scuttled out of the kitchen. The ottoman had strayed from the club chair so she had to tug it close to prop up her feet. *Why was that failed Turkish Empire used to name this plump, round footrest?* She'd Google that later. Now, she needed to rest her spirit, aching feet, and back. Her emotions were building up while her body was winding down.

She picked up the small devotional and began to read, soon snoring with peace. Reverence was compelling after good wifely entertaining exhausted one.

A half-hour later she turned on the computer. Her positive attitude replenished, she prepared a Christmas letter for their friends and family with a photo of their Sunnybrook as masthead. She didn't write about Brandon's job loss – that was his news to share - or the blue cremation canister, which was now safely in the back of her pantry beside the stash of weed. Steve's grin-and-bear attitude had pulled him through to accept the road trip responsibility that had initially creeped him out. He'd even joked about the ash stash – after Widow Braghorn and Pastor Rankin left – but none of that was fodder for the letter:

Dear Ones,

How are you? As snow whitens the Michigan landscape, we are pleased to share the joys of the season and the news that Steve and I intend to travel around the USA in the coming year. We are heading first to the Alamo Bowl in San Antonio, Texas. Go, Spartans!

Right after we unwrap our Christmas gifts, Steve will be wrapping his arms around the wheel of our new Winnebago, hauled behind a bright red truck, sort of like Rudolph's nose lighting our way. Brandon will be taking over the micro-dairy business, so we traded trucks for our lengthy adventure trip. Amy's still careering at the bank, so no grandkids yet. Brandon and Amy will watch our house, too, taking care of Sparty.

*Perhaps you would like a visit in 2010! We'll be taking a computer on the road, so you can email us at **Breedenbreeze@gmail.com**. We may just park in your driveway for a night or two if you live out West. If you live in the East, well maybe the next year. Let us hear* *from you!*

Blessings to you and your kin with prayers for safe travels hoped for in return.

Jackie and Steve Breeden

She considered emailing this greeting, knowing she should, to get rapid responses for formulating their trip plans, but union loyalty ran deep, and she just couldn't stiff the postal workers. Besides she'd devoted time to cutting-and-pasting the Sunnybrook brochure picture onto the letter. It was simple to make 100 copies onto the holiday paper frames she'd gotten on sale at Wal-Mart. *Waste not, want not*, her mother's voice said in her head, as she performed the task on the small desktop copier.

On Friday morning she switched to cocoa instead of morning coffee, part of her post-Thanksgiving Christmas letter ritual. She signed, and then stuffed the letters into envelopes, alternating hot cocoa sips with licks to seal them tight, pausing to kiss the envelopes of people she particularly loved. Tiny tears simmered in her eyes now and then. She hoped that she'd meet-up with some of these friends during their road trip to make up for folks she was leaving behind.

The Christmas letter ritual took up most of Friday, in part because she kept up the pretense of individual notes by hand-addressing every envelope. She interspersed rapid stabs at household chores, like dusting table tops, after realigning their clutter into artful color splashes of daily living, then sweeping the floors all around. When Steve came in for lunch, they, of course, savored the leftovers.

The next day she would drop the Christmas letters at the post office though it wasn't open on Saturday morning. She wouldn't head to the mall, never did, not enlivened by the crush of the crowds or the rush of nabbing great deals. She and Steve and Brandon and Amy had already exchanged gifts: the truck for a truck, the opportunity to make money for the opportunity to spend it.

Sixteen: Things are being Mapped

As Jackie walked into the kitchen, carrying packages of hamburger from their garage freezer, Brandon and his father sat together at the kitchen table, across from each other like the old days, elbows bent and fists at their temples to prop up their brains. They were studying the US map as if it were the Constitution. The map still showed its fresh pressed folds, so crisp that a dry cleaner might have been the manufacturer.

In fact, the US map was printed in Taiwan, imported in the belly of a giant container ship, and then trucked across America to their local AAA outpost. At least the longshoremen and truck drivers were union and American. *What kind of future did my son's generation have when even a map of our country was manufactured elsewhere?*

Brandon was garbed in football jersey as always, hair unruly. He grinned, lifting his recently pervasive gloom to reveal his central tooth chip, the ruination of years of orthodontia that he called his anti-trophy, refusing its repair. He looked hungry, expectant of breakfast between dairying and mapping chores. Expectant of payment for his geography expertise, too. Today's kids were neither easy nor free, they with their entitlements.

Thank goodness Jackie had used the final four eggs to make a monster omelet, hastily pulling a second plate and popping more wheat bread in the toaster.

"Guys, I'm on my way to lunch with Principal Fran. Listen for the toaster pop and serve yourselves. I trust you to divide the omelet appropriately, and you know where the glasses and silverware are. We've got milk - I'll be checking for mustaches when I return."

Neither man looked up from the map, so Jackie pecked each on his ears, and moved to the Amana refrigerator. As she put the hamburger in its small freezer compartment, she retrieved some individually frozen sausage patties, calling, "Jimmy Dean's here if you want to heat him up."

She declined to sit and get hooked into the geography lessons. Steve had her list of preferred sites; let the menfolk fly their pencils and their mouths. She bustled upstairs to shower and ready for lunch at the Koffee Kup with Fran.

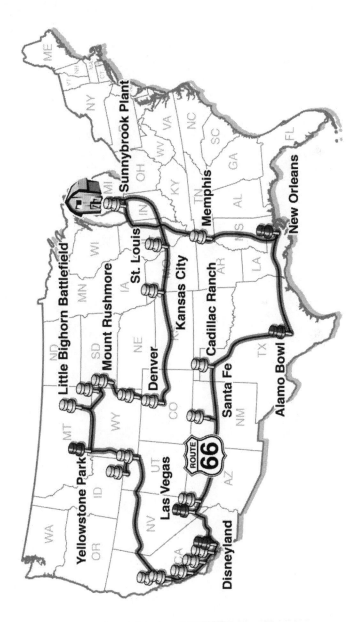

Satisfied with their endeavor, Steve and Brandon ambled to the garage, without coats and hats, to grab Dilly Bars from the freezer. They hadn't bothered with frying the sausages, and half an omelet didn't fill the bill.

Never mind about winter; they needed a cold treat, but couldn't pop a beer. Milking duties would be on deck soon.

Seventeen: Amy Sets Another Course

Brandon had left the house early as usual. I wasn't used to the twice-daily schedule demanded of a dairy apprentice. Didn't he get Saturdays off to spend time with me? I was getting lonesome, my euphemism for horny.

I called Andy in Chico, only able to leave a message, trying not to sound needy. He was probably out playing soccer in the sun. I wished I were there with him.

Then, I thought of Jackie, who I hadn't seen since turkey day. Odd, I sort of missed her. I longed to regenerate the closeness that we'd felt while we made popcorn balls last month – it wasn't in evidence during Thanksgiving. Perhaps Jackie was too distracted by that freaky ashes ceremony or the many chores of the feast. I tried to assist in the prep, again making Mrs. Molden's potatoes and mounding the biscuit basket, but Bran and I had skipped clean up, preferring to watch football on our super-sized TV minus the soundtrack of Pastor Rankin's famously brazen snore.

So the limbo feeling remained, seesawing with anxiety. I was doing my best to cope. Losing our home had hobbled my ego, and I was more than equivocal about living in the Breeden farmhouse. It was dreary white, inside and out, and had no sense of style. It blended with the winter scenery that I hated most. What if the old farmhouse wasn't well insulated, and we froze to death this winter?

I could navigate the big kitchen's cupboards and their contents – and I certainly remembered the pantry – pleased that Jackie had commented on my memorization skills. I was uninterested in cooking or appliances, but what could she do? Brandon wasn't starving; his paunch was highly evident. His side view looked like a Boyne Mountain slope, snow-covered when he wore his Spartan's white jersey, grassy when he wore the green.

Besides, I applied myself to making money at a real

job, not some old glorified 4-H hobby. My hobby was a different 4-H: head, heart, hands, and hash.

I knew how to read the instruction books stashed in a drawer near the stove, and pizzas got delivered, even way out here. There was more than enough milk in the barn. Best of all, Brandon's favorite food was Mac and Cheese, the blue box gourmet kind.

I couldn't square the vague sense of unease. Jackie wasn't having second thoughts, was she? The deadline for our move-out-in was looming, and I was feeling loss, needy of family now that my in-laws wouldn't be around - a surprise to my assured, self-contained self. *I've heard that absence makes the heart grow fonder, but they are not even gone.* I'd gotten used to my brother being far away and not having a clue where my mother was, but the Breedens had always been here, taken for granted, I guess.

I often wished that Steve was my dad: a brave, noble six-foot with dark eyes, hair, and mustache. His eyes had a glint in them, as if he was in on every cosmic joke. His hair had a glint, too - of white, airbrushed into the temples as if he were a Hollywood action star.

My unspoken wish intrigued me, a master of intrigue, since I'd not even known I had a father until junior high sex ed. Steve was a mellow, unperturbed man, someone that any person would want in her life. Maybe I married Brandon to get a dad, his dad.

But Jackie, Jackie was a challenge, a competitor for Brandon's soul. Psychology 101 had not prepared me for her, nor had Shakespearean plays.

I hadn't realized that my hands were folded prayer-like, with thumbs were atwirl until one scuffed my index finger, triggering an idea: I was VP of the bank, I had an Economics degree, therefore I could help Jackie and Steve budget for their trip. I knew when and where I was needed.

I got them an ATM card for on-the-road expenses and planned to show them how to use it to access their bank account, so it seemed right to add another banker favor to the cache of encouragement. I wasn't pushing them on the road, I was expediting. As usual, I had plans.

I grabbed my iPad…thought better of it because of its pot research, recalling that Steve had a desktop for the dairy business, and that Jackie regularly emailed her friends. Jackie knew how to turn the computer on, even if she'd never used Excel. I'd often heard Jackie say that she could only be competent in one room at a time, with a giggled, sidelong look at Steve. I wondered if Jackie would welcome being competent in more than one computer program, which were like rooms unto themselves.

It would be good to give the Benz another drive. I so dreaded giving it up, my precision German armor. Insult to injury of the loss of our trophy home. I couldn't pacify with new clothes because our cards were maxed out, but I wouldn't burrow into gaming, Brandon's drug of choice.

"Why Amy, hi! I didn't expect you!" Jackie said as she opened the door. "You didn't have to knock. This will be your humble abode soon. Did you come for more house-keeping lessons?"

"No, I actually came to offer my budgetary know-how, to help you prepare for your trip."

Jackie cocked her head to one side and said, "Nice coat. Let me hang it in the closet for you, rather than drape it over a chair back. We're going to be sitting a spell, if the women are going to do men's work."

"Men's work? Jackie, I am a banker, this is my forte."

"Well, Steve's done all of our budgeting for years."

"He's welcome to join us, if you wish," I ventured.

"He's out with Brandon delivering the milk, so I guess it won't hurt if we started. He and Brandon worked real hard while I was at lunch, planning the route of our trip. See that map pile over there? Move it over. Drop your purse anywhere you think will support it. Doesn't your shoulder hurt from carrying that big thing?"

Before I could speak, Jackie continued, "You always look like you could use a good meal, Amy. Want me to make you a sandwich or wanna snack on the box I brought back from lunch?" Jackie said with a kind face. That woman couldn't have a mean bone in her body; I imagined her as able to walk the clothesline outside as her Jesus walked on water.

"How about we snack at the computer, Jackie? I'm used to it," I said to her quizzical look, "I eat at my desk at work."

"Well, then," she said as she plunked the styrofoam box on the desk and pulled the ottoman over to sit beside me. Before she sat down, she dashed to the kitchen for a fork and napkin. I swear she would have tucked it in the neck of my blouse if I'd let her.

I turned the computer on, and as the screen came alive, I opened the box to half of Mae Kettle's club sandwich, a special of the Koffee Kup. Mmm-n. I clicked on the keys.

Jackie warmed to the task of budgeting for the trip. She was certain that Steve would be pleased with our contribution to get the show on the road; for some reason he hadn't gotten around to it yet.

A round tuit. Jackie shared the Breeden joke, looking shocked between her snickers, that I had never heard it mentioned in this house, the house that soon would become my home.

We got busy brainstorming a list of trip essentials and then dollar-signed numbers for each category based on the financial records that Steve had filed on the computer or scrawled on scraps of paper. We had debits, and we had credits, including Jackie's unemployment, a monthly draw from the business, and their savings. Jackie felt a little uncomfortable at my deft finger invasion of their financial privacy, but I calmed her with a reminder of how proud Steve would be. She marveled at how words and numbers could be moved with highlights, clicks, and drags. She felt like she was watching a magic act, she said.

Jackie gasped at the amount of Brandon's truck

payment, but kept quiet, patient, and seated. I recalled that she had been a daughter-in-law, too. She leaned in as I finalized a list:

1. Home equity payment
2. Truck payment
3. Cell phone and Internet fees
4. COBRA insurance payment
5. Truck and trailer insurance
6. Gas
7. Food and Supplies
8. National Park and Campground fees
9. Dish TV
10. Medicine

Number 10 had been a ginger topic, I noticed. I tried to be empathetic, silent. After all, I'd managed Mother's medicines from the time I was ten, the expenses as well as the pill shoving.

A click of a key added the figures. Jackie's chipper attitude evaporated, perhaps as stunned by the monthly amount as I was. She was unlike the confident farm homemaker she'd been as long as I'd been in the family, now a frozen dairy queen. I started to make a teasing remark, but changed my mind. I watched her get up and pace the family room, then return to the desk, her face ashen as its wood.

Perhaps there is a hook to grasp – like that topknot curl of a Dairy Queen cone: "Jackie, I have a confession to make."

I paused to make sure that Jackie's attention was with me, for I wanted to conduct this business in whisper: "I do Roller Derby. Do you know what that is?" I waited until Jackie nodded, to know she was alive behind those spacey eyes, "I practice on Thursdays, with a match every Friday night. Tessa's on the team. This fall we placed first in the mid-state league."

"Do you have a trophy?" Jackie's mind grasped what she could relate to, for all of Brandon's athletic trophies were still enshrined on shelves around the rec room.

"Not yet. What do you think Brandon will say when I bring it home and place it on a shelf among his trophies when we live here?" I said in a convivial tone borrowed from eavesdropping the koffee klatch at the bank.

"You haven't told him?" Jackie said, shifting in her chair. The wood joints of the chair squeaked. The clock chimed the time, its reverberation compounding the hollow feel in our stomachs. Though we'd each eaten half of the same sandwich, we'd also swallowed the same unpalatable spreadsheet.

"Nope. He was morose about the job loss and obsessed with online gaming. I just had to get out. I needed to yell and scream, and it didn't seem the time to smash plates when we had all that debt." I paused at Jackie's strained laughter, then explained: "I used to roller skate when I was a kid. Tessa mailed me a flyer."

Now Jackie's laughter stopped. The question was in her eyes: *Tessa?*

I continued, "When I found out the team colors were my favorite, cinnamon, I tried out on a whim, and re-discovered my finesse on wheels. Meeting up with wild-maned Tessa was a weekly bonus this fall."

"Jackie, I was coming over to tell you all this after we won the league championship earlier this month. It was late at night, and there was music loudly reverberating the front window. I stopped."

"The drapes were wide open. The sight of you and your friends lolling on the furniture, pointlessly energetic, giggling at the air instead of at each other, no TV sitcom on, stunned me…and I saw a Solo Cup held sideways to a guy's mouth. He held it there for a long time, and then passed it to the guy beside him, who did the same." Amy continued, lowering her voice again, "It was not Santa's pipe they were smoking. Jackie, do you and Steve do weed?"

Within minutes Jackie and I morphed our revealed secrets into plan B, for Business. Money was needed and any method was warranted to make it. Jackie, the churchly farm wife with scruples, had reservations, saying, "Is this truly legal? Sure hope there's never a warrant out on us."

"A doctor wouldn't give you a prescription if it wasn't," I stated emphatically. The subject didn't go any further. For each of us, I think, it felt good to be in cahoots with an accomplice, so we buried our edgy relationship for expediency's sake.

Later in the week, when Jackie visited the pot dispensary to buy an on-the-road supply, she committed several ounces of low-grade marijuana to making the initial batch of cookies for the Milkweed Goods enterprise, a sort of down payment for what was sure to be a lucrative, debt-solving solution.

Though our plan hatching may seem hasty, I had studied. I was quick. It was clear to me, the financial and pot farm expert, that the teeny portion of Jackie's stash was necessary because it could be three months until harvest of the two dozen plants, soon to be ordered online and ensconced in black plastic pots in the small barn's grow room. Brandon had been composting the cow manure to enrich the grow process, but every online site confirmed the time line. Nature was not quick.

With more time for curing beyond that, it unfolded that crop readiness would coincide with the arrival of spring. A grand metaphor was clear, but I didn't befuddle Jackie with such nuanced detail. She just knew that their road trip dream needed more cash, and that we'd cooked up a simple deal to get some. We were on a 'need to know' basis, as they say in spy movies.

And, Steve definitely did *not* need to know, she said.

Jackie brainstormed a bit, after recalling how Steve ate cookies from the small plate Brandon set out for Santa until he was eight. Since Christmas was approaching, she suggested a little pre-season sampler of Milkweed Good product, a pot cookie bagged with each quart of milk delivered.

I gaped at my straight-laced, pious mother-in-law –

who had conceived the bodacious promotional idea - and envisioned a surge of post-Christmas orders after mommies and daddies got happier! They'd get by with a little help from their friends, Amy and Jackie.

Profit potential was also looking up because Jackie shared her recipe for her new Breeden Brownies, which I figured could be sold for $10.00 each. To further our business communion, I shared my potcorn ball idea. Jackie immediately suggested researching recipes online – and, thus, we discovered the Stoner's Cookbook. We almost fell off our perches in laughter and delight.

Sure hope Steve didn't check his search engine's history.

Eighteen: Bad-Ass Amy and Wackie Jackie

Principal Fran looked up, startled at Jackie's bustling, intrusive entry. She was in the midst of a difficult phone call, grateful that she held the receiver to her ear rather than using the speaker feature. Fran's secretary appeared in the doorway, clutching at Jackie's apron, which was laden with pea soup blotches. No question what lunch was today.

"Fran, why not?" Jackie said, playing tug-of-war with the other corner of her apron, as well as with her facial expression.

Fran modulated her voice and continued her phone call, "Mr. Edwards, an emergency seems to have arrived at my desk. I assure you that I will give your concerns great weight and speak with Coach Uhrig about the matter as soon as possible." Fran held the phone a few more seconds, inching it away from her ear and into its cradle amidst the clutter of a busy principal's desk.

"Helen, it's okay. I'm sure our cook only needs a moment of my time," Fran accompanied her 'back to your desk' tone of voice with the movements of a traffic cop. Helen harrumphed, a staple of secretarial repartee, and bustled back to stand guard at her desk. Fran fervently hoped that seven other emergencies would emerge to keep the woman from listening at the door.

"Now, Jackie, what not why not?" Fran said as she reached her arms across the desk to air hug her best friend.

"I'd just finished serving the seniors, the motley crew, and needed a break from standing. So, I walked down to the teacher's lounge - you know I seldom go there – and I walked in on several teachers grousing about all the extra practicing for the Christmas Pageant and why were we having it when the Jews were complaining about equal time and the kids hadn't learned their math facts all the way through…"

Fran was reminded of the famous Clarence Darrow

tactic of letting the ashes extend as he smoked his cigar throughout his opposing attorney's remarks; she was distracted by the fact that her friend Jackie, the well-trained singer, had not paused to replenish her breath until now... She'd never witnessed a Jackie like this one. Not her cool-headed confidante and cohort in problem solving, the mediator of people and all things mid-Michigan.

"And gas prices were going up, so why were Steve and I gallivanting off in a Winnebago when their husbands were losing their jobs and kids needed gifts, and the children in Africa are starving," and now Jackie looked Fran in the eye, "so they decided not to have a 'fare-thee-well' party for me."

Fran was astonished. She prided herself on knowing just about everything that was everything, at the school and in town. "I'm sorry, Jackie. I've been busy, too, and I guess I counted our Thanksgiving feast as farewell. You know I'm not good at good-byes."

Jackie smiled wanly and listened as Fran continued with excuses. The fact was that the staff was fussed about many things and there was no mood for a party. Jackie was beloved for her food and would be missed, but the football and road trip fervor had grated nerves aplenty. There's a time and season for everything, the Bible stated, but this was not Jackie's time.

Then Helen knocked and stuck her head in the office, insistent that several school crises required Principal Fran. Fran dismissed her friend with a hug, promising a call later.

Jackie hung up her apron, not bothering to unload the industrial-sized dishwashers of the pea soup-making bowls, pots, and utensils. Let the student helpers take care of the trays. Let them earn Santa's bounty this year. Bah Humbug and Holy Crap! Jackie went home in a hissy fit of hurt.

When she got there, she slammed her keys on the granite counter, rather than depositing them in her purse. She tucked the stray curls behind her ears and began to pace her home. She needed to vent. She knew the Pastor would proclamate prayer – and Bonnie would echo his sentiments: it was only a farewell party, after all, and not her funeral.

She couldn't trust her views with Maybelline, who would put it all on loudspeaker for everyone in town, especially with her beauty shop jammed with pre-holiday hair appointments. Jackie's mind was aflame and didn't need Maybelline's lighter fluid personality to spread fiery havoc throughout town. Jackie knew that their trip was already the talk of the Koffee Kup Kafe.

Her van had practically driven itself home, like a dog returning to its doghouse. Steve and Brandon were in the midst of the milk route, so who was she gonna call: the Ghostbusters? Jackie put the keys in her purse as her mind collected itself and, in almost the same movement, she scooped out her iPhone.

"Amy, you are not gonna believe it!" Jackie overlaid tears of frustration with a gush of words. "Principal Fran says there can't be a farewell party for me because the whole school staff's just too involved in the holiday program."

"I overheard staff members in the lounge, grumbling that they just can't make time for it, for me. They're upset with me! With the economy downturn they are all traveling farther to Wal-Mart and Dollar General Store, trying to find bargains to be able to have a Christmas, and the price of gas is going up... They're jealous of our trip. There's not gonna be a Goodbye-and-God-bless-you party. Those snarky snits!"

Jackie didn't allow Amy time to say sorry – *as if Amy would* - she was barreling ahead. The drive home was a hot one, melting the snow off the van from the inside out. Jackie didn't want *sorry* anyway; she wanted restitution.

"Amy, I've been a cook most of my life. And, my momma honed a habit in me of moving from worry-to-do pretty quick. So," Jackie paused for effect, "I have a plan."

Amy must have put her phone on speaker and

grabbed some pencils for her desktop stash because Jackie heard a circus drum roll after she said Amy's magic word, "Plan." Amy rat-a-tatted pencil erasers as fast as she twirled her thumbs. Jackie savored the build-up and took a deep breath to tell Amy the rest, the best, the *piece de resistance*: Jackie's big-finish, fast-track restitution.

"I have access to a huge kitchen with a super-size mixer, oven, and counter space worthy of a fundraising project. Amy, we're gonna make the weed cookies in the school kitchen!"

After a shocked silence, Amy finished her drum roll with an "All right!" as cymbal crash.

Jackie hung up, shoved her phone in her purse, and headed to Wal-Mart with the ingredient list. She'd pick up a roasted chicken for supper. It was all good.

The deed took two nights, under cover of winter's deep and early darkness. Jackie contemplated the death of innocence, plus the void of nature the season represented, hoping that God didn't withdraw His grace from her, like she always imagined He'd done to winter.

It was easy to slip away while Steve and Brandon were engrossed in the evening chores. Milking demanded ritualistic thoroughness, and sometimes the men extended the evening with jokes and a celebratory beer – or one of the frozen treats stashed in the dairy barn fridge.

Jackie drove to pick up Amy with the Wal-Mart bags of baking supplies still stashed in the van. She'd not taken them into the house – even butter kept in the temperatures they were having daily. She had the needed ingredient, the weed, a large pot, and utensils. Her clothes were blackout, which wasn't easy for her, the Spartan fan, but Amy suggested the movie-themed tactic.

As if the duo needed more drama.

Amy emerged from her house as Jackie parked. She seemed to be at the van in three leaps, so long were her legs, wearing a jacket that shadowed her face with a hood like the grim reaper. Jackie looked at her own black slacks, which were dressy as a man's tuxedo, while Amy's looked like stretch pants for yoga or skiing. She wondered if Amy and Brandon skied, which she knew was an expensive sport, then re-focused on the here and now.

"Amy, what the hell are you doing out here? Aren't we going to make the pot butter? I brought my vacuum sealer so the house wouldn't smell. Wasn't that the plan?"

Amy turned her head away from Jackie, so that hood fabric muffled her reply. When she turned back, she said, "I'm on edge. I confess I forgot. Remind me why I give a rat's ass about a stinking kitchen when the bank is repossessing?"

"Because you need your J-O-B, Amy," Jackie reminded her while trying not to shake her head. "My son needs to eat more than the milk he's getting from our cows. Let's get to work. We both need our sleep, and I prefer not to get caught and do it in a jail cell."

Amy left her flakiness outside with the new fallen snow and got down to work when the two were inside, coats flung over the La-Z-Boys. She had watched online videos of how to do this stuff, so she was the lead. She communicated in pantomime how to carefully retrieve the weed and break it up into gallon-sized plastic bags. When Jackie wondered why they were quiet, Amy responded that they were practicing for work in the school kitchen.

When each woman had her baggie of carefully combed and culled weed, Amy added the butter, in measured amounts as per the Internet recipe, and sealed the bags with Jackie's $25.00 appliance from Wal-Mart. Such a deal!

Now they popped the bags into boiling water in mega-capacity pots ordinarily used to make pasta. Jackie's mind flashed on canning vegetables with her mom, noticing that, while her pot was brown with food residues burned to the surface, Amy's pot was pristine.

As expected. *I can't call her kettle black.*

As if she read Jackie's mind, Amy said, "Double, double toil and trouble; fire burn and cauldron bubble." Amy leered, then smiled when Jackie exclaimed: "Macbeth!" She knew a wee bit of Shakespeare, too.

"So, are we the Weird Sisters or the Witches?" Jackie quipped. The butter and weed mixture needed to boil for a couple of hours, and the noise was already getting on her nerves.

"How about some Roller Derby names? Like Bad-Ass Amy and Wackie Jackie. If you add Terrible Tessa, we might be the Witches," Amy added. "Maybe we'll have to recruit her when our sales territory expands upstate."

Amy stopped the topic to open cupboard drawers as if she didn't know where the hot pads were. "Hey, I've got an idea, Jackie. Since we have all this down time, while the brew bubbles, let's pre-measure and mix the ingredients for tomorrow night's adventure."

So they did, powdering their black clothing well. Jackie knew that Amy had many pairs of black slacks, but she'd be laundering the slacks she wore – or getting out the shoe polish kit, like Fran had jokingly suggested when she's complained about the gray hairs that had strayed onto her head.

At two hours exactly, they strained the hot canna butter mixture through a Mr. Coffee filter in a leggy pasta strainer. Jackie wondered how Amy knew the mixture was done; because she'd been cooking and baking so many years, she just knew by the look of things when they were done, but pot butter was new. It just looked liked eggs whisked with herbs before hitting the hot breakfast skillet.

The night's tasks completed, Wackie Jackie drove home, arriving seamlessly to join Steve in front of the TV for the 10:00 news, no questions asked or answered.

Drama was new to Jackie, but apparently not to Amy. Drama seemed to open her up like a can opener as they drove to the school for Phase Two of Plan B.

The two women chatted more than they'd done in the several years that they'd known each other. Amy coached Jackie in deep yoga breathing – natural childbirth hadn't been the practice when Brandon was born - and prattled about dressing Goth while in high school. Their ghoulish garb tonight was reminiscence for her, while it was a Halloween nightmare for Jackie.

Just like a movie script, they drove into the parking lot without lights, clandestine as a Bond arrival. Each loaded arms with bags of baking supplies, one with the pot butter Baggies stashed in the bottom. They were weighted – ten pounds of flour weighed, well, ten pounds, and that was just one of the ingredients in the plastic gallon bags. Hurry! Holy crap!

Jackie fumbled a bit with the keys, performed better when she set her bags down, and then allowed Amy to enter first while she held the door open with her butt. Amy made brave entry without the lights until Jackie elbowed them on. She'd scouted the route purposefully in daytime. Jackie's bad knees shook with nerves, but didn't buckle, which she took as a good sign.

The cafeteria was down a lengthy hall past rows of cubicle lockers. Jackie rehearsed her cover story with every step she took, its rhythm and rhyme making more sense as she scurried along with her armloads. Though they were dirty white, not black like the rest of the burglar ensembles, at least her tennis shoes were soundless. Amy, of course, wore black suede boots with soft soles and no heels to clump.

The kitchen looked different, but, perhaps, that was because of the eerie silence that shrouded the entire building. Jackie felt like a sneaky school kid, working on a private dare to herself, using the kitchen tools and appliances when and how she wanted, against all the rules, living life without concern of consequences. Amy's "strong, smart, and bold" attitude had been molded in the Girls Inc. after-school programs in Costa Mesa, California, and she infused the attitude into Jackie for the night.

They poured the pre-measured ingredients for the

pot cookies into two massive stainless bowls, careful not to spill any of the flour mix. *Wouldn't want the janitor to think he had Anthrax to sweep.* Though each longed for music, they disdained to be on alert for noise outside their clandestine operation.

They oozed the canna butter into the big bowls. *Ooh, can ah butter ya'all's biscuits?* Jackie practiced for her travel down South until Amy capped her with a rap-rhythmned offer to butter her ass.

While the big Kitchen Aid machines mixed the ingredients to a potent batter, Jackie and Amy argued a bit about cookie prices, finally deciding that $5.00 matched dough dropped into rows on identical aluminum sheets by the ice cream scoops, like sailors aligned on an aircraft carrier deck.

Four ovens baking pot cookies made a putrid smell. They had not entirely anticipated this.

"Phew – it's worse than a hog lot!" Jackie said. Amy's comparison was from her dumpster diving days as a kid. It was other worldly rank, belying the euphoria that its products created. The phrase, "strong, smart, and bold" returned to mind, as the stench of baking the pot cookies almost overwhelmed them. They regretted that they couldn't hold their noses – alas, that's when Jackie remembered her wood clothespins in the laundry room at home - because their fingers busily made gingersnap cookies from on-site ingredients as stench antidote.

"The staff lounge will have a sweet surprise on Monday," Jackie giggled. "Hey, it helps to breathe through your mouth, Amy. Try it! My friend Fran will consider me a martyred hero who didn't mind not having a party after all, not suspecting that I am a United States felon. I am going to have multiple reasons to smile during my last week of work."

Four cookie sheets, working in shifts in double ovens, made the baking swift. Jackie and Amy were savvy bakers, proud to be equal to their former assembly line men. They kept the kitchen doors shut, and the windows opened onto a breezy night. Never mind that it was a little chilly. They were fueled with purpose and the inner heat of semi-guilty consciences. Their sense of smell acclimated, thank God.

The industrial dishwasher was sloshing the utensils clean as the cookies cooled atop the vast counters. Jackie looked at the clock, ticking obnoxiously to remind her that they were in the wrong place at the wrong time, doing a wrong thing. She was amazed that the noisy kitchen clock was still ticking on weekends – no recess? Its noisy presence couldn't be ignored. It reminded her of the "Telltale Heart"; or was that her own heart trying to thump its way out of her chest?

Amy pulled her away from useless thought loop with an aptly timed whisper, "Calm yourself, we are almost done, Wackie Jackie." The comment was better than a hug.

Amy had screwed up her nose when Jackie rinsed and dried the plastic bags, but now she smiled as they bagged cookies in them, carefully counting them into groups of 30. They would beat the clock. They would beat the world at its game, credit scores be damned.

Jackie brought out Extra-Strength Febreeze and rags, and discovered that Amy was a great little cleaner after all.

"I imagine the white knight, Mr. Clean, working alongside me, smiling his approvingly broad smile," Amy said. "He's our cohort, our cheerleader - and our protector if the janitor shows."

"He's slimmed-down in the ads these days." Jackie laughed. "Maybe we will be, too, after all of this effort. My wrists hurt more than my knees."

Giggles overcame them as they re-loaded their bags, hefted them into the van, and drove away from the school. Giggles were a better sound track than the dishwasher, ticking clock, or the thud of their heartbeats had been.

They beamed when they got back to the farmhouse and tiptoed under the security lights to complete their tasks. Brandon and Steve were long done with their chores, both probably snoring their own nighttime sound track, and each women wanted to join her men in relaxed slumber.

It was all good: 350 cookies good. 50 were cellophane wrapped, ready to be attached to quart bottles of milk with an order form for more of Santa's Special Sweets. Aligned like soldiers onstage for the Nutcracker Suite – no, the Potcracker Sweets – in the garage fridge. The rest were in storage bags in the freezer, behind hamburger and pork tenderloin packages. Bad-Ass Amy and Wackie Jackie had the munchies, so they cleaned out Steve's Fudgsicles and Brandon's Dilly Bars.

The next day Jackie went to Wal-Mart and copied the school building and cafeteria keys to leave with Amy after she and Steve left town. She didn't go to Handy's Hardware because the keys were clearly stamped "DO NOT DUPLICATE". Things could be complicated by Handy's inquisitiveness and his tendency to share news in this tiny town. The man managed other people's business as well as his own, his store the male equivalent of Maybelline's Beauty Salon.

The Wal-Mart kid had a nose ring and barely lifted his eyelids while he worked. Confidentiality fostered by stupidity. Jackie hoped he had fingers by the end of the day, working as absently as he did.

The plan seemed confection perfection. After all, the school was out in the country, and the elderly custodian didn't work weekends. The baking schedule could be worked around school sports practice and games when the monthly schedule was posted on the school's website. *God, it felt good to be devilish!*

Nineteen: Amy Ups the Ante

Jackie and I, the new dream team in town, settled into a second task over mid-Saturday morning coffee: arranging an impromptu send-off party for Steve and Jackie's trip. We set a date and decided on a restaurant or gasoline gift card shower for ease and practicality. Portability, too. Jackie and Steve didn't need more earthly goods; they needed less for the compact space of their tin can home. Jackie hoped for Cracker Barrel and Mobil, in that order, but didn't ask Steve for opinions – nor Brandon, though they would be driving his beloved truck, which guzzled premium, as I recalled from our credit card statements.

We made quick work of it because Jackie had house cleaning to do, though I did not. I'd been on strike since the bank had stolen our house.

I prepared and sent e-vites to everyone in both of our address books – theirs was long and ours was short – to the school's personnel, the congregation, and everyone on Steve's dairy route. Jackie persisted with mailed paper invitations to her less-tech friends – that would be, all of them. I think she had a thing about sticking stamps on envelopes, which she admitted, trying to explain something to me about Green Stamps with catalogues to get stuff for free, important in her newly-wed days. When she began to name the items she had acquired with Green Stamps, using all her fingers to cite them, my eyes crossed, and I changed the subject.

I suggested that the party could be a secret promotion for Milkweed Goods, so I conferred paper and postage costs as business expense, as well as our Starbucks coffee. To convert this on-the-road woman to my addiction, I installed a Starbucks app to the iPad to show every store in the US.

Business expense. *Oops,* expenses. My party-planning euphoria dissolved into banker reality. I lifted my hands as the download completed, thumbs wiggling in mid-air, ready to help me think, but my right hand reached for my purse like a robot. I retrieved the Benz car keys and made a hasty exit to the bank. Jackie was already dusting, so we didn't hug good-bye.

Yeah, we were hugging like Roller Derby champs these days.

No one thought much of seeing the Benz speed through the small town and park in front of the bank, despite the fact that it was Saturday. Inside my office, undisrupted by the cleaning crew just yet, I turned on my computer, trying to remain calm while I waited. I hummed Christmas songs, liked I'd heard on the car radio, but even I knew I sucked, so I stopped.

Finally. I clicked onto the spreadsheet of expenditures I'd made for Milkweed Goods, prior to the past few heady days of Plan B. I'd never tallied the line items into a total and hovered my index finger over the keyboard a moment, frightened of the financial sinkhole I suspected. I'd not opened the Master Card bill envelope on the countertop at home either, seeing it in my mind's eye, buried under Merry Christmas cards, junk catalogues, and grocery store circulars, lurking like a shark under the surface of our happiness. The bill with all of the pot farm start-up charges on it, and there it was, glowering at me online.

And thus it came to pass that I forged Steve's signature to increase the senior Breedens' credit line to $100,000.00. It could be done, it had to be done, and it was done. 'Twas the season to be needy as well as jolly, and I felt like Santa Claus as I gifted the business with necessary funds, from the benevolence of the land.

Twenty: Shopping Cart

Lordy, now I know why Charlene's always gushing about retail therapy! Jackie thought as she navigated her cart across the vast acreage of Wal-Mart. The aisles stacked with food packages and cans, toilet paper, clothing, and gadgets were like mini Grand Canyons. Each item seemed to puff out its chest and say, "Choose me, Jackie. I'm essential for your trip."

With all of that choosing, the cart was soon stacked as high as an Egyptian pyramid. Jackie's arms wrestled the cart along, the drudge of muscle power overwhelming the delight of purchase power. She flinched as she glanced at her watch: she'd been shopping in Wal-Mart two hours.

Just as she spied a short check out line, the Muzak switched to 'Jingle Bells' and she hummed along. As she unloaded items onto the conveyer belt, her eyes locked on the cashier's florid face atop moldy green garb. The young lady's nametag framed 'Veronica' in smiley face decals to suggest a perky attitude, but she must have left it on her bathroom counter when she'd made-up for work this morning. She scowled with unseasonable humbug.

Jackie decided to share her abundant holiday cheer, so in her best Ellen DeGeneres voice, she said, "Do you think that I have enough food? My husband and I are traveling around the USA in a Winnebago and you never know where a Wal-Mart is."

Veronica's gaze remained fixed on the cluster of cans she was marshaling in steady cadence across the price scanner. Its rhythmic 'boop' sounded like submarine diving bells.

Jackie found herself picturing empty bubbles sifting up through water, then over the heads of cartoon characters. These images dissolved into the huge flakes sneaking out of Veronica's center-parted hair, so like the snowflakes hurling themselves at Wal-Mart's huge window panels. Jackie heard herself blurt, "Do you recommend the store brand shampoo? I got it because of the price savings – and it was the same color as the Prell." *So lame - how am I going to meet new people when we travel?*"

Zero response came from Veronica, so Jackie busied herself with swiping her new Master Card through the countertop device, fumbling like a kindergartener, proud to scrawl her name with the stylus. Her mouth crept toward a smile, but Veronica had already turned her back to Jackie, so she saved it for the Salvation Army Santa outside. Jackie paused to give him some coins, and pushed on toward the van with the heavy, adroitly loaded cart, into emerging winter.

The bags were an easy swing from cart to van and Jackie was soon behind the wheel, welcoming the friendly chatter of the radio DJ as compensation for Veronica's snub. Though she could see the snow deepening its slick on the roads, she felt safe with the extra weight of the road trip staples stowed behind her in the van. Each gearshift took her further from Veronica's anti-holiday sulk toward the safety of home – and the promise of new adventure – and Jackie began to pity Veronica. The young lady was still stuck behind a counter and Jackie wasn't because she'd taken that job and shoved it! Just like the shopping cart a few moments ago.

It was 3:00 when Jackie got home. Her guys were busy with milking chores, so she toted all the supplies directly from the van into the RV by herself – *sigh!* Lord knew she needed all of the exercise she could get.

Jackie pulled into the garage, stashed the keys in her purse, and began the trek, pausing to retrieve an old shower curtain and carefully lay it atop the new plush carpet of the RV. When all 20 bags were in the RV, helter-skeltered on the tiny swath of linoleum kitchen floor, Jackie stretched out on her new couch.

Perked up in twenty minutes, Jackie began stowing the supplies in just the right cubby. Her mind turned to meal planning, as reverie to her mother, and she became wistful. What would Mother think about all of this? What would she think of parents escaping to explore America, leaving the responsibilities of home and farm to young adult children? As she moved into arranging and re-arranging the staples, Jackie wondered what Amy observed in her bending and unbending of the rules and rhythms of life.

The reverie stopped with a single honk of a late migration Canadian goose. She'd left the RV door open...and then she flashed on how she'd left herself open by taking part in a *fakery* business. And, Lord forgive her, Jackie had to figure out just the right place for the weed stash.

Just as Jackie latched the door of their new home, the great idea hit her. She ran inside and up the stairs to rifle her closet for the two dainty padded hangers: one a be-ribboned pink, sallowed with age, and the other a jaunty black that fairly growled with its tiger ribbon. Both had held Valentine apparel from Steve.

The gowns were gone, but the hangers remained, a metaphor for a longtime marriage in there somewhere. For now, she wouldn't follow the emotional trail of that issue. Jackie was long-practiced in the practical. Besides she felt vindicated for her semi-pack rat tendencies, which always gave her a buzz.

Jackie took down her sewing basket and retrieved the seam ripper from its space, carefully slicing open the seams of the hangers, then fished out the padding with an embroidery hook. Her mother had last used that tool. What would she think of Jackie's purpose? Surely heaven didn't allow her a judgment any more than her lifetime did.

Then Jackie brought the measuring spoons up to the bedroom – she was not performing this operation on the spacious granite tops in the wide-open kitchen, no siree-ma'am. She and Steve lived, like most farm people, without locked doors. She measured their weed stash into four judiciously equal amounts, then double-baggied and triple twist-tied them, flattened them into cigar-like shapes, and threaded the bags into the hangers' fabric. Too bad she couldn't enter her project in the county fair under either Crafts or Sewing or the new area, Life Style. Jackie hung both of her good church dresses on these hangers and took them out to the RV closet pronto. There she admired the reverent dignity of her camouflage operation. It was going to be a good trip.

Then she remembered her Playgirl magazine stash.

Quickly she wheeled in the tight bedroom to explore the nooks and crannies within and discovered the storage cubbies under the bed, praying thanks that God truly loved sinners, as the Pastor said. Jackie vowed to put more money in the collection basket at church as thanks. Maybe she'd return to Wal-Mart to give more money to the Salvation Army Santa after church.

Jackie grabbed her purse and headed into the house. Playtime was over and the meal-planning reverie had to shift from future to present because she heard the milk deliverymen putter into the garage. She put on her 'how was your day, honey' smile and hurried in to be in her proper place in the kitchen.

Twenty-One: Cheap Sunglasses

It was the first day of Jackie's conveniently fired status. The closet looked twister-torn, starting with the scarves and heading for the shoes, so that head-to-toe Jackie's wardrobe contents splayed in colorful mayhem. Sparty was spending a rare day inside due to the deep cold snap, but after a brief foray upstairs, he'd tucked his tail and scampered to the laundry room. If he could have spoken, he would have said that his mistress had an air of heedless determination about her, and he didn't want to be covered by the wrong pile.

Jackie had only interrupted her frenzy once, to fetch one of Steve's yellow pads for her two lists: Goodwill and Go-on-the-road. The yearend was rapidly approaching, and she needed to get this task done. There were half-dozen heavy coats already headed to the church's winter coat drive, some with hats or scarves to match. She didn't think she'd need any of them, since they were headed south to the Bowl, then through Texas and the Southwest, on to sunny California, the land of the beach and Disney. If she needed a coat she could buy a new one because she knew that Wal-Mart was everywhere. There was an app for that on their iPad.

She peeked out of the closet to the dresser's mirror where she'd taped the Alamo Bowl game tickets, so they were the first and last things she saw each day. "Go, Spartans! Go, Clothes!" She got up for an impromptu cheer for her favorite team, upending herself as the rug slipped with her high kick attempt, then her knees buckled to remind her that she was no longer young, but she was still foolish. She picked herself up, checked for scrapes and rends, then scurried back to the closet, glad that the only observer was her mirror. She'd forgotten her bad knees in her new lightness of living, in looking forward to the road trip.

Gosh, this was like shopping in reverse. Oops, that reminded her of the lesson that Steve had promised, a threat to Jackie's peace and serenity: learning to back up the truck with the Fifth Wheel attached. That was Saturday's chore, and she wasn't looking forward to it. She hoped that Brandon and Amy would not come over to witness her embarrassment. She knew that she could silence Steve with a look – or a threat to withhold his meal – but she had no such control of the young'uns.

She turned back to the closet-clearing task, returning to a kind of high-colored magical confusion that her sensible, farm wife self had never allowed.

"Jackie, where's lunch?" Steve asked as he climbed the stairs. If she'd turned around, Jackie would have seen his stupefied look as he sighted only a few patches of plush carpeting visible among the colorful confusion of clothing piled throughout their bedroom. "Jackie, it's 12:15," he continued. "A starving man stands behind you, cleaned up from dairy duties and wondering what the heck you are doing. The floor looks like a map of the United States, with California on the edge of our bed, about to fall into the ocean after the big one."

"I'm sorting clothes for either our trip or Goodwill, clearing our closet for when Amy and Bran move in here. And," Jackie whirled to face him, "Steve, I'm already scared of twisters, so don't bring up the earthquake potential of California."

Steve sat down on the bed, suddenly no longer hungry, as he processed the scenario that accompanied her words. Whether by twister or earthquake, their lives were in mighty upheaval. He'd never considered that his son and daughter-in-law might be sleeping in their bed. He suddenly knew how Mama and Papa Bear had felt after Goldilocks had lurked into their home, messing with their possessions. This road trip excursion had as many layers as his wife's lasagna.

"Anyway, you ought to be sizing up what you can and can not take on the road with you. Perhaps it is time for lunch and a look at the push-pin road trip map," Jackie said. "We're having leftover lasagna for lunch, okay?"

Steve's eyebrows rose in suspicion at his wife's

apparent mind-meld prowess again, knowing that she'd contemplated the bed situation and might have something to say over lunch.

Jackie and Steve had a fondness for leftovers, a convenience when lunch was abbreviated by the intense pace of farm life. The plastic salad bag's zipper afforded easy open-and-toss of lettuce bits alongside their lasagna slabs, to make their plates respectful of good dietary principles. They were both so hungry they almost didn't need forks to inhale the food; they certainly didn't bother with napkins. That's what Clorox was for.

Steve was surprised that Jackie had no comments about the kids' move-in complexities. He retrieved the map from its bulletin board berth, mindful that their future was in his hands. He got a couple of her bulging cookbooks to prop it on the kitchen counter as if on an artist's easel. Red pins were the places that they'd agreed on, mostly national parks like Grand Canyon, Yellowstone, and the Grand Tetons. Hollywood, California was also marked in red as well as Disneyland and the Disney for adults: Las Vegas. And, of course, San Antonio, though Steve had already learned that the Alamo, for which the Bowl game was named, was belittled by aggressive urban architecture and no longer heroic looking.

Steve's yellow pins seeded the USA like sunflowers. There were few blue pins, which denoted Jackie's picks. She got up to retrieve the box of them from the desk, bringing the high stack of mail that Steve had retrieved from the mailbox. The postman was as regular as Steve, and they enjoyed their ritual wave with a bit of country gossip. She talked as she walked back with both hands full, saying, "Let's go through our mail to see who's responded, wanting a visit during our trip? I'm hoping for Jack and Leslie in Ft. Collins, where we could go on the brewery tours they've told us about. That's probably near where we'll spread Big Braghorn's ashes, right? And, how about going to visit the places where our Winnebago and Amana were made, in Iowa, Steve? That sounds sort of homey and respectful, doesn't it?"

Steve waited until Jackie settled into her chair. He swiveled toward the map and plopped the pin box near it, eager as a student teacher in front of a class. Then he pointed his finger at Iowa, which was surrounded by a forest of pushpins but was bare itself.

"That's a wholesome idea," Steve said, "but it's not close to any of our major destinations. And I've already plotted over 6,000 miles for our trip. We've gotta start getting practical about our expenses."

Jackie's face colored as she recollected Plan B; she turned toward the cupboards so Steve couldn't see as he continued with his propositions, "Jackie, our RV was actually made by Sunnybrook, a company that Winnebago recently bought. If the Sunnybrook plant in Middlebury, Indiana, is open between Christmas and New Year's, we can stop for mid-morning coffee and a tour? And, how about New Year's Eve in New Orleans? I've figured out the travel time from here to San Antonio. We have time if we leave early on December 28."

Jackie decided then and there to let Steve do all of the trip planning. Learning to maneuver the truck and RV was going to be enough to tackle, a potential tempest in a truck cab. She didn't want to tether her spirits to more frustration. She had to pack their provisions, which would be enough.

To change the subject, she suggested a quick trip to Wal-Mart, telling Steve of her family's ritual of getting cheap sunglasses before each trip.

"Come on, Jackie, put on your sunglasses. It's time to learn how to back up the truck and Fifth Wheel," Steve said, a coat, hat, and gloves for her already in his hands. "I pulled one of your coats out of the bags that are going to Goodwill. Weren't you a little overzealous in your giveaway? Pastor Rankin might withdraw his trip blessings if you arrive in a frozen state to church, and he had to compete with the chattering of your teeth during his service."

Jackie kept her mouth shut, for she could see that he'd loaded all of the bags of donated items into the truck. If she retorted, he'd go poking and notice that she'd looted his clothing drawers, not merely her own. She chose to compliment two initiatives: shoveling the sidewalk and his consideration of retrieving her coat – and to practice the deep breathing that Amy had modeled.

Jackie put her new sunglasses on, glad she hadn't mentioned hefting the give-away bags, for he was sure to tease about the hefting another bag: *me. Not the way to begin a tutorial.* The climb into the truck cab was a bit tough due to its height, but being settled into the soft, smooth seat was a worthy goal, augmented by a tap to the heated seat button. Mmn-n, that was welcome.

Jackie switched on the radio to ease her nerves after Steve's thoroughly high-geared instructions about how to back up the tandem vehicles. His words were too speedy for apprentice ears... "Hey!" derailed all her effort to comprehend.

As Pink Floyd's rant about instructional rigidity continued, she tried to shrug it off, not wanting to think backward to her school career but forward to her road trip aspiration. She regressed to age 15½, when her father taught her to drive, an epic struggle that rattled even her cool-minded mother. Her mom had awarded her a trophy, probably left over from the county fair, for surviving his ten lessons.

"...brick in..." not until then did she see the wall of their garage looming near the back of the Sunnybrook, in huge mirrors, in place on both sides the truck. Steve was a madman of shaking limbs with a red face contorted by fear and shouting. She hadn't seen him look like that since Brandon's high school football days.

She thought she'd heard no impact, no shatter of plastic or scrunch of metal. He had to know that she loved the Sunnybrook and would never intentionally hurt it.

She recalled he'd given her the 'Come on back' hand signal. She was certain, she thought.

She shrugged into herself for the chore of facing down Steve. She untucked her State sweatshirt from her jeans and, after she put the truck in park, she tugged at her belt buckle to remove its bind from her lap. She'd have removed the seatbelt, too, but that was what was holding her from flying at him.

"No dark sarcasm in the truck cab," she snapped as Steve opened her cab door to bark orders, with some other general observations about her competence and his not wanting to be killed. He folded his arms as he ended, "I thought all you women knew how to look in mirrors. Use your mirrors! Watch my signs!"

Jackie cleared her fury as Steve stepped into the cab, signaling the end of the back-up lesson near his garage. As his wife, it was her obligation to shift them back onto a positive track, and she accomplished it as safely as she drove to town: "I brought our ATM cards so we can try them at the bank. That's where the Goodwill station is located, so we'll kill two birds with one stone." Steve gave her a slow burn, so she swallowed and continued, "Oops, didn't mean to say kill."

Steve let a beat go by, and then responded, "A cup of hot chocolate sounds good, too. We'll ease down the streets of town – remember to drive in the middle so the tree branches don't scrape - and into the bank parking lot. You can practice parking, and Starbucks will be our reward."

"Our reward, what are you doing to earn a reward?" Jackie sassed.

"Riding shotgun to a wild woman and living to tell about it," said Steve.

"You're not allowed to tell anyone about this practice run," said Jackie. "Swear it or I'll swerve this rig into a culvert. Swear."

"Okay. Just promise to use all the mirrors, my dear," Steve said as he unfolded his arms and relaxed his hands to his lap. He kept his boot ready to hit the invisible floor brake, however.

They both tuned back into radio play. Christmas songs were interspersed with the rock-and-roll they favored, and the mood lifted in the cab, especially when the barking dogs performed "Jingle Bells." Jackie's driving skills increased as Steve's blood pressure decreased, and soon the rig was safely parked, albeit across multiple spaces, at the bank. Matter of fact, it had been parked a second time for good measure, both making a mental note to always seek a pull-through RV campsite throughout America and back home again, safe and sound.

They shared the chore of giving the Goodwill donations to a volunteer dressed as Santa. Jackie was careful to hand Steve the bags that didn't contain his cast-off clothing. She stuffed the receipt in her pocket and after a little small talk with the man, the couple moved to the bank's ATM. There was a small enclosure, in case of inclement weather, that made the machine look enshrined.

Steve mentioned that he had seen actual shrines during his service in Vietnam. "I recall thinking that Buddha's belly would be a great place to stash stuff. I wished I could stash my gun and run away, but I couldn't do that, so I hoped that I'd make good money after I returned home in one piece. To enjoy life with you, Jackie. We still are, aren't we? Our road trip proves that."

Jackie hugged him in agreement. Hugged him heartily, knowing for certain that she'd passed the truck driving test. Though the act of walking across the small town street didn't really require looking both ways, Jackie and Steve swiveled their heads in unison, grabbed each other's hand, and got their Starbucks reward.

Jackie knew Amy would be proud, but didn't mention her name to Steve. He still regarded her as a semi-she-devil.

A hour-and-a-half later they returned home from Jackie's parking trials, with success in the bank, the church, the school, and Wal-Mart parking lots. Alive and well-chilled. Jackie wheeled into the kitchen to make more hot chocolate, and Steve headed for his iPad. He'd already downloaded 22 travel-related apps in the moments before Jackie delivered a mug to the desk. He lifted his head at the clink of the cup and smilingly pointed at the screen with the colorful little icons mustered for their trip. Their precise rows reminded Jackie of the classrooms she was leaving behind.

Brandon banged into the house and found his parents hovering over the computer: "Why don't you just put the apps on your phone, Dad?"

Jackie and Steve exchanged a look. They hadn't thought of that, but who'd admit it to their kid? "Because the screen is too small, my helpful son," Steve improvised.

His reason held the floor, so Brandon changed the subject with a turn to his mother: "May I have some hot chocolate, too? Got any chocolate chip cookies to go with it?"

Jackie quickly moved into the kitchen so her face couldn't reveal the secret cookie project. She didn't know if Brandon was included, but she knew that Steve wasn't. Not now or ever because he wouldn't approve of breaking federal law, no matter what Michigan statute said. His pledge of allegiance was thorough and true.

She bustled about, mentally searching for a way to re-direct her men. She knew that Brandon had computer tutorials in mind, and that Steve would be receptive. She was done with lessons for the day.

"Brandon, does Amy's bank have one of those coin-counting machines? It's rumored that each staff member will give me a roll of quarters, and I'd rather have the bills than the weight of coins. I expect the sound of those coins colliding down the metal chute would prime me to hear the jubilant tumble of coins when I win big in Vegas."

Steve smiled her way; he probably thought that she accredited his lectures on extra weight and fuel economy when packing the Fifth Wheel for the trip. Jackie was suddenly chagrined, knowing that her booty included stash of coins she inherited when Steve emptied his pants pockets each night.

But she smiled back and said, "Call in a pizza order for dinner? Invite Amy over, Brandon. She and I can discuss stuff while you two do the evening milking."

Brandon and Steve exchanged looks, shrugged, and sat down at the table. It was be a paper napkin night, manners not required.

Twenty-Two: Seasonal Changes

Jackie enjoyed decorating a Christmas tree, but only after Steve circumnavigated the irritating bristle of the branches with lights. He argued little, but harrumphed a lot when she insisted that he secure each light to a tree branch with a twist tie. The white pine, cut from their small woods, was the state tree. When they dumped it in a few days, they'd symbolically dump their state for their entire country.

Steve announced that he'd toss the damned twist ties, all 52 of them, into the trash bonfire, too. After all, Jackie had saved them from the bread wrappers. He was done with saving and into spending. It was his turn.

Burnished rivers of ribbon soon floated over the white lights that twinkled their readiness to showcase the family's treasured ornaments. Many were handmade and, with their special stories, were carefully uncrinkled before placement on the tree. Jackie's face lit up at the memory of the silver tinsel strands her mother insisted she toss on the tree just so. That tradition from childhood Christmases had been abandoned, though she couldn't recall when. It truly saddened her, because the entire ritual of tree decoration seemed to be about remembering when: the year when Brandon made the construction paper handprint Santa, then the year when he'd made a popsicle stick reindeer, and on and on, memories paired with visions of Brandon's eyes glued to her hands as she opened his tissue-wrapped trinket, then his whole face spread into a smile to match hers. The fact that the reindeer had only one google eye to peer down from his high branch berth reminded her that Google had meant something else a dozen years ago. The world had changed, at what seemed like a manic pace.

Nostalgia overtook her and the morning passed in internal reflection through the sweet filter of Christmas past. It was simple; it was safe and contained; it was over.

And so was the morning, as she looked up at the

blast of cold air that could only mean Steve had come in from the barn, and it was time for lunch.

"Hi, honey. Time to put the angel on top of the tree?" Steve said brightly, almost as if his voice could help warm his body if he amped up its volume.

The winter walk from the milk barn was brief, but the atmosphere had been chilly out there all morning. Brandon's aptitude with milking and clean up wasn't what Steve had hoped for in his former 4-Her. He hurried, didn't cajole each animal to avoid balks; he balked a bit himself. Steve caught him gaming on that damn phone once in a while. The kid sulked; and so it went. Steve had to admit: Brandon was a slacker. Perhaps Amy wasn't the only one who wasn't cut of the country cloth.

So throughout the morning chores, rather than count to ten, Steve envisioned the sweet treetop angel to evoke his father's rule to never curse in front of a lady.

He lost the argument about whether to put up a tree with their travels set to start in a week, so he asserted his right to top it with his mother's heirloom angel. Tradition reigned, needed all the more, because they were leaving home for a long, long time. Wandering the USA merely had roots in a map, not terra firma, like their lives did. Their whole lives had been lived within miles of this spot, with the exception of his tour in Vietnam.

Steve dared not mention misgivings to Jackie, especially not about handing over the business to Brandon. She might go over the edge. He overheard her constant phone chatter, alternating between nostalgic sadness and elation. He planned to extinguish his concerns and homesick feelings when he burned the pine tree with the trash Sunday night.

"Yes, sir," Jackie said as she eased her body up from the floor. "You secure your mother's angel on her lofty throne while I put the leftover soup on to heat and make you a sandwich. Hey, you're tramping snow in here!"

"It'll melt in a second, you've got the heat up so high

in here. Shall I call Sparty to lap it up?" Steve replied as he went to the pantry to retrieve the step stool.

He almost didn't need it because the tree was his height, but the lower branches were filled with Jackie's precious memory ornaments, many placed where younger Brandon had put them when first made. He knew if he jostled the tree branches he'd earn a second admonition,further delaying his meal. Didn't Jackie know what energy it took to set up, milk, then clean and sterilize the equipment, let alone put up with her spoiled-ass son? She had already slowed 10 m.p.h. in the several days of her pseudo-forced retirement.

The afternoon passed in peaceable rhythm, as Steve returned to outside chores and Jackie prepared elements of their farewell party. She'd given a little pause to the fact that she and Steve were feting themselves, but their home had become game central in Spartan football season. She felt certain that their friends' vehicles could have auto piloted them to and fro, a convenience for people getting older and high on sport.

Even Steve's brother and ferret-faced wife were coming from Alpena, willing to do so, it seemed to Jackie, only after Steve offered them a place to stay. Claire was sure to step into the Sunnybrook to pass judgment, as she always did, but Jackie was into her 'outta-here' persona and was determined not to care.

She had thought, however, to call their partiers to warn them against a request for special brownies – Claire and David would not approve if anyone got *baked*, of that Jackie was sure.

The glory of having stay-over guests, an unusual occurrence, was that she got to finger her bed linen stash, including hand-embroidered pillowcases two centuries old. She rifled through the hall closet, front to back, making piles on the wood floor with memories to match.

Jackie jumped when the doorbell rang. She looked vainly at her wrist for the time, and then recalled that she'd purposefully left her watch atop the dresser in celebration of her unemployed status. She fluttered past the bathroom mirror, raking at her hair with her fingers to correct some of the skew of her curls. She descended the stairs to the tune of someone sitting on that doorbell. Not many people rang a bell like it was at the gate of St. Peter. Jackie peeked through the peephole to see...

Two blatantly beige people planted like statues on their square concrete porch. One was a carbon copy of Steve, though with twitchy, gloveless hands in and out of pockets as if in vain search for a match to set their house afire. The woman beside him stood so close she was almost tucked in behind, to meld her body into his, yet it was her finger that was glued to the doorbell.

Jackie struggled to unwedge the cloth draft stopper from under the seldom-used entry door and took a deep breath before opening it to greet the guests.

That same breath exhaled a word torrent: "Hi, David and Claire! Come in! Come in! Don't let the cold air filter into the room. Come in and give a hug. Where are Tessa and Kenny?"

David stepped in first and stood inert except for his fingers flitting like a bird from perch to perch. This allowed his wife only inches in the hall. She moved in to speak, "The kids stayed home. Tessa's baby-sitting. Kenneth still believes in Santa and was afraid if he wasn't home, he wouldn't get gifts."

"Well, It's so good to see you two, though we'll miss the kids. I made up the twin beds in Brandon's room for them, but never mind. Steve's out on his milk route and should be home soon. Brandon'll be with him. Did Steve tell you he's grooming up well to take over the dairy while we travel?"

"Humph, glad that's settled. I was concerned he was inviting us down to leave the business in my lap," said David.

As if. Jackie knew little about fishing, but she knew fishermen always wanted to fish. The business would fall off David's lap as he left to go fishing every chance he could.

She couldn't say that, but she didn't know what to say. Jackie had never been comfortable with small talk with small people, so her mind worked like a Wurlitzer, scanning old records to find a soundtrack for the conversational dance. The duo infected others with their fussbudgets, fidgets, and criminally conservative views. Steve called them problems-without-solutions professionals. They always ensnared others in a loop of angry chatter as pointless as Sparty chasing his own tail. Steve sometimes wondered aloud if he and David had had the same parents and Jackie agreed, although tacitly. In those moments, she was glad to be an only child.

Jackie hoped that if she kept her mouth in motion, they couldn't open theirs...that plan worked while she helped them slide arms off their coats. Jackie noticed that Claire had deftly untied and swirled the big square scarf from her head, and then held it in one hand, so that it was tubed in her coat's sleeve, a clever stowage move. Jackie finally had something to admire Claire for. She admired the scarf, too: red floribunda roses on taupe silk. Couldn't have been from David, that screwed-up scrooge.

Claire's wiry-haired head, brassy as the pot scrubber under the kitchen sink, whipped around, searching for something to critique. She'd looked almost pretty when the scarf was on her head; now she looked as harsh as her tongue.

David got right to the point, "We came to see my brother Steve's folly, the Incredible Hulk Hotel." Must be Steve had told him that the vehicle was Spartan green, but David perverted the color's significance.

She'd never been so glad to see Amy as when her daughter-in-law arrived early, visible through the wide window as she aimed for the kitchen entry. Amy stepped carefully on the shoveled walk, balancing two large platters covered in foil. A basket filled with wine and festooned with a red bow of enormous holiday proportion hung from one elbow. If she'd had a red cape, she would have been Red Riding Hood arriving at

Grandma's house with the basket of goodies.

As she opened the door for Amy, Jackie couldn't resist: "Well, Little Red Riding Hood, what big platters you have!"

"The better to feed the partiers," Amy's words came out in white puffs of frost. "I ordered extra for the bank holiday party, expecting to bring the leftovers here. There are more in the backseat of the Benz. Whose car is that in the driveway? Are Brandon and Steve here?"

"No, but Claire and David just arrived and would be glad to help, won't you, dear family members. Thank goodness, your coats haven't been hung in the hall closet yet, so they're ready to put on again." She danced around behind them to assist them with shrugging on their coats, not waiting for agreement. "Thank you for helping Amy. You two remember our dear daughter-in-law, don't you?"

As David and Claire fastened their coats, caught off-guard by this call to duty, Jackie turned to Amy to mouth 'Thanks' with a complicit wink.

When the trio was out the door again to fetch the rest of the holiday goodies, Jackie went to the kitchen, opened a drawer, reached in, and then began to work a holiday dishtowel with her hands to wring away the tension that had tightened even her knuckles. Her wedding rings reminded her that her bond to these awful people was accompanied with the reward of being married to Steve. *Ah, Steve, how you must have suffered till you met me.* Jackie smiled and smoothed the dishtowel atop the counter.

Soothed, she turned to the pantry to retrieve popcorn, paper goods, and matches to light every candle in the house. Their farewell party was going to be stupendously festive and successful.

It deserved to be. Texas Tech had fired its coach Mike Leach. Though Michigan State had had its own scandal when players were suspended for premature celebratory drinking, Steve was punching the air with his fists, shouting, "We've got a chance!" at regular intervals. This road trip had made her quiet man come alive. Go, Spartans! Go us!

Twenty-Three: Things are Adding Up

The next morning, heads propped in one palm, while the other arm pumped coffee like a transfusion, Jackie and Steve stared at the cards mounded on a tray in the center of the table, looking very much like a church collection basket. The stack proved that the party was over, the adventure was imminent, and their vagabond dreams would be realized.

Steve made the first move to poke a calloused finger in the tiny gap of the seal to rip the envelope and pull out a card. Taking turns, they opened the gift envelopes to reveal the bounty stuffed inside before their houseguests were up.

There was even a $200.00 card from the choir. Jackie was sure that Pastor Rankin would be unbiblically envious of their collection if he knew – until she opened his card with two Cracker Barrel gift cards. Glory be, it stirred a woman's soul and made her wistful. They were leaving so much behind, and she wondered if their abandon was worth what was ahead.

"A thousand dollars in gas cards! Are you serious? Wow!" Steve exclaimed.

"Keep your voice down, Hon," Jackie punctuated her whispered mandate with both hands coming down like the last curtain after a play. "If your tightwad brother hears you, he'll be asking for one to repay him for driving all the way down here. Are you sure they know we plan to leave early Monday morning?"

Brandon and Amy weren't coming to say final good-byes during a last Sunday supper, having had several "how-to" briefings of the magnitude of going to war. The chumminess of the two couples warped as Steve tutored his son. Jackie knew he could get a little pedantic, especially about how his micro-dairy should be run.

Brandon responded with more than a little peeve. After all, his 4-H championship ribbons were chained around the ceiling of his teen bedroom; though fading, their colorful prowess was still evident. One day he'd even stormed upstairs and coming down wearing several pinned to his ever-present Spartan football jersey. Jackie had quietly replaced them after removing from his jerseys to launder them.

She quit trying to referee and Amy ducked the scene - so much for time together. Jackie reminded herself that Amy had already demonstrated her memory of where the cooking and cleaning supplies were, and then sighed as she reckoned that the young career woman would likely never use them. Jackie wondered again how it would feel to come back home, but it just wasn't worth looking forward when she didn't even allow herself to look back.

Jackie was relieved that there would be no ritual departure drama, no movie-worthy handkerchief scene. She was queasy about the layers of farewell: to her son and her newly chummy daughter-in-law, her home of thirty-odd years, and her extended family of friends. Steve had a heavy heart for the business and his family land, but she could only handle her own feelings just now. Nostalgia and novelty were an odder combination than chocolate mints and peanut brittle, which she suddenly craved.

What had seemed like the best party this side of Vegas had ended with such a cluster of hugs that she and Steve had felt as if they were in the midst of a rugby scrum, moving back-and-forth across a determination of go/not go.

Gifts and brains fully open, they reminisced about the party, taking turns between continued sips of coffee, for a lazy half-hour. Then Jackie got up to make a second pot, while Steve fetched their trip maps, and they reflected on their future.

As Claire and David floated into the kitchen – both fully dressed; *how did they accomplish that without a sip of coffee?* - Steve rose, not capable of chat at the moment. He had much on his mind; a mind that was mildly hung over, like hers was, Jackie knew. She watched him stash the gas and restaurant cards in plastic cases that would reside in the truck's glove box. How handy that she'd found the yellow and blue pencil cases in the school's lost and found bin. Then he marched upstairs to inventory his clothing that she'd pre-selected for the trip.

She turned back to their guests, with their buttoned to the neck, long-sleeved shirts. Both wore sweater vests over khaki slacks. *Did they shop in the same department?* If they did, they wasted no money on color. They remained resolutely beige, like a pale version of shadow people, the black metal outlines propped against many houses she passed on country roads. Just as thin and rigid, Jackie knew from experience.

"What would you like for breakfast? We have to clear out the refrigerator, so be generous to your stomachs," Jackie said, already reaching for coffee mugs.

"Do you have Jimmy Dean sausage?" David asked. "That's my favorite. I sure liked that guy's grin, didn't I, Claire?"

Jackie always thought it strange that David seemed to feed Claire her lines to speak, so she turned to Claire with a whimsical grin, eager to hear what she could want for breakfast.

"I'd love an abundance of your dairy cream in my coffee," was all Claire said.

"Well, pour yourself a cup. It's fresh. I'll get out the cream, and sugar's on the counter. After you've dosed up, would you like to visit our new residence for a year? It might be best before Steve brings his clothes in and messes up the tidy space." Jackie hoped she didn't sound negative. She didn't want to trigger Claire's natural proclivity for pickiness.

As they bundled into coats, hats, and gloves, David quipped, "I just love to walk in the country because you can't step on a crack and break your mother's back!"

What a cheerful childhood companion David must have been – not, Jackie thought. Claire and David were well suited to each other, living in an enclave of negativity. Each reminded her of the Charles Schultz cartoon character that perennially had a squiggly cloud of dirt over his head. They were dirt magnets, not for their outer selves, but for their inner selves, ready to shovel it out on anyone and anything. She'd already listened to their Obama diatribe, replete with racial slur that extended to include blacks in sports, film, and music. Apparently *they* were taking over the world, acrobatically remaining on welfare rolls while taking home big salaries and not paying taxes or giving back...aargh. Jackie fervently hoped she wouldn't hear it all again because she'd heard it all before. These two were a broken record.

Jackie put in her imaginary mouth guard - a ploy she'd adapted from watching Brandon play football - because tact was necessary to expedite the requisite tour, just as Steve descended the stairs with his clothing bags. Reprieved, she ran to help him and hurry them all out to the Sunnybrook to complete the onerous show-and-tell. With Steve as leader of the band, she could be a deft, demur Vanna White, opening cupboards and cubbies on cue, adroitly avoiding discovery of any of the stashes. Jackie wanted a gold star when it was over.

The tour was over before it began when Claire stumbled with the first step into the RV despite Steve's admonition to "Watch the step. It's a little high and narrow." Her spill featured flailing limbs, racy red underwear, and was punctuated with expletives. She could no longer masquerade as a pious little twit, patient behind her man. She'd goddamned-it-to-hell blown her cover.

Already inside the vehicle, David may have begun to roam on his own, but he rushed back to see what was up, then down. The first thing he did was to clamp his hand over Claire's mouth. Then he felt her pulse. Instead of soothing Claire with words, he turned on Steve, "What were you thinking when you bought this thing?"

Steve was still outside the vehicle and pretended not

to hear, his upper body tensed in emergency mode.

As a volunteer fireman, he had special EMT training; so he was ready, set, go. Jackie squelched a laugh; Steve looked like a hunting dog after a quail...*except it was a turkey in a trailer.*

Claire's limp body wedged the doorway. When blood started to spurt from her nose, it was Steve that stuffed his handkerchief in, though not so very tenderly. David's nervous hands had retreated to his pockets.

Which was good, because if he'd said more, Jackie would have stuffed them down his throat. She tried to summon sympathy, but her thoughts were on her new plush carpeting, fearing a permanent red spot in its precious fibers, right at the entrance of her new home. It was un-Christian, but she couldn't help herself. *I did not desire Claire's blood as a trip sacrament.*

Jackie sighed, knowing the trailer had a first aid kit. But Claire blocked the door and stepping over her body seemed more disrespectful than helpful. She'd have to run upstairs in the farmhouse—*the farmhouse? Yikes, she was already detaching from her longtime home —* to get medical supplies from the bathroom.

Claire was soon on the mend, ensconced in one of the club chairs, feet up, icepacks mounted on elbows and knees. At least this kept her out of the way of final packing and trip preparations. David was napping on the couch, as if he'd done a great deed. Jackie had half a mind to ask Pastor Rankin to re-bless their road trip, but all of the commotion left no time for church. Please, God, let the meddlers go, without a lawsuit in mind, was the prayer she lofted on her own.

Sunday afternoon, when David carefully backed out of their driveway, without a wave or a smile from him or Claire – well, Claire had waved off an ER visit for her injuries and that truly sufficed – Jackie felt a mixture of relief and rapture.

Then apprehension overtook her like an early blizzard. She was leaving her nest, her home, for adventure in a box. How would this Christmas gift unwrap?

She channeled her fears into a frenzy of anticipation, like a six-year-old on the first day of school. In keeping with the season, she imagined herself as Mrs. Santa, helping her man check his list twice to assure all provisions were aboard his sleigh. In fact, the fully-packed Fifth Wheel mounted on the F-150 could be imagined as Santa's full bag of toys on his sleigh: the RV was their toy and its bags were full.

Only it was two days after Christmas.

Twenty-four: Steve Revs Up

Monday, zero dark thirty. Steve stepped into the cab of the shiny red truck and busied himself with dashboard gauge reading and dial setting, adjusting the mirrors, to avoid his son's eyes. He'd checked Brandon's milking procedures one last time; the cows were faring well, his turn ended as their keeper. Jackie waved like a float queen from the passenger seat while Brandon firmly held Sparty's leash and collar to prevent a gallop after the truck.

What a rambunctious travel companion he would have been, Steve thought. But they couldn't figure what to do with him while they went to the bowl game and, besides, Amy wanted him. *Good-bye, Sparty buddy. Bye-bye.*

Steve sighed as he punched on the truck radio, then the ignition. He was leaving so much more than a beloved dog and son behind, but it felt peacefully right. He'd already had the free fall of job loss, followed by the buoyance of new beginnings; this was just another floor on the elevator of life. Whether up or down, or roller coaster-like, the trip's experience was yet to be determined. He was living the best life he could; he hoped he wasn't going to hell with this plan.

Steve watched his farmland diminish, and then disappear from his rear view mirror as he drove toward the Interstate south. It was surreal to leave his farm, though, truthfully, he hadn't felt like a farmer since his father died.

He got downsized at the GM plant in August 2008, and whether from depression, aging, or lethargy, his body began to upsize soon afterward. He hadn't been expecting the pink slip stating that he was dispensable. He went from automaker to autonomous with a single piece of paper. He often wished he'd made it into an airplane to soar into the trash. That action would have had power and invention in it! Little children never consider that bold-colored birthday balloons may pop either – and that's how Steve felt: like the child whose

Disney balloons flew away to snag on telephone wires, joy obliterated by communication's cusp.

Soon enough he would be in Disneyland. Perhaps he'd buy some balloons to symbolically release his broken dreams. Jackie would love the balloons and never know their secret intent.

Steve's one tour in Southeast Asia had at once short-circuited his personal growth and hastened it in ways that he never completely understood. The war itself had made so little sense that his participation in it hadn't either. Ironically, he was proud that avoiding his duty had never crossed his mind. Drafted soldiers invented *Just Do It.*

But the experience had scarred him in ways that didn't show. Every year, he tore up applications to join the VFW, despite Jackie's urging about their great Memorial, July Fourth, and Veteran's Day parties. He did not do it out of shame, but to avoid remembering, which he knew to be the subtext of the parties. He didn't want to imbibe that elixir.

He'd been almost a child when he went to work for GM, though childhood had been beaten out of him by that single tour of duty in Vietnam. He had his first legal beer with the guys on the line. Part of the celebration was that he had all his limbs and that he was able to walk into the auto industry as a legacy, just like his dad who'd gone to work there after his turn at war. Working two jobs was penance for having lived through the war, his dad said; working more than full time was necessary to mend the country, though he meant his soul. Steve wished that he'd complimented his dad on his wisdom. He'd give anything to even hear him swear again.

War, then work. The wife came next and Jackie was a good one. They'd grown together, had a kid and a dog, and years of peace and prosperity. Pink didn't seem a manly color for blowing up their life, especially not when it was a mere slip of paper. He and his buddies had laughed at the word play, while crying inside at the joke that was on them.

Better the green of grass with brown cows munching and basking under the blue bowl of sky. So, what had been his kid's 4-H project became his own soon after the county fair ended. Brandon had gotten married and moved into town anyway, so the chores' shift had symmetry and moved Steve forward in life. He got a handshake bank loan for a few more cows to make a herd. Neighbors and fellow church members signed on eagerly for organic milk. Soon it had become more business than hobby, and it kept him content.

But 5:00 a.m. milking could be hell, especially if the cows kicked up a fuss and happened to hit your defenseless knees. Knees that suffered through the sustained crouch expected while one hooked the udders to the machinery, day after day, night after night, year after year.

It certainly wasn't the hour, because the alarm remained set where it had been for thirty years of factory work, sometimes seven days a week. He relished the milk delivery, recalling the clink of glass milk bottles dropping in the aluminum bin on the porch in his youth. In his child's eyes the deliverer was venerable, for in his gray uniform and cap he looked similar to a policeman, a guardian of good health and clean living.

Steve smiled at himself in the rear view mirror where he saw a half-faced superhero. It's what Jackie said to him after they brushed their teeth every night. She'd point to his countenance in the bathroom mirror and say, "You're my superhero."

Well, this superhero may have played his radio a bit loudly on his delivery route. Were there radios in the delivery trucks that he recalled in childhood memories or did '50s men drive in stalwart silence after their war?

His short route became routine, and there were no people to mix with like he'd had at the plant: rocks on a dirt road were not convivial. You could commiserate with a radio; "As Good as I Once Was" suited, especially when his superhero costume felt faded. Sing it, Toby Keith, a beer-drinking good old boy if there

ever was one. Steve admired his commitment to troop
entertaining, but had never seen him. Perhaps he'd seek
out Toby's Las Vegas bar.

Jackie's songbird tendencies broke him out of his
reverie. The Sirius radio song was "Roadhouse Blues,"
his pleasantly-plump wife in an odd duet with Jim
Morrison, the dead, black leather bad boy. If Jackie's
curls were flung out with gel, they would create a mane
like Jim's. A glance at his watch after a sign for
Middlebury, Indiana, revealed that he'd been on road
trip reverie for a while, and he had to admire her quiet
patience.

"Keep an eye out for the Sunnybrook Plant, Jackie.
We'll see if they'll give us a pit stop and tour to work
the legs a bit."

"I was wondering when you'd remember that you
had a passenger. One that might need an un-coffee
break, if you know what I mean," Jackie said. "Oh,
look, there's the Village Inn. Doesn't that look like the
restaurant in New Lothrop? We've been a hundred
miles, and it still looks like home. I wonder if that's
what the whole country will look like?"

As it turned out they had a nice little late-morning
meal. The diner was still decorated for Christmas; a
small tree at the cash register was dappled in
decorations and ringed in tinsel strands. Its lighted star
topper blinked on and off in a syncopated rhythm, as if
it had given its all for the holiday and wanted to be
boxed away. Matching tinsel streamers swagged across
the windows that fronted the diner, though some
swagged more than others – *just like the butts of my
friends and me,* Jackie said when she pointed them out
to Steve. As a wise husband, he didn't laugh.

It was Monday, December 28, and all workers at the
Sunnybrook plant were on obligatory holiday furlough,
facts learned in overheard conversation in the nearby
booth. The couple groused about the shutdown when
they had Christmas bills to pay. No plant tour today,
Steve's first burst balloon.

Since there were few people in the restaurant –
with the cook and waitress, the number was six – and
there was a wait for two sunny-side-up eggs with toast
and bacon, Jackie leaned out of their burgundy leather
booth to say "Hi." She'd made a vow to meet others on
this trip, as if it was a line item on a report card to her
Maker.

"How are you this fine morning? Did you enjoy your
Christmas?" Jackie said. She'd heard their grumblings
and wanted to divert them to pleasant conversation.
This was the first day of their dream trip, and she
wanted to start it right.

"Oh, yes, we had a fine Christmas. All our grandkids
came over to show off their presents. My name is Sue,
and this is Glenn. Want to see a few pictures?" Sue had
her phone out and walked to their booth before Jackie
could shake her head either way. Jackie didn't even
glance at Steve; she scooted over. She was good at
vicarious oohing and aahing, and, perhaps the kid vibe
would convey to Amy and Brandon back home.

With the females aprattle about kids and recipes, just
like over the proverbial back yard fence, Glenn came
over to shake Steve's hand. "I saw youse drive up and
park. Mind if I take a look inside? I helped make that
rig."

Steve scooted out of the booth, sending his white
paper napkin aflutter like an angel. Glenn called over
his shoulder to the cook, visible in his dingy window to
the dining room, "Hold the eggs till you see the whites
of our eyes, will you, Joe? We're going for a tour."

Steve opened the door with a flourish and followed
Glenn, who pointed out his handiwork within strides.
Steve had to admit that, as he ran his hand over the
spot, he couldn't feel the weld, let alone see it. He
complimented Glenn on its secret excellence, but Glenn
launched into gripe about the company. Steve re-
directed his grumbling by allowing him behind the
wheel of the Ford F-150, only the fourth person on the
planet to do so, he announced. Now Glenn ran his hand

along the dash, with its jillion dials underneath, eyes closed as if in meditation.

Steve didn't share the fact that he'd worked a line at GM for thirty-some years. He wasn't into being competitive or conversational; not with a man whose glumness threatened to thwart his own good mood. "We have to hurry down the road to San Antonio for the Alamo Bowl," he said, "so we've got to eat our eggs and get our show on the road."

"Thanks for the tour," said Glenn. "I'm going to be proud all day." Back inside the Village Inn, he retrieved his wife and paid his bill, as well as Jackie and Steve's, they learned at the register. Goodwill and Godspeed, too, because Glenn had left a Sunnybrook magnet with the waitress as an added gift.

They had their first road trip souvenir. It reminded Steve of Brandon's artwork, photos, and sports schedules that used to coat their refrigerator – and set him on another road trip reverie as they drove through Indiana, enjoying the look of other farmers' land on either side of the Interstate, while Jackie fiddled with the iPad.

No calls from Brandon yet – Steve was equivocal on the subject, not daring to mention it to Jackie; he felt certain that she'd cry. She and that other lady, her name already faded like his blue jeans, had talked a lot about children. Since Jackie only had one, with no grandchild prospects, he felt certain that her tear box was filled more than the Kleenex box in the truck cab could accommodate.

Twenty-Five: Amy, Andy, and Another

"I can't believe you abdicated good-bye, Sis. You, the queen of vamoose," Andy said.

"You are fortunate that you are out of reach, Brother, or your butt would be kicked thousands of miles further west than you are. I was working. I avoided Sparty, the pounce-upon-me hound. I'm sure he was out of control when they left, slobbering as much as Brandon was blubbering," I said, intending the disrespect.

"Probably irresponsibly bred," said Andy. "Should be outlawed for dogs that run with the Budweiser Clydesdales. Did you know that they were sometimes trained as sniff hounds?"

I said nothing, thinking fast. I didn't like hearing my little brother's references to booze and drugs. If he blew his sports scholarship, I'd feel compelled to add his college expenses to my debts. We were close. I'd always fended for my brother, which often meant *funded.*

After all, our whacky mother had named us after her twin childhood dolls, Raggedy Anne and Andy. The dolls may have been Momma's only friends, so close did she clutch their faded cloth bodies and furtively protect their button eyes and rag mop hair. I was jealous of those dolls, wishing that Momma would squeeze me like that – so, when I filled out my college application, I changed my name to Amy. Whiteout and controlled lettering altered my teacher's recommendation and the scholarship form; Amy was born in an envelope on the way to Michigan.

"So the in-laws are gone. When does the party start?"Andy said.

"Andy, this is not a campus. It is a farm town."

"Describe it to me, Sis. I'm bored."

"Go out and check your crop, Grow Master. How's the pot business?" I quickly clapped my hand to my mouth, relieved to see that my office door was shut. I'd forgotten where I was. Medical marijuana might be legal in Michigan, but I was in a bank.

As if on nefarious cue from the gods, my bald hulk of a boss lurched by my office with its wall of waist-to-ceiling glass. He seemed to stalk to the restroom twenty times a day. I waved back.

"Sorry, Andy. My boss beckons. Talk to you soon."

I slid my smart phone back into its pocket in my purse, trying to re-group my pixie look. It was my masquerade even as I commanded small town business at the bank with the finesse of a corporate pirate.

Soon I was engrossed, grinding my teeth on year-end statements, no post Christmas vacation allowed. While my posture was focused, my mind niggled at a conundrum, one that my merchant clients would have relished: too many cookie orders. The 350 cookies stashed in the freezer might be fully depleted several weeks before the pot plants could be harvested and dried to perfection. Holy shit! It could be bad if business was good.

I noticed one of Sparty's long white hairs on my pant leg and cast it off. Sparty was valuable as guard dog presence, but I begrudged the cost of his board – $40.00 in dog food and chew toys/month – as much as his manners. It was going to take a lot of yoga breathing to handle my aversion to his Marmaduke behavior and his expensive doggy breath.

I took a moment to renew my yoga class series online before I returned to the drudge. I wryly thought of why I didn't like Sparty – because I couldn't dominate him like I did other males. And, Sparty was more persistently demanding – and more universally loved – than I was. He had no time but the present, and it was always the best. I had to admire the dog's life.

Yoga sign-up prompted a downward-facing dog that I hoped would clear my mind - just as my boss floated back by my office. He quickly opened the door, braying, "May I help you pick up something?"

"No," I said coolly as I stretched upward. I stared him out the door, the old goat. Probably eager for some cleavage. I had a mind to moon him – soon.

Not that I'd kept yoga a secret, but it was an awkward posture to be caught in, for one who relished professional status. I could feel a red blush, which mimed the math on some of the year-end Profit-and-Loss Statements that I struggled to complete for my clients. Some of their numbers didn't add up, but I was paid big bucks with expectation to do it. *Just do it!* It seemed easier to fly to the moon and back. Made me want to stash some weed for office work when the crop came in.

I almost wrote that on a Post-it note. Holy shit.

I knew I couldn't call Brandon for reprieve. He was in a bodacious funk. Even his football jerseys looked frayed – if and when I saw them. That guy was scarce to everyone, even Coach Uhrig. Probably scared, too. He and I fought demons, the same, but different.

He'd better pull his fool head out of his games and watch the grow You-Tubes and the weed farmer sites my brother recommended.

The small clock on my computer screen began to tick like a time bomb as the hours of December 28 passed away. Finally, I decided on the dumbest, most erstwhile thing I could think of as diversion: a cruise through the local Wal-Mart for after-Christmas deals. I did not let the door hit me in the ass as I strode out of the bank.

Driving Jackie's van wasn't bad. I liked feeling above it all, invincible in a different manner than the baby Benz. But the reduced guardedness when parking in a lot was a bigger bonus. Because I didn't have to park defensively to avoid door dings, there was less slush to trudge, with that awful road salt that sullied my boots. These alligator beauties couldn't be replaced by Wal-Mart stock.

I whizzed into the store, struggled a cart from the impound area, and pushed over to the free coffee bar, chastening myself for the smile the greeter evoked. Bolstered with caffeine, I guided a clicky-wheeled cart up and down the aisles, an aimless seeker. I put little in my cart. I couldn't interest myself in this plebian drivel; I shopped online and didn't poke, paw, and peruse. Most of all, I didn't like caring what items cost, with scrimping money inherent to the hunt.

"Not shopping in the food aisles, buying all of the butter and flour off the shelves?" I looked up at the ruddy face of a young woman who beamed with familiarity.

I almost flinched. Fortunately I was practiced at the fine art of furtive nametag reads from Chamber of Commerce events, so I could address the woman by name, glad for the cart's shield from the hug that seemed to be jumping from her arms. "Hi, Veronica. Do I know you?"

"Not really. I've only seen you shop here once with your perky mother-in-law, Jackie. She introduced us, remember? You bought so much baking stuff, I was really intrigued," Veronica said.

"I bake cakes for weddings and birthdays to make extra money for my car payment," Veronica continued, eyes glued on my face. "I thought we might have something in common. What do you bake?" As she raised her eyebrows in expectation, a silver ring untucked itself from a Smurf Band-Aid.

"Just cookies. For my husband." I squeezed the cart handle, determined to wheel away fiercely to avoid a conversation, but Veronica's bright smile broadened.

"Wow, you must love him a lot. Wish I had someone like that! Hey, I was just headed to lunch. How 'bout if I treat you to some pizza? It's yummy here. And it's free!"

My hunger answered for me, and I abandoned the unwieldy cart to trail behind Veronica's perky insistence. I'd never done anything like this in my life, never let anyone be my Pied Piper. I'd adhered to Leader or Loner paths, never following someone's behind, as in the 'L' I disdained: Loser. I reminded myself that I was in the palace of losers: Wal-Mart.

I certainly hadn't wanted to go behind the scenes of a Wal-Mart either. Gray concrete block walls emblazoned with scenic motivational posters to emulate windows with a worldview. Framed statements of regulations and labor laws in miniscule print to assure that no one read them. The walls echoed the sounds of our boots. The place was as sterile and void as the Wal-Mart shopping space was cluttered. A length of gray employee lockers, so very high school, and six white Formica picnic tables completed the decor. Over-full trashcans underscored that Veronica's lunch break was later than others.

Thus, it came to pass that I dined on cheesy pizza with the texture and taste of freezer pizza cardboard. As a former dumpster diver of some repute, I wasn't squeamish, but I wasn't in the mood to reminisce. I could barely swallow.

"I'm intrigued by the Smurf Band-Aid, Veronica," I said to avoid tasting.

"I'd rip it off to show you the body jewelry," Veronica mumbled, "but I can't ruin the stick'em. If it's exposed, I get fired."

I almost giggled. "I wear Miss Piggy Band-Aids as needed after a Roller Derby practice or meet. I relish the secrets under my clothes as much as I relish Miss Piggy's attitude."

Veronica's rosy skin tone reminded me of the country ham that the bank had given its best customers. The pig affinity did not flatter Veronica, but at the Band-Aid mention Veronica cracked up, almost capsizing the picnic lunch table.

"I like your laugh," I said, thinking that Veronica's seal-like bark contrasted with her perky demeanor to imbue friend potential.

Our opening conversation was as gangling as teenager talk. As we cycled through topics, I relaxed. Both of us had someone with which to be human. It was all good - except for the pizza.

I was soon to inherit Jackie's wonder world kitchen, so I decided to become what Veronica initially thought I was: an accomplished baker. I was eager not only for an indoor hobby, but also for a compadre in this town. I belatedly realized that Jackie was a semi-ally now far away, soon as far as my soul mate brother.

Brandon was far away, too, though he was here.

There was Terrible Tessa, which named her well – she was an over-emotional, complaining teen. Roller Derby season was in full tilt, but it wasn't non-stop. I had time on my hands, mental anguish to dissipate.

I began to watch the Food Network, wanting to be the Barefoot Contessa as soon as I read the show title, and then liking the woman all the more for her similarity to my plump mother-in-law, Jackie, albeit more expensively clothed and coifed. Maybelline's establishment couldn't have hewn such silken tresses. Clairol didn't have colors like that.

I needed someone to be proud of me in this endeavor, so I called my brother. I wasn't sure I was prepared to hear Jackie's gloat or Steve's guffaw – and I wasn't sure I was related to Brandon anymore.

"Andy, have you seen the show 'Diners, Drive-Ins, and Dives?"

"Sure, what guy hasn't? We emulate him by wearing sunglasses like a low-down, bass-ackwards tiara when we don't need them for the blinding sun," Andy said. "And, hello and how are you, Sis? What brings this up? Got a crush on Guy?"

"No, Veronica does."

"Veronica?" Andy said. "You been watching cartoons on Nickelodeon? Call me later, will you? I have to run."

As soon as the van tires crunched the gravel parking lot in nearby Potterville, Michigan, Veronica and I were hooked. The headlights gleamed off a shiny white chicken posed in mid-strut in front of the plain structure. It was twice as tall as Brandon would ever be, with a chest three times as broad, so the chicken had to be a guy. Photo op! Veronica adjusted her beret over her eyebrow bling, and I snapped our photo, pausing to email it to my brother. I hurried to catch up with

Veronica, who was already inside the restaurant.

The sizzle and smell of frying swarmed our senses, so that the menus that the hurrying waitress shoved into our hands weren't necessary. There wasn't a seat at the counter or any table. The lack of hubbub and conversation was not what you'd expect of about 100 people, most of them portly and pleased to be so, because they were focused on their plates. There was a guy walking around with a handheld mic, trying to speak with people, followed close by two guys, one with a shiny umbrella and the other with an on-the-shoulder camera.

Trying with little success. *Don't bother me. I'm eating,* like Brandon would say if I tried to converse during one of our infrequent meals together. At least he didn't say, *"Don't bother me. I'm gaming."* His mama trained him better than that.

"Deep-fried Oreos! I believe I've arrived in heaven," Veronica said.

"I'd rather dunk Oreos in milk, but I don't see milk at any of the tables," I said, swiveling to look around the room. "Maybe we can talk to the manager and get him to order from us."

"Do you ever turn off that business shit, Ms. Banker?" Veronica said. "Maybe they'd like to order a cake/week from me. I could use the money," Just then, the waitress seated us at a table and took our order, in a fluid series of moves.

"They don't mess around, do they? This is my kind of place, direct to the palate," Veronica quipped.

Within ten minutes, two piled high plates appeared. Soon Veronica and I were as silent as the rest of the room, though our tasting was a bit tentative initially. When the waitress came back we ordered more napkins and beer, but that was the most that we said. Until the mic, umbrella, and camera guys sidled up. Then we talked – to keep the camera focus somewhere besides our breasts.

A half-hour later, I called Andy: "Watch the Guy Fiero's show tonight, Andy. I think Veronica and I are going to be on it because we were in Joe's Gizzard City Restaurant when they were filming."

"Wow. Really?" Andy said – and then he softened, "It'll be great to see you, Sis, anyway I can."

I ended the call before Andy got all mushy new age male. I assembled a 'to-go' box for Brandon. He could eat it whenever, I didn't care. *Don't bother me. I am sole support.*

Twenty-Six: On the Road

Jackie woke up, wondering why she was scrunched in near fetal position in a triangular third of the bed. A glance over her shoulder confirmed her suspicions. Steve's body bisected the mattress corner-to-corner to accommodate his six-foot frame. Now her neck crinkled. She punched Steve's side in retribution, and rolled out of bed onto all fours, aware of her age. She squelched a laugh out loud as she recalled the last time she'd crawled on all fours to a bathroom: after Steve's drunken celebration upon return from Vietnam.

The bathroom was spare utilitarian, alcoved at the back of the bedroom, as if an architect apology. To coincide with the overall look of underachievement of the Motel 6 room, the toilet flushed meekly, yet echoed throughout the open space. A five star Las Vegas hotel suite this was not.

Nor was it their motor home where they'd slept off the road wearies the first night of their fresh-start vacation. They had accomplished what looked simple on a map: twelve hours travel from Michigan to Memphis. Jackie drove an hour for every two of Steve's to keep them fresh, on track. When one was at the wheel, the other was checking for gas stations on the iPad, reloading the CDs of traveling music, or fishing bottled water from the cooler in the back seat.

Neither had envisioned the incapacity that this much driving would bring to their thoughts as well to as their bodies. They'd been as fussy as four-year-olds as they pulled into the Cracker Barrel parking lot. The Motel 6 across the street had an attractive, neon-signaled price.

"Jackie, how much and how far is the Graceland RV campground?" Steve said as he eased out of the truck cab.

"I don't want to bring the iPad into the restaurant. I'd leave it for sure," Jackie said as she rounded the cab and put her hand in his to walk across the lot. Even though the wide wood plank entrance only had a single step, Steve steadied her. She felt like the Tin Man from the Wizard of Oz.

"I know," Steve said with energized spirit. "We'll ask that Siri girl on our phones."

"You ask her, Steve, I've heard she's nicer to men. I'm heading to the restroom as soon as we're set up in a booth."

When Jackie returned to the booth, Steve looked as satisfied as if he had already eaten. "What did she say?"

"Graceland RV Campground is 40 by 40," Steve said.

"Is that a crossword puzzle clue, a test, or the size of the stupid place?" Jackie grumped.

"It's the distance and the price. I vote that we stay at the Motel 6."

"You're not gonna cheat me out of Elvis, are you?"

"No, but I reserved a room and have a good plan for tomorrow, I promise," Steve said. He picked up his menu.

Jackie picked up her menu, too. She was too tired to argue. *I won't arg you if you don't arg me,* as Brandon had famously said as a child. "What did Siri sound like?" she said behind the menu's fortress wall.

Forty minutes later, while Steve screwed his shoulders into a knot trying to park the lengthy duet of vehicles, he cursed as hard as he turned the truck wheels and vowed for a new plan. He'd heard that Motel 6 had shorter beds, but hadn't figured on smaller parking spaces, too. Miniature prices had consequences; they had a long road trip ahead, but one lesson was already learned.

Recalling his exertions, Jackie forgave his monopoly of the bed. *Forgive and forget* - she hoped their bodies would. In the middle of the night she remembered that some Wal-Mart parking lots allowed RVs, and she couldn't wait to remind Steve. Jackie lay there, wanting to sleep in her own bed, which was just right, like Goldilocks said.

As Jackie turned on the coffee pot, a weird single serving machine with an outer spacey blue collar, she worked on her kinky neck. She turned on the shower, to add its noise to the melody of morning, just as Steve kicked back the covers. He got out of bed in a heaving maneuver that she watched in the mirror without a word. She knew she was going to have to drive.

So she began to hum Paul Simon's "Graceland" as she kissed Steve good morning.

"Steve, we better get going so we can be the first at Graceland. How you feeling this morning? Like a warm shower will stretch you back to six feet? The water's hot, so why don't you step in first?" Before he could answer, Jackie threw on a coat, grabbed the keys, and walked out to the rig. She had to retrieve the day's clothing, and she'd heard his good morning farting before.

Much later, Jackie and Steve were *done* with Graceland. "That man had a lot of money and talent, but god-awful taste." Jackie sighed. "I don't know what I was expecting at Graceland; maybe more grace."

She was happy to be walking into the plush splendor of their motorhome, away from Graceland's over-wrought décor and the dank simplicity of Motel 6. Their Elvis experience added emotional whiplash to necks that were already kinked.

"Well, his cars, bikes, and plane were good to see, but that gaggle of broads sobbing and flailing long white scarves at his grave in the side yard was obscene," Steve said. "You're not allowed to miss me like that when I'm gone."

"What makes you think I'll miss you when you're gone?" Jackie said.

"With those words, you get a turn to drive."

"I will when we get out on the Interstate, OK? There's too many cars and not enough lanes for my driving sanity," Jackie said as she strode to the passenger side. She got in the truck and buckled her seatbelt before Steve could arg her.

Steve sighed as he put the key in the ignition, but he shrugged it off because there was no other choice: seldom was in his life.

As the truck engine hummed in greeting, Jackie saw Steve's smile widen with the above-it-all, expansive view out the truck's windshield. With a gearshift he said, "God, it's a glorious, sunshiny morning. Bet it's snowing bushels back home."

Jackie rewarded him with a smirk that agreed, and they were back on their couple track.

Scenery was soon whizzing by their eyes. It was sort of like watching the big screen TV back home, on hyper-speed simulation on an old Star Trek show. They found themselves turning to each other and smiling in unison. The road trip no longer felt like the effort of yesterday. They were a day and night further from the farm and closer to freedom.

Jackie reached into the glove box and pulled out the iPad, punching on the AAA app. Soon she was calling out directions to Steve, who gripped the wheel at 9:00 and 3:00, casually, like it was the morning paper in his hands. Jackie read aloud about the topography, history, and people on either side of the Interstate. Steve smiled, nodded, and occasionally interjected comments into the travelogue.

Soon they agreed to trek through Clarksville, in search of Robert Johnson's Crossroads rather than Elvis' Tupelo. They already knew as much as they wanted about the King of Rock-and-Roll. A second magnet, a Las Vegas white-suited Elvis who kissed up to a microphone, graced their refrigerator, both a reminiscence and reminder of what was to come.

Steve pulled over at the intersection of Highways 61 and 49, glad for the AAA app's assurance that they were at the spot. At least someone had erected a sign, a high glory festooned with double guitars, each neck pointing down one of the legendary roads. For some vague reason the guitars were sky blue. It seemed as good a place as any for the obligatory photo. Jackie urged him to pose with his arms spread to the sky, as if to invite God down to re-take the intersection where Robert Johnson had famously sold his soul. At least that was what they'd say when they showed their trip photos back home. Especially Pastor Rankin.

Clarksdale's struggles were mirrored in the barren, yet burly-looking fields that surrounded it. They rumbled through the small town with a main street not much longer than their Ford and Fifth Wheel parade, Steve thought.

Their destination, the Delta Blues Museum, came into view near the end. A smiling black man opened the doors and motioned them in with as much infectious good humor as the Wal-Mart greeter back home. "You're lucky I got here early," he told them with a grin. "Go ahead, be my guest", after giving them the AAA discount on admission.

The man never stopped smiling as he calculated their change without punching a register key. He pulled their change out of his left pants pocket, having put both of their twenty-dollar bills in the right one. "Take all the time you want," he said as he pulled what looked like Grandma Bree's old piano stool under his ample ass. He looked set for the day.

Inside Jackie and Steve perused the exhibits of blues folklore while they stretched road-weary legs. Muddy Waters, John Lee Hooker, Charlie Musselwhite; names as imaginative as the music that accompanied their museum stroll. When Jackie spied the normal name, Turner, in an exhibit, "Proud Mary" started its refrain in her head, complete with a visual of Tina Turner's high-geared motion, re-igniting her resolve to experience the turgid river.

Steve had nixed this in his fevered plan to get to the Alamo Bowl. It was six hours still to New Orleans, yet Steve readily agreed when Jackie threatened to belt out the song in Tina-imitation.

When they arrived, the Mississippi River was rolling

along, mighty indeed, swirling in muddy eddies, the color of Jackie's morning coffee with cream. Neither of them had envisioned that color. Michigan had many lakes, but they were a steely color of gray/green, appropriate for a state made by the auto industry, a state whose citizens were now singing the economic hard time blues.

Nor had they imagined a river so congested with flat barges laden with coal piles or containers as large as the captain's wheelhouse. The Mississippi River was a muscular thoroughfare, boding better for this state's economy. Jackie pulled up the iPad maps again, to trace her finger over the lengthy river and share the names of river towns with Steve. Colorful names like Vicksburg and Natchez, which raised thoughts of America's people at war with themselves.

At a scenic overlook, Steve parked easily because no one else was there, which was good for Jackie's intention. She carefully stepped over a guardrail and scampered down the bank to dip her toes into the hurrying river water. The sun-infused air felt like Michigan in May. Steve could not resist it either, and soon it was a baptism for their accelerator tapping toes, their new lives of freedom.

They missed Sparty dog - how he loved a romp – and felt a creep of guilt. Sure hope Brandon took care of him because they agreed Amy wouldn't, though she was the one who demanded that Sparty be part of their deal to live on the farm. Jackie wondered why; Steve only shrugged.

Jackie couldn't blame Amy for her aversion. Despite Amy's height, Sparty always managed to jump high enough to paw and slobber her clothes, leaving tongue tracks like a snail in Jackie's garden. He once licked Amy's face so hard that one of her favorite earrings flew into the flowerbeds. But would he fetch it? No.

Nor did Amy. Jackie had to devote an entire Saturday morning, scrounging in the beds at Amy's insistence, and she told Fran all about it when they met for lunch.

"You should have invited me to help, Jackie. I'd have pulled a weed in the name of each school board member while I searched," Fran said. Jackie's mouth opened and then shut, as she tucked her curls behind her ears. Fran apologized: certainly there were no weeds in Jackie's flowerbeds – as there were no cobwebs throughout her house.

Thoughts of Sparty and the house inspired Jackie to call the homestead, but she was only able to leave a message. Before lonesome could overtake them, they put on their shoes and climbed back to the truck to continue their trip.

Steve had wanted to get into their RV camp before dark so that he could do the hook-ups with light left in the sky and energy left in his body. That was not going to happen, though they both had noticed that the skies didn't darken as early as in central Michigan. As with any new skill, the techniques and timing of their road travel were a lesson underway, but Jackie knew that she couldn't interject with advice yet. Not yet.

So they used the park's facilities.

Twenty-Seven: New Year Revelry

It was now December 30. They'd been three days on the road. The truck was hauling the Sunnybrook, smooth and easy. Jackie's trepidations were gradually dispelled with each successive turn at the wheel. She sometimes forgot that the RV was trailing them, though Steve was inclined to remind her to glance in the mirrors. Incessantly. Now she knew how Brandon must have felt during the dairy tutoring sessions.

They were four hours away from their RV Park. With luck they'd be there in time for a walk in the French Quarter, where Steve hoped to see and hear the Preservation Hall Jazz Band.

When they switched drivers at a rest stop, Jackie slid in the CD that they'd bought after the band's concert, recalling the middle-agers' mob that clamored the table set up in the basketball arena reception area. Like they were jostling for a rebound.

Steve's toe pressed the gas pedal lively with the opening trombone slide. "Man, State had great concerts!" Steve said. "We were sure lucky to live close by all those years, weren't we?"

Jackie was glad she couldn't see the speedometer. She brought up a topic to re-direct her mind: "Steve, I've been thinking about names for the RV. Winnebago is just too Native American, and Sunnybrook, Winnebago's subsidiary, reminds me of our farm. I just can't wrap my arms around calling it a 'The Fifth Wheel' nor its model name, the Titan. Sounds like the wrong sports team to be backing." Steve nodded his head and, maybe just maybe, Jackie could feel him easing off the gas pedal. "Got any ideas?"

"Let's call her Rebecca, like in your favorite childhood book," Steve said with a wink.

"What makes you think this RV is a she?"

"Every man's vehicle is a she," Steve said. "That's just the way it's done."

"What's the rider mower's name?" Jackie asked. "He was mine before he was your she, and I called him

John Deere."

"And all these years, I thought I was your only man," Steve said, taking his eyes off the road to flash a grin her way. It was becoming obvious to Jackie that his aches and pains were dissipating with each mile away from farm chores.

"Just for that, I'm going to call this vehicle Robert Redford," Jackie said. "He likes it out West where we are headed."

"How about Sundance? No, I've got it: John Wayne! 'Remember the Alamo' was one of my favorite movies as a kid."

The iPhone chimed "Born to Run". Jackie laughed and pulled it from the handy side pocket of her purse and said: "Remember the Alamo!" to Brandon.

And that's the story of how the RV got its name: Alamo. The Alamo was in San Antonio, and they were headed for the RV's namesake Bowl. Brandon agreed because he was holding down their fort, their farm. It was all good.

The Big Easy earned its name with big, prevalent interstate signs that flowed through the city and to their destination. Jackie used the binoculars as advised by a friend, so she could read the smaller street signs to provide timely directions to Steve.

They'd found the French Quarter Park among those cited on the Super Bowl website. The desk clerks, used to rabid sports fans, smiled at their Michigan State shirts. Jackie and Steve took a little ribbing that they were at the wrong game site, but could give as good as they got, so fast friends were made. Staffer Larry pulled out bus line and walking route maps to take them to the French Quarter after breakfast. Man, city folk were accommodating!

"Steve, we're already missing the intent of our trip," Jackie ventured as they explored the French Quarter hand-in-hand.

"Whaddaya mean?" Steve said as he kept his eyes on

the sidewalk, wishing he could sweep them. The city streets were dirtier than anyplace he'd ever been, populated with cigarette butts, glass chards, colored drink straws, and bits of paper strewn like wild, uneven bits of confetti. Even freshly plowed fields of dirt had orderliness about them, he thought as he waited for Jackie's next sentence.

"We were going to emulate our hero, Charles Kuralt," Jackie continued. "Every Sunday morning he took us someplace we'd never been and showed it slow and simple. Clarksville was supposed to be our 'off the beaten path', but it was more commercial than I'd expected...and tweakier."

"Well, I just don't have another word," Jackie said as Steve raised an eyebrow of inquiry. "Thanks for taking me to dip my toes in the Mighty Mississippi. But, otherwise, I'm feeling whirlwindish and not refreshed by our travel, like I'd hoped."

"Jackie, we drove by Indiana and Illinois farm fields lying flat as a Lake Huron flounder, all similar to our Michigan scenery and that was enough of that", Steve said. "Mississippi scared me just a little; so starved were the roadside fields that I didn't want to meet the people to confirm my impression of who could farm and live there. I'm craving some height to the land, some reach to the clouds," Steve proclaimed, "like mountains, even the sides of a football stadium." He raised his eyebrows to emphasize football.

"And, I'm not liking daylight New Orleans, so let's come back tonight to party. Let's go back to the RV, take a nap, and catch some CNN. Did you know CNN started in the South?" Steve grinned on top of his grimace.

"Condolence for starting the Civil War?" quipped Jackie.

Steve's hearty laughter echoed in empty streets as they turned around and headed 'home'. The Quarter had a different timeframe than a farm.

Their 'On the Road' rampage had erased memory

that tonight was New Year's Eve until Larry mentioned it in greeting at the park. Jackie and Steve looked at each other: the famous party style of this city would anoint their freedom after their Mississippi toe-tapping baptism. They ate lunch, napped, and headed back to the Quarter.

The Preservation Hall Jazz Band, in its own concert hall, demanded their attendance, it's lively music vying with the dark, voodoo vibe that pervaded the Quarter.

Steve noticed it first - he had an affinity for trombone from listening to his father's occasional play: the trombone player was white. That didn't seem authentic to their preconceived notion of an all black band, but the unjustified prejudice dissipated when they heard the group – the trombone player was good. He made frequent eye contact with Steve and came over to chat when the group took a break.

"Name's George. I see you folks are from Michigan," he said as he pointed to their shirts. Steve indicated an empty chair at their table, and George sat down.

"From Michigan State", Steve replied, then looked down at his chest, where the same words were written on his shirt. "We love your music. Can we buy you a drink?"

"No thanks, I'm working. But I'll buy you one if you'll bring me up to date on what's happening in Michigan. I haven't been home in years."

Steve and Jackie looked at each other and back at George, feeling almost hoodwinked. They couldn't believe it. Here they were, heading away from a home that this man longed for. They couldn't imagine where to start to tell someone about Michigan. Their lives were as straight forward as the shirts they wore, with no exotic traces like New Orleans.

George turned on his entertainer's charm and plied them with questions, listened raptly to their answers, then began to spill his own details. He'd been in the Michigan State band, boasting his national anthem solo before a football game, which was tricky for any instrument, but particularly for a slide trombone. He was as thrilled as they were that State was in the Alamo Bowl and promised to watch for them on TV. Oops – the game was Saturday night – so Steve promised to email game photos.

George walked back to the stage as if he'd been given the best Christmas gift in many a year.

George's gift in return was to hail a taxi that carried them to the Maple Leaf Bar as soon as the band's set was complete. He promised them the best party in New Orleans.

What new feats! First, they were following the tip of a relative stranger. Secondly, they were on the first cab ride of their lives; it felt good for both be passengers - *smooth.* Finally, the Maple Leaf Bar was aflame with sound, a multi-sensory blast that almost upended them when they exited the cab. As Steve paid, he took the driver's card as suggested, so they could call him for return to their RV.

The Maple Leaf Bar was on Oak Street, the first incongruity. Another was the architecture. At street level, it had a scrappy ramshackle look, almost without paint, with a unibrow-like covered porch to greet guests. Above the brow line, the second story was a yellow cottage laden with white lacelike wood accents, as if a tornado had plucked it from Cape Cod. The total effect was similar to an elderly church lady adorning herself with a new Easter bonnet.

The loudly infectious music was Zydeco, George had told them, and its rhythm made you forget it was late night. When Jackie and Steve walked in the door, the odor, music, mixed apparel of dancers who moved like a squirmy worm, all drunken and sideways of themselves, was like nothing whatsoever of home. There were men in fedoras and jeans, a few women with low-shouldered ball gowns lofted to show bare dancing feet, and teenagers that looked like Halloween skeletons. Some folks looked sensibly wholesome, like Jackie and Steve, but no one sported an MSU shirt.

Soon they were dancing like the others, beer bottles in hand, to the chunky funk of the band. Jackie marveled at a band member's plump, bouncing fingers of hair, pointing all over the bar. The washboard he clasped was like her grandma's, though this one seemed electrified by flying hands. Everyone was trying to match this man's furtive, wild-armed rhythm. No one in the bar sidelined himself or herself. It was synergy sincere. *Everybody dance!* echoed in Jackie's head, a refrain paraphrased from Saturdays at the skate rink when she was ten.

Jackie thrilled at the serendipity. She wondered what the Maple Street Bar would have been like if she'd opened up their stash. She was on vacation. She was having rowdy thoughts, busted loose by Zydeco.

Steve couldn't wait to check-in with Brandon and tell him of this, their first marvelous, unexpected adventure; subterfuge for checking up on the micro-dairy handling.

Twenty-Eight: Game Prep

So used to farm ways, Jackie and Steve awakened at dawn, just a few hours after they'd collapsed into bed. Holy crap! Their buddy Advil was called out to alleviate body aches generated by binge dancing, but they were going to need toothpicks to keep their eyelids open, dammit darn. Zydeco washboard scrubbing still buzzed their ears, threatening to climb into their temples with headache. Stiff coffee washed down a second Advil dose within minutes.

They lumbered through therapist-prescribed stretches, Jackie in the bedroom and Steve in the living area, hoping to divest body aches further – and divert the headaches with activity, a method that worked on the farm.

"Steve, I didn't work up a sweat," Jackie said as Steve came to the bedroom, "but it wouldn't be prudent to bypass showers as body massage." She knew his plan to be underway before the camper neighborhood came alive.

Steve nodded, gulped more coffee, and flashed into the cubicle to model a quick shower for his achy missus. Thank goodness for liquid soap and towels within arm's length when you're in a slapdash hurry.

Nine hours of highway travel beckoned. While less than yesterday, they had an unwanted lesson about the ravages of age and would keep the Advil in the glove box, wedged between the gift card containers. They'd also eat breakfast cereal out of its box, set between the truck's bucket seats.

The endless array of campers was silent, comatose, seeming as hung over as their drivers, the New Year's Eve revelers within. Jackie and Steve were reminded of the dealer lot where they'd purchased their RV – *was it truly only a couple of months ago?* They almost felt guilty for starting the truck's powerful V-8.

Though it might have been a holiday for some workers, hundreds of drivers clogged the Interstates that wove a 'Y' through New Orleans, more cars than they'd ever seen in one place—except maybe at Michigan State stadium. Sipping coffee in Spartan travel mugs to wash down handfuls of cereal, they promised to take turns at driving and napping, hopefully in the right order for safety. It was the first day of 2010, their new year of freewheeling.

Soon they were speeding by Baton Rouge and Lafayette, names that figured in the songs at the Maple Leaf Bar. That led to reflecting on the magic of New Year's Eve. With caffeinated enthusiasm, they regaled each other across Louisiana, which was shaped like a boot walking away from Texas, Steve noted, unlike their travel route toward.

They made up novel toasts and recalled old ones, topping their coffee cups when they pulled into rest stops - which, of course, were increased by their religious imbibing - eating vendor food to speed their highway progress. By nightfall they'd reached San Antone and wheeled into the Whistlin' Dixie RV Park.

The next morning, they slept past dawn for the first time in years, taking it as a sign that they were finally on a vacation, not a dream. They had arrived for the main event, the bowl game that routed them to Texas rather than some Florida beach like the other Michigan Winnebago Club members. Their other trip obligation, distribution of Big Braghorn's ashes in Colorado, lay down the road.

Before they left for the game Steve had instructions to give Jackie, as he always did. Sometimes he reminded her of her father, not her friend. After all these years, Jackie acquiesced to this aspect of his love: the tutor in his heart.

"Jackie, you gotta remember how much beer makes you pee and how far away the bathrooms are gonna be."

"What do you mean? More than the coffee yesterday?" Jackie said as she stuffed the game tickets in her fanny pack along with Kleenex and Purell.

"This stadium is bigger than State's, the aisles are going to be crowded with people and vendors and such.

If you leave your seat, you may miss most of a quarter and all the best plays, so I'd strongly advise against drinking and eating anything. We had our share of junk yesterday."

"You have got to be kidding," Jackie said, but as she looked at him, she knew he wasn't. He was reading the news on the iPad, in between his random lectures, so he didn't acknowledge her comment. To be perverse, she snuck into the stash, extracted a dash of weed for their scrambled eggs, and returned to the kitchen. She'd tell Steve it was parsley if he said anything, which he wouldn't.

Soon they would both be feeling no pain, so beer wouldn't be necessary to bolster their rowdy game attitude and enjoyment. *But being high made you hungry, so how was this going to work? Too late, guilty conscience. We'll deal with it as it comes.*

"And, you know how much you love the marching band," Steve continued as she served breakfast, "There will be a fabulous half-time show. This is going to be spectacle like you never imagined. You may even get to see the Goodyear blimp. You don't want to miss a thing. Certainly not the TV cameras when they pan the bleachers. Brandon, our friends – and George – want to see us!"

Jackie smiled as she buttered toast. She knew Steve was right. While she jumped at things, he contemplated. He researched. This kind of stuff explained why he drove in near silence for miles, something she had not had occasion to witness in Michigan. The sole history of them riding together was to church and back, a distance of only twenty miles. His lengthy solitude and the scenery were a duality of new experience. Jackie planned to call Brandon later about some free download games suggestions, to occupy herself on the iPad while Steve drove.

They inhaled their food, eager as kids on the first day of school. Jackie rinsed the breakfast dishes, loaded the dishwasher, and wiped the small counter, smiling at how rapidly kitchen chores were achieved. Steve made

the bed – how could you not in such a small space –
and squeegeed the bathroom, looking at his Timex:
"Let's boogaloo, Jackie. The Spartans await!"

They opened the door and stepped out of their home-
away-from-home…into a flurry of vehicles and people
garbed in school colors, a real-time emulation of
Michigan State tailgating. People were milling about in
small groups, and Jackie was sure she heard the fight
song from multiple vehicles. They'd arrived late last
night, too weary from their marathon drive to wonder
what the game day scene might be. BBQ smoke gave
the aura of a rock concert stage, and the sound level
was like Marshall amps set at #11. After deep inhales,
Jackie and Steve descended the steps to join the others
on the parking lot stage.

"Where are you sitting for tonight's game?"
bellowed a fellow as big as his voice.

"I hope not in front of him," Jackie whispered to
Steve as she unzipped the fanny pack to peek. *Silly to
not have taken notice of the letters and numbers on
their tickets before this!* Now she was stoned and the
fuzzed-up figures marched around the ticket perimeter
like a college band. Previously it hadn't mattered: going
to the game was going to the game; where she sat in the
stands was just a superfluous detail. Jackie was here
and happy, light and loopy. Her knees were not going to
hurt no matter how many stadium steps they had to
climb.

The barrel-chested man swooped the tickets from
her hand, held them alongside his, squinted, then
handed them back, shaking Steve's hand in a series of
gestures that made Jackie's eyes go bleary again.

"Name's Denny. Class of '69. Sitting on the 40-yard
line with other former football players and family. This
is my wife, Pam. She was head cheerleader."

Pam raised her arms as if they held pom-poms and
extended her right toe to complete a classic pose. Jackie
and Steve mumbled their names, almost in contrition,
then remembered that they had a football hero son and
made mention, working hard to pronounce every

syllable precise.

Denny beamed and clapped them on the back, rapport firmly established. "I was on the team that went to the Rose Bowl in '65, but didn't get to play. Must be why State lost that game, don't you think?" Then he winked at Jackie to cut the bravado in half, to show that he was kidding. She tried to wink back as they stepped into line together for the bus to transport them to the stadium. The green and white colors seemed to move *on their own*, Jackie thought, as she scanned the crowd – *wait! Oh, yeah* - there were people in the clothing that was moving. *Have to buckle down to be able to converse with this boom-voiced man and his cutesy Bo-Peep wife.*

Jackie needn't have worried about conversing. It wasn't necessary because Denny talked non-stop, and Pam broke out in spontaneous cheers if he paused for a breath. Jackie found that smiles worked, for the two hyper-fans merely wanted an audience. Their boisterousness filled the stadium shuttle bus like a hot air balloon that could carry itself to the bowl game.

The din on the bus reminded them of school bus days, especially when Jackie had driven the fan bus to Brandon's games back in the day. There was an uncontained emotional perfume to the air that made conversation sail around like paper airplanes, bits of this and bits of that: player stats and team reports from purported insider sources, newspaper hype, and rumors about the coaching switch at Texas Tech, seasoned with regional Michigan accents. At least that's how the chatter reverberated in Jackie's head. It was as if Ma had put the kettle on and everyone was bubbling, ready to let off steam.

Jackie was also ready to pee, wishing she hadn't enjoyed two cups of coffee. She'd been swept into conversation with Pam the cheerleader and forgotten to venture one more time to her glorified closet of a bathroom in the Sunnybrook. She teased open the zipper of the fanny pack to assure herself that she had remembered to pack tissues and hand cleaner because she was going to lower her standards and line up for the first port-a-potty when the bus stopped at the stadium.

Yup, there they were, stashed behind a bag of peanuts that Steve said would likely get confiscated, but what the heck? *You couldn't blame a girl for trying!*

To which Steve always added, "Yes, you are very trying, Jackie."

She began to recite the alphabet, forward and backward, to occupy her mind just as she had done when she was peeling potatoes or serving cafeteria food back in the schoolwork days when there often wasn't a proper morning break time. When the fight song erupted on the school bus, she joined in, though not with her usual gusto.

This mental game kept her mind and body engaged while Denny and Pam prattled on. And kept her attention away from the fact that Steve was right, *so right* about not drinking much liquid throughout this mega-crowded event.

She wished she'd bought adult diapers at Wal-Mart.

Twenty-Nine: Game On!

"Gosh, it's looks like we're at the Christmas Bowl!" squealed Pam, as the bus neared the stadium.

And, it did, Jackie admitted. There were intense swaths of Spartan Green and Raider Red clothing, swarming out of vehicles lined in a parking lot as large as farm fields. *Shouldn't the partisans been separated?* As she looked around, she spied bold yellow security jackets that could have been stars on a Christmas tree as the guys stood in broad-legged stance, windmilling arms to herd vehicles into parking spaces. Since their emphasis was on speed, the obligatory blue of police enforcement presided over this universe. The Guinness World's record of conga lines funneling into the giant stadium reminded Jackie of the garlands on her Christmas tree back home.

There was more noise than was possible, Jackie thought. As they walked along, she jerked Steve's hand so that his head came down to her level. "I've got to pee before we climb to our seats," she stage whispered.

"Me, too," said Steve, putting on his drollest face, "Remember, Jackie, when we get up to our grandstand seats, there will be no leaving them until the end. This will be our last stand at the Alamo, so to speak."

"Steve, you may stand, but I sit when I pee! Quit trying to make me giggle and wet myself," Jackie said. "A wet crotch won't sit well. Or maybe I'll sit in your lap and share!"

Steve laughed and pointed out a place to meet beside a bevy of drinking fountains that looked like they had been yanked from their old high school. They'd long since lost Pam and Denny amongst the surge of football-hungry fans.

When Jackie ambled to the spot, Steve was flipping through a game program. "What's a Valero?" he asked without looking up. As always, this signaled rhetorical. "Sounds like some Spanish cowboy or maybe a sexy dance?"

Then Steve looked up, beaming, "Was that the name of the song in Bo Derek's movie '10'?"

Jackie looked around and shrugged her shoulders, looking squint-eyed at Steve. She hated that movie and he knew it. *Cornrows didn't belong on a woman's head.* No one in the crowd resembled a cowboy, but she did see the boldly capitalized word, Valero, preceding the Alamo Bowl name on the programs.

It was confusing, but she let the thought flutter away. Valero was the title, obviously important to some corporate group. It reminded her of the pushy schoolyard prank that the class bully pulled to be first kid out to recess when Brandon went to kindergarten. Brandon often told her of being shoved aside, which was happening to them amongst this rude crowd. She put her arms akimbo on purpose. *Lord, let us get in and out alive,* she added to her prayers for State to win.

As they followed directions to their seats, Steve and Jackie recycled game-related chat to kept their wits about them: how the Spartans were going to play without a bench, since a dozen players had been suspended for outrageous partying in their dorm, before the team had even left campus. Had the suspension of Texas Tech's coach, Mike Leith, given their opponents a rallying cry equivalent to 'Let's win one for the Gipper!' or was the team relieved at his release over alleged abuse of one of his players?

Jackie and Steve had fretted endlessly around those topics as they packed to end their lives in Michigan and begin their new lives on the road. Brandon had added some back channel gossip then and they wanted to call him now, but they could barely hear each other in this rambunctious cacophony. At least they were rid of Megaphone Denny and Pam and could talk their own topics.

Jackie held tight to Steve's hand, but, even so, several times they were almost wrested from each other. They'd never experienced such rudely bawdy behavior – well, maybe a few times in their local bar and well, maybe it had been their group, but the crowd numbers here were exponentially larger. Jackie felt mildly endangered until they got to their seats, solid firmament on which to perch for the next few hours.

"Look!" Jackie pointed to the field. "The band is playing way down there and we can hear them way up there. It's our first game miracle!" She turned around to shush the crowd, shocked to reality. She didn't recognize anyone. No one in their home crowd had bought tickets. Farm chores were relentless, not having much off-season. Some wanted a sunny beach in Florida in winter, but with two days' drive down and back again, the trip wasn't feasible. If envy wasn't one of the seven deadly sins, she was sure their friends would have wallowed in it.

Jackie sat down and listened for all she was worth. While Steve introduced them to people on either side, above, and below them, she just smiled. *This is my game and I'm in it.* She wished Brandon could be here instead of at home with his money all spent - his home, job, and self-esteem lost. *Hope Amy lets him watch the game at least.*

Steve punched her side: "Damn, we lost the toss! But look – Texas Tech deferred to the second half. We got the ball first! Hope Quarterback Cousins has his best game on today!"

The scenario played out all day: Steve punching her side and shouting commentary and explanations that Jackie didn't necessarily need. *I know everything there is to know about football. Well, according to Maybelline and the beauty shop women.* Tech scored first, then MSU and, at the half the score was 20-14, in the Red Raiders' favor.

Jackie poked Steve in the ribs when the band marched in peacock finery and fluid formations at half-time. Gotta love the brassy sounds, sexy saxes and coquettish flutes, all supported by a drum line that stood like farm lane fence, with Sousaphones as big as baby elephants. The sound euphoria could surely be heard all the way to Michigan, and the stadium was lit up like high noon.

"I checked where the Texas Tech team's Red Raider came from," Steve said.

"Why do you care?" Jackie hissed, her eyes glued on the field. "Can't you see I'm busy now? Go call Brandon if you want to talk. Then go to the bathroom for me, would you?"

"That must have been a helluva half-time speech," Steve commented when Michigan State's quarterback Cousins carried the ball up the gut for a touchdown, and State was quickly ahead in the third quarter. "We've got a shot!"

The game continued at a high energy level and Jackie was sure she was losing weight from all the up-and-down motion with nothing to eat. The munchies feeling that followed imbibed weed, hitched like the Fifth Wheel to the Ford, wasn't masked by activity like their headache trick.

As Steve warned, the peanuts had been confiscated before they entered the stadium. She'd felt a little like a kid caught with a snack behind her mommy's back then, but now she was cranky. She searched her pockets for a Lifesaver or a mint and came up with one, not pausing to share it with Steve, who was fully engrossed in the game.

His last remark "shot" seem ill-advised when the Red Raiders quarterback left the game with an injury. Steve didn't need the sin of bad sportsmanship, since Jackie was almost a smuggler.

But then they both added cussing to their sins list, when Texas Tech's @#$%^&* replacement quarterback marched the Red Raiders down the field to take back the lead, adding another touchdown later to secure a Texas Tech 41-31 win.

Glum. God, what happened? Jackie looked up to the heavens and saw that it was black dark above the stadium lighting – what time was it anyway? She didn't look at Steve for she feared his eyes were watering, perhaps from all the bright lights. Was this burst balloon #2 or #3?

Nobody dressed in Spartan green wanted to remember the Alamo, and tried as best they could to empty the stands, sadly, unobtrusively, in a steady stream. The Red Raider fans doubled up on cheering, whooping, and gesticulating their Valero Alamo Bowl game win. That Valero could stuff it, whoever he was. Damnation.

It was a long, long walk back to the bus pick-up stop, everybody around them staring at their shoes, feeling more fatigue than grief. Nobody was talking much, not even the braggadocio Denny with cutesy pie Pam. Jackie was glad not to talk because she'd shredded her voice. Besides, her mouth was busy, chewing fingernails.

As dejected as Jackie, Steve, and all Michigan State players and fans had been, when Texas Tech beat State – "TEX ASS!" Steve shouted, raising his fists to the heavens, their funk was eclipsed by the post game gabble of Pam and Denny, when the couples climbed into the same crowd transport bus. Each was an expert: Pam on the cheerleaders (with all of the money we alumni give them couldn't they afford bigger banners to chase around the field when we scored?) and Denny on the game. With his boisterous, play-by-play deconstruction, Jackie began to wonder if State had won or lost. *I'm losing my patience.* Blah-blah-blah. Jackie wished she could sneak a tissue out of her fanny pack to fashion earplugs.

"Glory Days," Jackie and Steve mouthed when they had a chance to engage each other's eyes, then flinched and looked quickly away. This might be Brandon in a few years, if he didn't find a life to sate him like sports had for two decades.

Now Jackie wished for mind plugs. Worse yet, she was starving. She wished that tissue morphed into manna from heaven.

"Brandon, wish you coulda been there!" Steve shouted in the phone.

"Dad," Brandon held his phone away from his ear to check the time. "Why are you shouting at me? I did all the chores; it's past midnight."

"Whaddayamean? Oh, yeah, I don't have to shout. It was loud in the stadium."

"We expected a call hours ago, but figured you and Mom were depressed," Brandon replied in husky whisper. Didn't want to awaken Amy. She was a viper if caught mid-dream.

"Sorry, but we didn't even think of phones at the game."

"You didn't take any pictures or video any plays?"

"No pictures, Kid. After the game, we waited in line over an hour to be bussed from the stadium."

"So, are you headed west tomorrow?" Brandon wanted to move this phone call along; bringing up the road trip seemed the way to do it.

"Yeah, Gonna head out in the morning. Your mom's on a grocery run with another gal we met. She's exhausted and her voice is gone, but our stash of beer and snacks needed replenishing." Steve added, to Brandon's bemusement, "It won't be long. It's a grab and go grocery stop, so she doesn't need to talk, though you know she loves to."

And then he paused with a long inhale to shift the tone and topic, "Everything cool with your move, Bran?" Steve caught himself referring to his son by Amy's preferred name for him, a sure sign that he'd become accustomed to that girl.

Brandon sighed. Would this call never end? "We done moved, Dad."

"You left your home empty?"

"Yeah, the bank owns it, so why should we care?"

Steve stared into the RV wall, trying to visualize his son and wondering how he'd become a debt-dud? He took a deep breath and continued, "Well, sorry we can't be there, but you know we wouldn't be much help anyways with our beleaguered body parts. Well, wish you luck. Bye."

Only when he snapped the phone off did Steve recall that he hadn't asked, and Brandon hadn't offered, anything about Amy. While mothers are renowned for good listening ears, Papa Steve was intuitive, too. When his son went silent, something was wrong.

Steve sighed again. He guessed that he ought to call his brother David and his twirping wife Claire to wish them a Happy New Year. They were his only kin. The Michigan State Alamo Bowl loss, and his direct witness, was set-up for serious ribbing. But how would that be different than any other interaction with the King of Gotcha? He girded his resolve to get through the next few moments with grace, proud that he knew to do it without Jackie's coaching.

"Hello." David picked up the phone, as he always did as commander of communication for his household. He had a sullen teenage girl living at home who was not allowed to touch the device without his permission. Since cell phone coverage was spotty in the area, Steve knew that she was cut off like Rapunzel had been in her tower in the woods. Tessa's hair was long and tangled as overt symbols beyond her father's control. Steve had observed her sullen spirit a time or two; relieved that Brandon's personality was more upbeat. Well, it used to be.

"Did you watch the game? State gave us a start to the new year that we'll have to rise above," said Steve.

"Did watch the game. Didn't see you in the stand. Did you go?" said David.

Steve could just see his brother's hands twitching to punctuate his short, terse sentences. "Yes, we went and we certainly appreciated the Spartan seat cushions you gave us for Christmas. Thanks again."

"Alumni catalogue was crammed with game stuff. Seemed perfect for ya."

"What did you get yourself?" Steve asked, for David always treated himself well at Christmas.

"New Cadillac. Black. Looks sharp."

"What did Claire get – a ride in the car?" quipped Steve, though he knew this would go over David's head.

"A new coat. Cloth, not fur, like our other fool friends. Half the folks are hunters up here. It's no wonder they like fur. Say it's warm, but I say it's a waste."

Steve could hear David winding up, incredulous as always that anyone related to him could be that judgmental and punishing of others with words, so he sped to "Happy New Year" and prepared for good-bye, knowing that he'd receive no thanks for the gifts Jackie had given, just as they hadn't when proffered during their brief Christmas visitation. He also tallied a lone question; one question to show interest about his life was a gift from his carping brother.

"I'll never hear right again," rasped Jackie when she returned from the store. "But it's okay. As you can see by my arms being full of groceries, I broke my rule of never grocery-shopping hungry. It was a nerve-wracking day. Only after I eat all this crap, can I die in peace. Do not leave a note for my Weight Watcher's counselor."

"Jackie, don't wish that on yourself, even if you are saying it in whisper. I have need of you here, woman. You are especially attractive when you have monster bags of groceries in both hands. Open. Open." Steve grinned and wrapped his arms around her after she released the bags to the couch. *What a day, what a wife, what a life!*

As he released her from his bear hug, Steve shelved his desire to talk to help Jackie shelve the road trip supplies, munch snack, and guzzle beer. They'd huddle about the problems of family dynamics while driving. Perhaps they could dump all the problems over the rail at the Grand Canyon or stuff them in the cars at the Cadillac Ranch.

Thirty: Together and Apart

In fact, Brandon and Amy were drifting apart since the day Brandon lost his job, as hinted by the body language Paul Rankin and Fran had noticed at Thanksgiving. It was the topic of their first lunch date, though Fran doubted that the pastor would have called it a date.

Paul, who had a counseling as well as seminary degree, shared that the scenario was classic and all about power, about having and having not. The salary imbalance probably polarized the couple primed for it by their respective personalities as much as by Brandon's understandable depression. His super-hero complex deflated by sports-related injury, no job prospects, and nothing to help his generation of displaced human beings.

When he'd called to check on Brandon, as primed by Steve, the kid was either active at cow-milking duties, hung out with Sparty ,or his worldwide gaming community.

Which meant that each call had been terse, unembellished with emotive content except, perhaps, for what was unmentioned.

Fran added, "In my experience, Brandon acclimated well to routine and rulebooks. Lunchroom hang-out was his best subject, which he could do with straight A's."

"Great at Catechism memorizing," Paul tagged on.

Hang out - it had been a singularly male pre-occupation in their generation's day, they agreed over pork tenderloin sandwich bites. The community experts wondered what you'd call what Brandon had done since his job loss. It was certainly not hanging in. They had seen Brandon's facial expressions collapse into a mask in a few weeks, though not of Halloween type. Everyone in the area remembered a time when Brandon had been a god among a large group of friends - and wondered what had happened to the entourage?

Brandon had taken to communicating by cell phone, even when he was in the barn and Amy was at home, according to emails from Steve. This practice kept conversation brief, and he never had to consider where Amy was, something that he seldom knew and didn't care anymore. Milking chores took a lot of time before and after Amy worked, and he gamed all day while she worked at the bank, Steve guessed. Steve hoped that Brandon was at least abiding the dairy business and that, if not, the cows would kick his son's ass. Paul Rankin had promised to pray on the kids' behalf.

Fran had always known that Brandon was not cut out for a life of independence. She figured that all 30-somethings would have denied it, saying instead that they reveled in the chance to be grown-ups. Paul Rankin called Brandon a cocoon kid, grown in the unearned self-esteem of motherly love, bolstered by fatherly spending to assure an unfettered equable life.

Steve had shrugged off the description. As an athlete, Brandon had soared higher than any butterfly could – and he wasn't done. Besides, didn't athletes live by the creed: no pain, no gain? He'd seen Brandon in plenty of pain after games and workouts. Anyway, Steve had replied, there was nothing to be done about it now except to see the process through to the grave.

"Thank goodness the two Breeden couples have the family plan for their smart phones," Paul said. "The number of minutes called back-and-forth must increase at the rate of the national debt."

With that remark Fran was glad that their lunch bill came; Pastor Rankin was famously libertarian, and she was decidedly not. She paid her share and hurried to the high school - to confer with Coach. She now had clear purpose for continued meetings with Paul: divine intervention that Jackie and Steve would second.

Thirty-One: Amy's Game at Home

I invited Veronica to watch the Alamo Bowl on the big screen at the Homestead, which is what I called our new abode. It might take a long time to feel at home here; and to release the feeling that we had been pulled from center stage for a second act re-write before the rug-pull. At the moment, the Homestead looked like a hoarder's home because of all of the haphazardly stacked boxes and furniture.

Our belongings shared space with my in-laws' left-behinds in a cluttered vagrant-like mix, which embarrassed me. I had worked extravagantly to surmount my street child roots. I reminded myself that the best part of the move was making an outsized donation to Goodwill, which had been my childhood store of choice. With that congratulatory self-hug, I turned to the football event and whipped my injured pride into team spirit.

Carefully picking among the trash bags I'd dumped our dresser drawer contents into, I fervently hoped my vanload to Goodwill hadn't included my best jeans. I was determined to enjoy myself tonight. Tomorrow I'd tackle unpacking and all the attendant chores, in Scarlett O'Hara style.

Yeah, I read that book, even though it's old. I spent a lot of time in the public library. I often pretended that I was my own personal Pac Man, eating all of the books in my path. Reading got me a college scholarship.

After sliding one of Brandon's State football jerseys over my lanky torso, I completed the ensemble by stuffing my jeans into Uggs. I winked at my image in the mirror, a childhood habit to bolster myself, before I turned into the kitchen to answer the loud door knocks.

Three yards inside the door, Veronica began cheering in a distinctive megaphone voice. Brandon didn't cringe because he was used to her volume, but I saw his two buddies lift their shoulders like turtles retreating into shells, reflexively protecting their ears. Tobin and Phil sat on the floor resting with backs against the couch where Brandon reclined, leaving the club chairs for the ladies. Each guy clutched one of the floor pillows like a shield when I introduced Veronica, then saluted us with a beer.

No one sat on Steve and Jackie's plaid colonial-themed couch, the one with wings atop the arm rests and a skirt pleated to floor level. Apparently it didn't look like it was ready for some football. It was too similar to their parents' couches, on which they'd jumped with pointless energy until their mothers' yelled, "Stop!" None could shake opinion that a couch was more indoor trampoline than comfort zone.

Perhaps they imagined sticky masses of chewed gum, jellybeans, or a frog cadaver spurting out from between the cushions plundered by marauding teens. I could only guess at this stuff from seeing families on TV or in the movies. A couch had been a wish in my childhood.

I was glad I had a girlfriend to invite – despite the fact that she wanted me to call her Ronnie, a boy's name. Even Sparty, invited inside for the special occasion, was a male. I didn't shoo him off the floor pillow he slumped on, relieved that he hadn't jumped to greet me. I noted that Sparty didn't search out Brandon for a pat or scratch of the head. Maybe he was crowd-shy, but I was not about to gather the feelings or opinions of a dog.

Veronica dubbed the group the Spartan Six and pushed homemade hors d'oevres and cold beer, even letting Sparty lap some in a shallow dish I found after opening up every cupboard in the kitchen. I opened the varieties of chips, bags as bowls, and tallied the Frito Lay ads throughout the game.

Why, that company must own the universe, we Six agreed in crunchy, full-mouth mumbles. Drinking and munching didn't interfere with the tug-of-war on the screen, but who was ahead did get confusing. While I didn't truly care about the outcome of the game, I knew that my in-laws did. *Better call them outlaws now, since they're up and gone. Gosh, who knew I'd miss them?*

Veronica seemed as disappointed as anyone that Jackie and Steve weren't on TV, only louder. She projected as a one-woman cheer force, dressed in compatible colors when she attended my Roller Derby matches, and today as an instant Michigan State fan, cheerful to the end. She was the one who cajoled Brandon out of his funk when he abruptly turned the TV off, foregoing the post-game commentary and second-guessing. She grabbed a cold beer for each hand to hydrate his pouting. Veronica was good at being a sidekick; being dressed in Wal-Mart chic must do that for a woman, but I'm not about to abandon my garb.

Throughout the past week Veronica had provided empty Wal-Mart boxes and packing expertise for our move. Early Saturday morning she helped us load boxes, then drive in caravan to the Breeden family farmhouse, with a not so hidden agenda to meet Brandon's friends. I watched my friend savor the heft of the refrigerator into the milk truck, then into the future grow barn. I was glad that all able bodies were so busy checking each other out that nobody questioned the need for a fridge in a barn distant from the home and milking arenas. Except Brandon, of course, but he never questioned anything much.

I approved as Veronica wheedled Bran's friend, Tobin's assistance to ferry the unneeded two-seat sofa to her personal abode, which she promised was less than ten miles away, so that they needn't secure the small sofa tightly. Maybe because she'd treated the moving crew to super-sized pizza, Tobin quickly said, "Hell, yes."

I awoke, groggy from an alcohol-brined evening, and scanned a room. The bedside clock was not familiar to the eye I'd opened – then I remembered. It was the first morning of being mistress of the house, Brandon's parents' house, sooner than I had intended.

Steve especially welcomed our move-in just days after he and Jackie departed when Bran informed them, saying something about pipes freezing. Bran used the phone's FaceTime, so we could see his mom and dad, who were boogying down to New Orleans. I watched Jackie's frozen face, her emotions hidden like icebergs, apropos given the season. What did I have to swear on, to assure her that I'd take as good of care of her home and earthly goods as her son? Didn't I help her throw a farewell party as good as any damn Mardi Gras in New Orleans?

The spectacular loss of the Alamo Bowl game would live on despite my hangover, I guessed. It coupled well with the loss of our home. Straining to be celebratory, Bran and I had toasted our move with a bottle of champagne near midnight. We'd kicked everyone out soon after the game coverage ended, including Sparty, who whimpered at returning to his habitual abode in the barn. His tail went from wagging like a pom-pom to half-mast in a hurry, but I wasn't backing down. I didn't want to wear dog hair on my pajamas.

I thought it a grand gesture to toast the move with champagne, but when Bran insisted on drinking the entire bottle, with a 'waste not, want not' finger shake at my face, I drank along.

With each sip the finality of the foreclosure burst into my every failed attempt to surmount my crap-filled life. I'd wanted a lot and worked more…instead I got wasted, just like my schizophrenic mom. And I allowed myself a good cry, two minutes long, folding into Bran's specialty bear hug. That he performed like his dad.

When the bottle was upended in the trash, we fumbled with the decision of where to bed before finally opening the door to his teenage room and its twin beds. On the walls, buxom movie starlets still co-mingled with football hero posters. In the moments before I crashed, I blearily wondered why the poster people hadn't coupled since he'd left home, a thought that morphed into the dream I now recalled. While the football heroes wore bikinis, the starlets wore numbers – tattooed on their breasts. Sparty led a group parade into the barn and then…

I flung the winter covers back and yawned into the quiet. I knew Brandon had been up since before dawn to be a milkman, even on a Sunday, even after the move, the football game party, and toasts. As recompense, now we lived only 50 yards from the barn, and he had a half hour more to sleep. To sleep off the loss of our dream home. Oh, shit!

When I caught sight of myself in the mirror, I giggled at my flamingo pajamas, a garish allusion to the vibrant sunshine that my in-laws were probably enjoying while I was stuck in mid-Michigan winter gray. Though I was alone in the house, I still felt it necessary to creep down the slippery oak stairs, stealth to balance my sense of intrusion. As I passed by my own king-size bed components and numerous boxes stacked along almost all the walls, I began to feel a little more secure.

The phone ring startled me; the caller ID reassured me. It was Veronica, perky as ever, saying, "I got lucky. Did you? Come on over, let's bake to celebrate."

I left a note for Brandon; sure that he'd spend the day on micro-dairy chores. Veronica didn't live far. With gas in the van, I was ready for anything to defer unpacking the crap, especially trying to nest our cookware and dishes amidst those in Jackie's kitchen. Where were our clothes going to go and would we, like Goldilocks, try every bed in the house before we got it just right?

Veronica's little house had a gingerbread storybook look, perfect for a devoted home baker. As I entered, the scent inside the door was something altogether different: swarthy and potent with earth, yet not of a farm, something like – yeah…I recognized that pungent smell from the massive cookie-making session in the not so distant past. Perhaps Veronica baked on several levels.

Veronica's hug was heartier than expected and, as I drew from the embrace to take off my coat, I saw glazed eyes under half-staff lids. It looked better on

Veronica than it had on Jackie, perhaps due to some shimmery eye shadow, perhaps due to pro versus amateur status.

"Welcome to my fakery. Want to join me in some weed?" Veronica crooned with a fluid infomercial arm gesture, then walked into the kitchen.

I couldn't even speak – as a businesswoman, I was determined not to partake of the product, to literally eat my profit, but this was Veronica's stash and not mine. The little devil inside my head whispered, "You need perking up." My roller derby athleticism, as well as yoga principles, dissuaded me from soiling my lungs with smoke, so I hoped for an edible high, my business resolve crumbling like a cookie.

"I made pot roast, if you get my drift." The words sifted from Veronica's lips as if slowed by a DJ working a dance party, so her drift was easy to get. And there was that aroma...

"I brought the salad like you suggested. Hope you like Caesar," I said as I set the plastic bag on the table.

"Yeah, Caesar, a great Roman who died too young," Veronica replied over her shoulder. She was peering into the oven. Her wrap-around apron covered most of her clothes and almost touched her toes in this bent-over stance. For a moment, just a moment, she wobbled, and then bobbed up to look at me.

Veronica seemed circumspectly lucid, but I was in a mischievous mood, so I said the craziest thing that came to my mind: "Don't you think it would be awesome to have a pet giraffe?"

"Cool, do you have one?" Veronica didn't skip a beat. "Does he help eat the cookies you bake *just* for Brandon?"

I recalled the day when I'd gripped my Wal-Mart cart and tried to put the insistently perky woman off with that statement, but I mentally loosened and rewound my thoughts. As always, an agenda formed in my head, one written in bullet points with an accompanying spreadsheet.

And so, over salad and pot roast, the fakery business

brought in a new partner, one with a whole new customer potential, the infamous Wal-Martians. We businesswomen plotted to convince the greeter to sell cookies on the side...or something, whatever.

I began to sing, "There's no business like grow business", as I drove away, now high in the van in more ways than one. Relief saturated my loopy core; I'd never felt secure with the plan to use the school kitchen to bake, especially after seeing how crowded the school's schedule actually was when I'd gone online. Further, the farm's electric bill might be higher than I was at the moment; even with the cushion of the Home Equity Line of Credit (*HELOC: what an acronym*) for expenses, my banker self had had qualms. I had to agree with Brandon's grumpy comment that, if phones were so smart, why didn't they pay their own bills?

The plan's momentum floated me over the snowy, rutted roads in anticipation of Brandon's arms. Maybe we'd have sex in the kitchen tonight. In my eagerness to smother my cowboy with kisses, I didn't even register Sparty barking as I garaged the van and ran into the house – *hey, where was my wholesome hunk of a man?*

My mind now acknowledged and worked to shut out the noxious bark as I explored the lower floor, cycling back to the kitchen. I grabbed a cookie and milk snack as substitutes for sex in the moment, alternating a bite and a sip in cadence with my climb up the steps. I didn't bother with the room lights as I crashed on the twin bed and snuggled against the pillow that had last cradled Brandon's head. When he came to bed he'd lie down beside me, take my clothes off for me, and then we'd have some fun.

Meanwhile, back in the gingerbready house, Veronica was singing, too: "My lips are sealed!" She'd promised to be a very silent partner, but she was already spending the profits in her mind. She needed a new car and so much more. She recalled one of her mama's favorite songs: "Oh, Lord, Won't You Buy Me a Mercedes Benz!"

Thirty-Two: Brandon sings "I Love This Bar"

Brandon whistled softly throughout the morning, as contented as his cows. The rhythm of the micro dairy chores had become as sweetly fluid as their milk. He took a break and walked into the kitchen when his stomach signaled, seeking lunch and a hug from his bride in his new old home.

Instead he found a note on the table. He frowned as he grabbed his phone and found an equivalent text. Hell if he was going to make a sandwich and eat it in silence, sitting in a tumble of cardboard. He retrieved his cell and called Tobin and Phil, "How about if I treat you to some beer and pool in town for helping us move!"

To declare Sunday afternoon suitable for beer and pool was a way of knowing for certain that he wasn't a kid anymore. He suspected that his dad wished it for years, but his mother wouldn't allow it. Sunday was sanctified as the Lord's Day, though Brandon never could square why God made cows that needed milking twice a day every day, a day of rest be damned.

The trio entered Darcie's Bar to a crowd swell of football coverage on the big screen TVs. Other sports were banned today: no Nascar, no basketball, and no damn golf for sure. Hoots and hollers, team jerseys, and bottles and glasses of brew layered into an extravaganza of testosterone. They found a small round table and jostled in so all could see a screen. This was easily accomplished due to the brilliance of HDTV as well as the eight-point deer head mounted over each, as if to crown it for showing the sport of kings.

The only women in sight were waitresses who kept shutters on their senses, keeping their minds focused on their car payments and kids at home. A brunette appeared at Brandon's elbow, careful not to block the views. She held a tray against her side but no order pad to further keep her profile slim. However, her hair was escaping a thoughtless bun plunked atop her head, like a doughnut leftover from breakfast.

"Afternoon, gentlemen. Welcome to Darcie's. What can I bring you?"

"What's on draft?" Brandon said, sweeping his eyes toward his friends, who didn't turn from the screens.

"Bud, Bud Light, and Molson Ale." The guys now eyed each other.

"Hell, you're buyin', so you decide, Bran," Tobin said, ever the conciliator.

"Surprise us," Brandon said.

"I don't do that, sir. Darcie doesn't want to disappoint."

"Bring one o' each, so's we can surprise each other," Phil said.

The three guys broke out in grins. The waitress rolled her eyes, then her hips as she sauntered back to the bar.

Tobin put his hand in front of Brandon's face, "You're not allowed to look."

"Yeah, you're married, and it's Sunday besides," said Phil.

"Don't thwart me or I won't pay," Brandon retorted and they all turned back to the game.

Watching the game was cool for a few beers, but then Brandon began to feel restless, creeping with guilt for being in a bar on Sunday. He spied a guy rimming around the coin-operated pool table that commandeered the back reaches of the huge, open bar, carelessly aiming shots. Half time came and went before he got up and walked back, straining to keep an eye on the game.

"Not a football fan?" he said after several minutes.

"Guess not." A few moments passed and Brandon assessed the guy's play. The 8-ball popped into place as the bar erupted in dismay.

"Well, I ain't a fan now," Brandon said as he looked over his shoulder at the screens. "Brett Favre just threw a rookie interception. Old age definitely drained his stuff."

"I take it that means the bar favorite is not going to

win," the guy observed as he began to collect the balls from the pockets.

"Name's Travis," he said, not looking up from the task. "It was so purple in here, I was wondering if I'd wandered into a Prince concert."

"Mine's Brandon. Now that football is in the shitter, mind if we play a few games? My friends and me got loose energy."

"This here is a coin-op table," Travis said. "If you've got some loose coins to go with that energy, we're on."

At Brandon's whistle, Phil and Tobin sauntered over to join them. Though they groused at leaving their prime viewing seats, they agreed to play when Brandon lifted his empty beer glass to give their waitress, more hair fleeing the crown of her head, a cue to bring another round. She nodded in ascent, simultaneously blowing hair out of her eyes. Sort of odd, Brandon observed: wisps of hair flying up while her chin moved down. Like parts of her head were running away from each other.

When the beer arrived, Brandon said, "Travis, let me introduce you to three of my friends: Tobin, Phil, and Bud. They just helped me move and this is my payback."

"I'll bet Bud helped the most," Travis grinned as he turned to rack up the balls. "Pleased to meet you all.

The guys mumbled to Travis' back and winked agreement that he should be allowed to break since the table was operating on his coins. Crack! Balls scattered pell-mell. Each watched the trajectories. The head scratching to recall high school geometry began.

Mostly it just felt good to whack at a ball. Tacitly the guys agreed that there was a sound peculiar to pool that was satisfyingly male. Everyone stood on equal ground and in the long play pauses, you could swig, scratch, shoot skeet in a daydream, whatever a guy desired.

They were into the third informal game, when Tobin climbed into a groove and began to run the table. During this time of sideline observation, Travis took out a smoke and lit up quietly in the corner.

Brandon began endlessly chalking the pool cue to quell his impulse to question. This was a no smoking bar. The pool table was centered in a dark, cave-like extension of the bar, but still. The sign was posted just over Travis' head.

Then Travis swiveled and extended the smoke: "Want to meet my friend, Bud?"

Brandon shrugged and looked around at his friends. Without a word, they all declined. They'd already broken several rules today and wouldn't add smoking to the lot.

Play continued while the crew ignored their personal knowledge of the smoke aroma and tried to pack down their height, so as to not draw any more attention to the cave. They made no eye contact but soon found themselves in a wall, as in the old days of protecting the quarterback.

Brandon thought of the cloth screen that had shielded him the time he went to the Emergency Room. Its portable privacy had seemed healing though it wasn't magic enough to save his pro career. Then he thought of Harry Potter's Invisibility Cloak, wishing that he had one.

Thankfully Travis inhaled only a few times, and then tossed the cigarette on the concrete floor. He stomped the end with his boot.

After a few rounds of play, Brandon noticed that Travis returned to the spot, bent to pick up the stub, and put it in his pocket.

Brandon's mind clicked on the word 'Bud' – *hey*! He decided to float an issue that popped up on a weed website suggested by Amy's brother. He sidled up to Travis and spoke in the best ventriloquist dummy-speak he could muster: "Know where I can get some trim?"

Travis squinted, grinned, and looked at Brandon's wedding ring: "Not enough at home?"

"No, man," Brandon felt his skin heat up, glad the room was dark. He stumbled mentally for some circumspect, yet direct words, and then said, "My wife's name is Amy, and I love her a lot. I was looking for Mary Jane."

Travis took several moments to grin like the Cheshire Cat, seeming to enjoy Brandon's stew. Brandon held his gaze, not daring to search out his friends' eyes.

Then Travis responded affirmatively to the question with a slight dip of his cap brim. Perhaps because he'd enjoyed their play or he was just feeling generous on a Sunday. At any rate, he tugged Brandon to a corner and shared a few details, not inviting the other two men into the huddle.

Travis' on-the-q.t.-answer had Brandon wrap up the evening in a hurry to race home and tell Amy that he had found a grow partner. He didn't bother to text, so high was his excitement. Or perhaps he forgot because he clutched something about the size of his phone: Travis had given him the abalone shell incense holder that laid on the pool table throughout their game, as a totem of their business contract. Abalone fishing was illegal in the Great Lakes – what an exotic trophy for his shelves.

Brandon ended up keeping the knowledge to himself because Amy was asleep when he got home and he suddenly felt more tired than a month of Sundays could have engendered. It was simpler - probably saner, too - to shrug out of his clothes, letting them drop to the floor, and slide into bed.

He could almost feel his cowboy belt buckle give him the evil eye, and he evil-eyed it back. His habit was to assure that it clanked the floor, separate from his pants' fall. It was okay to give up a ritual now and then, though his athletic prowess had often seemed predicated on them.

He replaced it with a new one. Since the twin beds were close in the relatively small room, he reached over and patted Amy's ass. That was good enough for the moment. Tomorrow he'd share the good news.

Then just as suddenly, it seemed, it was dawn and he was headed to the barn. Damn. Nights were supposed to be longer in winter, but the alarm clock didn't adhere to the rhythms of the earth's rotation, and neither did the cows.

Amy went directly from work to the rink, so she wasn't home the next evening or many others, as her Roller Derby team rolled into championship play. The two were speeding apart, either in spite of or because of their disparate roles.

Their sole equalizer was avoiding the escalating stridency of the creditors' phone messages and the mail. When the registered letter arrived, neither recalled who pushed it into the trash.

This Monday was a fresh start. Brandon felt empowered, a little bolder and less forsaken. He had been tasked as keeper of the weed, as logical extension of his farm chores. Not only because the grow rooms and rows of drying racks were in the barn behind his micro dairy, but because Amy required deniability as a banker. He conceded her point, but Amy kept the books on her iPad, which was a huge divide because he had been forced to relinquish his. He didn't feel comfortable gaming online with the computer his folks had left behind, so he was relegated to the tiny screen of his phone.

Now his new bud, Travis — *get the joke?* - would come over to tend the pot plants, harvesting and drying with the skills of a professional. No pass-fail educational course for good old Brandon, who graduated for good when he left Michigan State. The plan was to exchange top leaf product to Travis for the marijuana plant clippings/trim, in well-measured bags. Trust was ensured because they'd work within yards of each other, Travis said. It was so like football, and Brandon felt like he was fully home again.

How the baking got done was Amy's part of the bargain because he couldn't stand the stench and had no desire for second-hand fumes, like that of the reeky clothing she stuffed in the bottom of the laundry basket from the initial bake session. He was the provider of the secret ingredient. He finally had something to control besides his video games and how he squeezed his toothpaste tube.

Thirty-Three: Cadillac Ranch

Jackie was already keying their next destination into the Nav system when Steve climbed into the truck. Before he could lean over to plant a 'let's head out' kiss, the female Nav Nazi's voice was making assertions, continuing her obnoxious chime every so often, to remind them she was on duty. As his peevishness mounted, Steve forgot that he'd wanted to discuss Brandon and Amy's move-in and marriage status. With the umpteenth admonition, Steve bolted his patience and said, "Damn, I'm sick of her."

"Then let me use the iPad. It keeps its mouth shut," Jackie said.

"I think I packed it in the Alamo 'cause I doubted any signal in the lonesome spaces ahead. We're going to see a lot of sand."

"I was just thinking that myself, glad that I'm free of housecleaning," Jackie said as she punched off the Nav system and cracked a window to listen to the wind whistle and nothing else. The clouds that pocked the blue sky were mute. There were no birds, no texts or calls…

The Nav Nazi may have been annoying, but she wasn't as demanding as Brandon.

"Wonder how long it took to clean up the stadium after the game?" Jackie said as she closed the window.

Steve looked at Jackie and smiled. He knew there wouldn't be silence for long; his woman wasn't built for stoicism. He took up the football refrain, recounting every play of the game, in mostly sequential order, talking into a handheld microphone. Jackie accompanied with shredded tissue pom-poms, occasionally grabbed the mic, actually a hairbrush from her purse, to cheer.

Steve changed the ending of the game: State won!

"We won!" they shouted simultaneously, raising arms in touchdown sign. Steve recalled Coach Uhrig's statement that history was written by winners, so re-configuring the game was copacetic in their cab. The game had been the impetus for this route; the long put off journey to see the USA was their win.

Steve quickly dropped both hands to the wheel, realizing what he'd done. To divert attention from his lapse, he introduced a new topic: "Let's talk about the Cadillac Ranch. I'd always heard Texans were ostentatiously weird, but who woulda guessed such a place existed? I have got to see a row of fish-tailed Cadillacs nose-dived into the dirt like they drove in from Mars."

"I think that having lunch among a bunch of upended tin cans is gonna be fun!" Jackie said.

"Jackie," Steve fixed her with a slow burn, "don't desecrate the crown of GM by calling a Cadillac a tin can. Besides, we're trailing what road warriors call a tin can."

As they drove away from the Cadillac Ranch, the ultimate serendipitous sight, Jackie felt compelled to comment. "Why we didn't bring one of those spray paints scuzzing up shelves in the garage? We could have had tagger fun like other people had obviously done."

Steve took his eyes off the road to look at Jackie's face. Who knew she had a tendency for anarchy? When he looked back at the road, he said, "Our stuff would just have been covered by the next tourist, perhaps the couple in the rig behind us."

Jackie strained against her seatbelt to look in the side view mirror but, with the Alamo behind, a glimpse was impossible.

"I think they are playing a different kind of tag, Jackie. Kind of like the grade school recess game. Makes drivin' fun. How many miles to Albuquerque? Can you look that one up?" Steve said.

Jackie stared at Steve. The sports theme had sparked conversation that made interstate miles gallop, and the eccentricity of the Cadillac Ranch had ignited a spirit for shared adventure. *Everything seemed to open wide with the miles, including Steve's mouth.*

Jackie did not risk airing that thought; she didn't want to shutter him with needless teasing. There were many miles ahead of them. She shared Albuquerque destination stats and nestled into nap position.

Steve settled into rumination again, something he savored. It was what he'd done when out with his cows, creatures that couldn't talk back. He relied on the practice to retain equanimity; no one disagreed with — or reprimanded him for — the thoughts in his head.

Steve drove for several silent hours, through barren terrain punctuated by mountains. This was unlike anything he'd imagined and trumped the unusualness of the Cadillac Ranch. Each mile and each new sight detached him from lifelong perspectives religiously trained by military service, General Motors, farming, and the wisdom of his deceased father. Steve found that he now craved discussion to certify their trip experiences. The game parody had been fun.

This time, when the other rig passed him, he waved.

Jackie awoke, perhaps triggered by a short series of snorts – at which Steve did not laugh - and took in the distant mountains. "Look!" she pointed out the right side window.

"I can't," said Steve, but he did turn to look Jackie in the eye. "Ready to take your turn at driving?"

With quick agreement to switch at the next rest stop, Jackie shifted from tourism into mission mode: "When are we going to distribute Big Braghorn's ashes?"

"When we stop we'll retrieve the iPad, to review where we've been and where we're going. We'll figure it out. But now, here's a riddle: how many miles from home do you think we are?" said Steve.

Jackie stared at the visor, where they'd strapped their stash of road trip music CDs. She could multiply the number of CDs by 70 m.p.h. to get a reasonable estimate, but Steve's mental math was easier with the trip odometer in view. She knew he'd enjoy being right, so she shrugged and smiled benignly. "Do you want me to phone a friend, or are you just going to tell me the answer?"

"1700 miles, almost exactly," Steve said. His eyebrow dance was so vigorous that, if he'd been wearing one of his caps, it might have fallen off.

"In a little over a week! No wonder my body feels permanently creased at the hip," Jackie said.

Steve looked over with eyebrows at different levels, one for comedic, the other for tragic effect. "Jackie, I'm concerned overloading our budget. We've already spent $850.00 on gas. Would you look in the glove box to see what's left of our gas card stash?"

Jackie rummaged inside, clicking plastic on plastic as she sifted through the gift cards, then looked up and said, "Will the truck run on Cracker Barrel food?"

Before Steve could grimace, a rest area sign loomed, standing sentry to bathrooms that Jackie hoped smelled better than the ones at the truck stop.

"Thank goodness," Steve said, "I'd begun to fear that my leg alignment with a foot soldered to a 70 mph gas pedal was permanent. It's a peculiar lop-sided pain." As he parked and turned off the ignition, he looked at her. "How you doing?" in his best Friend Joey imitation.

Jackie said, "My hips remain locked for a few seconds when we climb out of the truck. I've been riding in trucks all my life, but…" Jackie put in her imaginary mouth guard to not mention the probable spreading of her butt seated so luxuriously, yet so long.

A few Robert Frost poetry lines wisped through her head: and miles to go before we sleep in our bed, at home again in Michigan. Home sweet, no problems we hope, home.

After they rested, Jackie called Brandon to check in.

"Mom. I'm so glad you called," Brandon said in a gush.

"Is there a problem, Brandon? Shall I put your dad on the phone?"

"Well, I'm not sure," Brandon said. "Yeah, put Dad on the phone."

Jackie handed Steve her phone with a quizzical look that he matched.

"Hi, Kid. How are you? How are the cows and the dairy route?"

"Fine, all fine, Dad. Except I'm freezing my ass with milk delivery. Why'd you start that, rather than having folks come to you? Gas is going up, too, but profits are holding steady."

Steve could see Brandon stand a little taller with those words – he and Jackie had only been gone a week.

"So, what's up?" Steve said mildly, keeping his eyes on Jackie's anxious face. He noticed that she'd combed her hair while in the restroom, but curls were already wayward.

"You got a registered letter, Dad. Looks important. It may have accidentally gotten shoved among our bills, but it shook itself loose, almost like there's an insistent elf inside or a nag like Mom." Brandon neglected to state that the registered envelope caught a breeze when he was emptying the week's trash, practically laying itself atop his foot. "Should I open it and read it to you?"

"Sure," Steve said, with a look at Jackie. "Hold on while we open the truck to sit for the important news."

Perhaps Jackie had hoped that Steve might forget her promise to drive, but he opened the driver's side door and gallantly helped her in and then handed her the keys – all while holding the phone to his ear.

By the time Steve was seated, Brandon had a synopsis: "Dad, you got a brother besides dumb David! And, he lives in California – way cool! I'll scan and email you this letter."

Steve's jaw hung open as if he were the whale hoping Jonah would jump back out of his craw. He shut off the phone and shoved it in a pocket.

"Well, what?" said Jackie.

"Seems like we've got family to visit in California, Jackie. Did we get the iPad from the Alamo?"

"I'll go get it – you'll never find it where I stashed it," Jackie said.

While he waited for Jackie to return with the device to view the emailed letter details, Steve contemplated the fact that they were in the middle of country where Indians had reigned in harmony with nature. And then he thought of his childhood cowboy heroes, like the Lone Ranger and his silver bullets. He ran after Jackie to fetch himself a Silver Bullet from the fridge. This news required a drink, a toast to soak or suck it up.

He popped the top of the beer can and sipped as Jackie turned the ignition key. The iPad was on the floor below Steve's feet. "Hey, aren't you opening the wrong aluminum case first? What family in California?" she asked, then added, "It better not be the Karadashians."

"Never you mind. I have my priorities straight. We have about two hours until we stop for the night. Who knows how soon an email from Michigan will arrive? I'll drink; you drive." Steve said with his eyes straight ahead.

Jackie noticed that his jaw was set as firmly as his grip on the shiny can and willed hers set, too. She drove: "Hi-Ho, Silver! Away!"

When they pulled into the Walt's Wasteland RV Park, it was cocktail hour, so the extra money spent on automatic levelers for the rig was rewarded with speed to more Silver Bullets. They smiled as they popped the tops – sober was neither the question nor the answer now. The beer was cold and refreshing.

During dinner Steve joked at having gotten through Indian country without losing their scalps and Jackie laughed softly, not correcting his political incorrectness. She waited patiently, trying not to eye the iPad too often, now on the table between them. She shared her travel impressions, relishing the intimacy of shared experiences with Steve, knowing the news of the letter would come.

Chime! Steve pulled the iPad closer and opened the email. Jackie could see that his eyes swept the letter multiple times before he looked at her and said, "Seems like I got a brother in California, near a place called Turlock."

Jackie was glad that she wasn't mid-chew in a cookie, so that no precious crumbs were spit out as she said, "Who and how did he find you?" Jackie hoped that her words came out more lucid than her thoughts. It was if sand had drifted through her ears to clog her brain. She yawned as if that could open her mind.

"Well, he's been searching for years. Used an agency, a private detective, and the Internet. Found lots of online articles about Brandon and figured a connection. But – Jackie, you're not going to believe this – his local paper ran a story about our quest to deliver Big Braghorn's ashes. Remember when Widow Braghorn insisted on publicity for her benevolence? Seems the Associated Press picked up the story, and it's going around. We're kinda famous."

"Famous? Can he fix us up with a reality show like the Kardashians?" Jackie teased to cover up her dumbfounded anxiety. It was almost as if Steve had told her that his brother was a Martian. "I can't deal with this now, can you, Steve?"

Before he could reply, Jackie belted, "Do you know the way to Sante Fe?" at the top of her lungs, getting shushed quickly by the nearby camper's occupants. Steve closed the iPad, clamped his hand over her mouth, and scurried her to bed.

Thirty-Four: Do You Know the Way to Sante Fe?

"It's the start of a work week back home," Jackie said as she rolled over and saw that Steve was already awake. "Sounds odd, doesn't it?" Steve just grunted as she picked up his watch. "I like your plan of not setting an alarm, Steve, but we still get up early. Wonder when that will wear off?"

"Probably when we get back home," Steve said, "But it's a great personal statement, isn't it? We are work-liberated. Now get out of bed and fix me some breakfast!"

"Why can't I retire from making breakfast?" Jackie asked.

Steve agreed that Wheaties, the breakfast of champions, tasted better on the road. Besides, it was faster than bacon and eggs. Cheaper, too, now that they had begun to realize that economizing was needed. What was not needed was a traditional farm breakfast when the only chores were gas pedaling, map reading, and rubber necking.

Well, up to now anyway. Jackie convinced Steve to shop in Santé Fe with the promise of extra-hot salsa and chips at a local restaurant. She read the description of several from the AAA site, and he began salivating in anticipation. Each also secretly looked forward to strolling a sidewalk.

Jackie had to prod Steve to extricate the red truck from its green fraternal twin. She smooched him, adding a salacious margarita slurp, and danced him out of the RV to the task. What really convinced Steve was when they named the truck Apache Red; now it could strike out on its own, leaving the Alamo behind.

The Fifth Wheel unhitched, they changed clothes, and drove the truck into town to explore, their first foray 'alone' on the road trip. Steve was mildly uncomfortable leaving the Alamo at Walt's Wasteland, but the staff gave assurances in exchange for cash.

Jackie and Steve rode in silence to Santé Fe, feeling very conspicuous. No one here drove such an ostentatious vehicle. People who walked beside the road glared as they passed. Jackie and Steve weren't used to feeling rich and were relieved to arrive in the touristy town, park, and dismount.

"Steve, would you have imagined this?" Jackie said. "It's a town square, like our Michigan small town, minus a round-capped county courthouse. It's familiar, the same only different." The buildings color-matched the soil and largely stood single story, an invitingly human proportion.

The scale and palate of Santé Fe's square worked to Jackie's advantage, though she couldn't have divined it. Steve was so hungry for color that, by the time they went through the fourth tiny art gallery, he was ready to buy something, anything.

But what could that be, each wondered as they entered the fifth gallery. The Winnebago storage space was packed with supplies, and there wasn't wall space for one of the massive paintings that featured women with feet almost as big as their heads, seated in hooked nose profile. Jackie felt snubbed by Gorman's famous women, bold blocks of color with cold-shouldered, averted gazes. Besides, she was not fond of anything that celebrated heavy weight bodies.

They weren't fans of the renowned local, Georgia O'Keefe, either. Other artists' landscape paintings loaded up gallery walls, but, as dedicated farmers, they wondered where the animals were? The only hints were splintered cow skulls. Neither could admire rusty brown rock expanses, no matter how nicely these juxtaposed a saturated blue sky, just like outside. The sky was what they wished they could transport home.

By their count, there were almost as many jewelry stores as galleries in Santé Fe, sprinkled with a few restaurants and western clothing shops. Steve's brain sounded its tourist trap alarm, and he stationed himself at the door when Jackie stepped into the third jewelry shop. He'd already determined that, while the gleaming contents of the glass cases ringing each shop were small, the price tags were not.

He watched Jackie's reflection in the glass cases, her skin glowing like the jewelry, a cheery smile spreading across her flushed cheeks, wrinkles flattened as if ironed for Sunday best. Behind his back Steve's fingers were crossed in hopes that Jackie remembered their talk about economizing, especially now, with the unforeseen side trip to meet a surprise family member.

Jackie pretended not to notice and swept her eyes across the contents under glass, much like she did when she read the newspaper. Among the many turquoise pieces, Jackie spied a ring shaped like a triangle with hash marks on its silver mounting. These reminded her of farm fencerows - to meld back home with Santé Fe blue - so she brandished her Master Card before Steve could think *no*. The clerk slipped the ring on Jackie's finger before she handed over the signed receipt, which Jackie quickly stuffed in her purse.

"Thanks, honey, you are so happy for me. I've got a piece of that sky," she said as she extended her hand for his admiration. "I'll be all gussied up when we meet your brother."

Oh, no! Steve didn't look happy; he looked vexed. His hands were dithering about like his nerved-up brother David, and she knew she'd stepped into a mess. She took his hands in hers and drew him to her, but he averted his face. She knew this was a subject that wouldn't be discussed for awhile, so she just hugged him with her hands high on his shoulders – so she could admire her new ring herself.

They enjoyed a fine Mexican meal – only one margarita each, so they made them Cadillacs, and toasted that silly auto ranch outside of Amarillo, Texas. They were feeling no pain – but yes they were... The flirty waitress overheard this remark and winked when she mentioned Ojo Caliente Mineral Springs.

Jackie felt destiny. She craved a new experience. Steve could soak away his concerns while both eased their road weary bodies.

They returned to Walt's Wasteland to retrieve their suits. Steve walked into the Alamo without a word.

"Jackie, what's this stuff under the bed?" Steve shouted as Jackie reached the Alamo steps.

Jackie reached the bedroom in five strides, knowing he'd found her magazine stash. She engaged his eyes with her best winsome smile. Then she turned to the bedside cupboard, fished out his swimsuit, and said, "May I trade you even for those?"

"Only if you say with all sincerity that I look just as good as all those guys," he replied, dropped the magazines, and stalked to the bathroom to change.

"Steve, there are changing rooms inside the resort, don't you think?" Steve didn't reply, but he came out laughing. Jackie stuffed their suits into her purse and pushed him to the truck, sustaining his laughter with tickling.

When they got to the Springs, Steve's confused look was a bad start. "What's this, Jackie? I'd imagined a building like the Alamo, white-washed Spanish with the vague squalor of history. Maybe staffed by sturdy squaws serving hot tamales and hot towels." The Mineral Springs building was straight out of a Hollywood movie set for *Gone with the Wind*.

Once inside the magnificent compound, the couple paid the AAA-discounted fee, went to the dressing rooms, and met at the double glass doors to the indoor pool. Winter was chilly in New Mexico even without the snow of Michigan. They couldn't imagine soaking outside.

But Steve balked at poolside as he looked all around. "Jackie, all the people's hair is white."

"Yeah?" Jackie said and reached to hold his hand.

"They're old," Steve said.

"So are we, dear. If you don't like this color of hair, we ought not go through Arizona, which is loaded with senior citizens."

"What if they are incontinent and peeing in the pool?"

"Hadn't thought of that," Jackie said and squeezed his hand tighter.

"Perhaps we'll just stick our toes in the pool and go to visit the little church at Chimayo. Perhaps we'll find our arthritic cure there. It's called the Lourdes of America."

"Or we could try to locate Site 51 at Roswell and get us an alien cure," Jackie warmed to the creative spirit of their road trip meander, but Steve shook his head. "Oh, Steve, let go. What's a little urine among fellow senior citizens?"

She stepped into the pool, sat on the bench seat, and Steve came following after: *you're in,* he grimaced.

A couple of hours later, fingers and toes wrinkled by the prolonged soak, they swore their knees felt better, so they skipped Chimayo. Pastor Rankin might question entry into a Catholic chapel, Jackie thought. No matter how tiny and remote it was, she was certain he'd get a bulletin of their whereabouts, beamed by God. She looked at Steve across the supper table. "The day after the Alamo Bowl was Sunday. We've been nine days on the road, and we're already heathens."

With repentance stirred, Jackie ventured the long-lost brother topic: "So your brother's a warlock. I hope he's not as bad as David."

Steve laughed, but not very heartily. Jackie waited, and then went to the refrigerator to get the Jello dessert.

"My mother had a kid while Dad was away at war," he said.

Jackie whirled around, glad that Tupperware had its famous seal, so that the Jello didn't slather her floor. She knew it was only linoleum, but it was new – and she didn't want to add mopping to her chores. This trip was supposed to be about freedom.

But, Holy bombshells, Batman! Mother Breeden, whom everyone idolized, the woman who baked every pie to perfection and more...the sainted mother of

Steve, Jackie's husband, her dear, sweet, wonderful, stable husband – Mother Bree had a baby and gave it up for adoption!

Jackie plunked down in the booth across from Steve and dropped the container between them. She didn't remove the lid; she'd already done as much as she was able.

"And, my new brother lives in Turlock, not Warlock, Jackie. It's in California. He wants us to come visit."

"Oh-Kay. We are headed that way. Where's Turlock? I hope it's near Disneyland because I'm headed there and then to the Pacific to dip my toes in water again. I've had to wear shoes everyday, and my toes are feeling cramped."

"I don't know," Steve said, suddenly staring toward his shoes.

"You mean you didn't look it up after you opened Bran's email and read the letter?" Jackie was incredulous. This was the man who had researched their trip destinations extensively. This was the man who built a successful small business after a career in automotive heaven collapsed. Steve was a church deacon. "Weren't you an itty-bitty-bit curious?"

"Well, maybe I'm stalling," Steve said. "This is harder to swallow than Amy's Mac and Cheese. I don't really like the brother I have. Why do I have to have another one?"

"Well, he's a Californian, so he's better already," Jackie said. "Let's look on the bright side: maybe he's nice and rich."

"But, it's another tie, another tether, another set of trouble," Steve said, still staring down.

"Is that what you think of Brandon?" Jackie said, skipping over connection to David because there wasn't any.

"You gotta admit..." Steve started.

"I don't gotta admit nothing," Jackie said, "I am his mom. I gave him life. He is precious, tall, handsome, and talented." She stuck out her chin and glared. When

214

Steve didn't lift his head, she stuck out her hand. "Steve, where did I go wrong?"

Steve grabbed her hand and gave it a squeeze. He looked into her eyes. Eyes that glistened with tears. "There you go again, Jackie, with that motherhood guilt thing. You didn't make Brandon the way he is single-handedly. Maybe we both did. You'd think that a kid who grew up on a farm would know better than to think that money grew on trees."

"Should we blame it on his athletic scholarship or his athletic supporter?" Jackie deadpanned.

Steve dropped her hand to hold his sides as his body erupted in laughter.

"Of course, I know about such things," Jackie tried to still his guffaws. "I did his laundry all those football-playing years,"

Steve was still laughing too hard to jab her with his thought: "Yeah, and you still do." He wondered how soon Wal-Mart shelves would empty of underwear in Brandon's size and preference now that Mama Washing Machine was gone.

He was still laughing as he turned on the iPad to look up Turlock, California.

Thirty-Five: Meanwhile Back at Amy's Ranch

Trying to get ready for work, my eyes watering and my nose scrunched, I was on my third attempt to affix my fake eyelashes. I missed the wrap-around mirror ringed with make-up bulbs in my lost house, which had showcased my face like the town's theater marquee framed its movie title.

I inhaled through my lips, and then bit the lower one, hoping to steady my hand. My forearm was aching as if it were wielding a woodcutter's axe.

Phew! I cocked my head to one side, now that the lashes were in place, and winked a positive opinion.

I checked the date as I clipped the Rolex latch – sure enough, the smell had been permeating my life for ten days. I was ready to plug my nose surgically to escape the perfume of manure. I'd always wanted a nose like Jennifer Aniston and figured that a re-shape might bypass sense of smell. Besides, I could recover somewhere else – perhaps Bermuda, where a renowned plastic surgeon was encamped. I was sick of the wind howling across the barnyard, carrying snow and fumes.

Brandon, the ever-chided and dutiful son, continually replenished the cow manure compost bin that his mother had built for her garden. Now I knew, literally, what a shitload was: what six cows made daily.

Brandon was sadly mistaken if he thought I would be tending a garden; I hadn't taken up his mother's recipes, so why would I do that? He was the farmer in the family, so that was his domain. I am the executive, the banker, the queen.

I hated to admit it, but I was reminded of the stench of baking the pot cookies – and that chore loomed. Now that I needn't steady my makeup implements, I twiddled my thumbs as I fretted. Perhaps I was not cut out for the full scope of the fakery business, and I'd ask Veronica to handle that chore - solo. I opened my make-up drawer and shepherded all the paraphernalia into it with my tired forearm. I sped into the bedroom and fetched my phone from my purse. I punched the numbers as I zipped into my favorite pair of boots.

"Veronica, how's it going on your Wal-Mart day off?"

"I'm busy making a three layer cake for a friend's wedding. Would you believe she wanted piped pearlized frosting dots on the white fondant three layer cake? It's going to look like I left the cake out in a snow storm," Veronica said.

I wondered again how I'd become friends with a Wal-Mart worker cum wedding cake baker, a feat right out of Central Mis-Casting. I couldn't even recall the look of my wedding cake, only that Brandon had jammed a piece in my mouth with more relish than a besotted groom should display.

But I got him back – I'd pulled his collar away from his neck and dumped the majority of his piece down the space between his tuxedo shirt and chest. After I slid my icing covered fingers down his tie, I turned to smile at the guests. I was not going to hug that frosted chest as they expected. I punched his gut with an upward arm movement that effectively lathered his chest with cake crumbles and frosting. The photographer snapped the series for posterity. I had it in on my phone and played the video when I felt down.

Jackie and Steve paid for the wedding and brought repayment up from time-to-time, directly suggesting that a grandchild would be appropriate. Shit! They were pushy, insensitive people. The wedding ended, then disaster hit with Brandon's dive into the honeymoon resort pool. Bye-bye plans of being an NFL wife. Bye-bye millions! You'd have thought that Jackie and Steve would have had more decorum. Were they not church members?

"And I've got to find a way to get the rose bouquet topper on the cake without freezing it," Veronica whined as I headed downstairs to retrieve my coat, hat, and gloves.

Hearing the slurp of Veronica's intermittent finger licking prompted hunger, so I popped a piece of bread in the toaster after a Rolex peek assured me that I had time. Veronica prattled on and on – even when the phone dropped out of my head-shoulder cradle as I stretched to punch the toaster handle down.

"The bride's colors are garishly unseasonal," Veronica said. "Maybe I'll go into wedding planning. I could use more money. My car is acting up, and I need to replace it."

I slid the toast in a baggie after it popped and shoved it in my purse. I wiggled into my coat and stopped at the mirror to adjust my hat. So pretty – in contrast to florid Veronica, who looked like a layered wedding cake when she wore that industrial strength apron. Her boobs were rather small.

I smiled at myself in the mirror. Somewhere I'd read that this behavior shaped a friendly voice, which I needed to foster my sales pitch. The method acting had been winningly effective at the bank.

I blew myself a kiss and said, "Veronica, do you have time to bake some cookies?"

"Sure, the oven's still warm. What do you need?"

"I think we need five dozen soon," I said.

"Sure, just bring me the recipe and ingredients," Veronica said.

"Can't quite do that," I said. "The essential essence isn't fully grown."

"And…" Veronica said, "I can feel another of your boots about to drop, Amy. Spit it out."

"Can't," I said.

"Can't?" Veronica said. "Oh, are you calling from the bank?"

"No, but the bank owns this phone – and it's call history. So, I'll give you three guesses, and the first two don't count. Sh-h-h. Think, Ronnie. You and I hold up the economy in our social circle."

"Fool! I thought you had hundreds in the freezer. What happened?"

"Uh, Brandon took a platter to the church bazaar."

There were several moments of silence as Veronica processed the implications and the irony of the fact, and then said, "Do you need me to swing by the church basement to snatch the plate back or, better yet, buy it and its contents? Loan me the cash, and I'll do it when I deliver this wedding cake. I'll only eat a few."

I put the receiver down, grabbed my wallet from the suitcase purse near my legs, and opened it to count.

"Veronica, I've got $10.00 on me and can finagle a counter check. Don't think the church will take ATM cards, do you? And, by the way, I heard you. The evidence needs to be back in the freezer to sell to customers. Got that straight."

"I was only teasing," said Veronica. "I'm a business woman, too, you know. I have more money than you, so if I have to buy the cookies rather than just swipe them, you can pay me back. Now I got to finish this frosting."

"Veronica, let the florist worry about the flower transport. Okay?"

I hung up and smiled into the mirror again. I flung the phone in the suitcase, hefted the bag to my shoulder, and jogged to the van.

Veronica carefully loaded the wedding and sheet cakes in her trunk and drove to Grace Lutheran, thinking that that was the name of her third grade teacher, the one who rapped her knuckles with a ruler and then twisted her ear. She rapped her own knuckles on her steering wheel to make the memory retreat, but didn't repeat the ear twist. She didn't want to dislodge the sparkly ear hoops that matched her new brow bling.

She parked in the lot, but, before sliding to the hall to deliver the baked goods, she stepped into the church office, where a blonde woman was seated at a desk smothered with books and papers. "Hi, Miss. I'm Veronica Childress, and I'm here with the wedding cake. I'm earlier than usual, so I'd like to refrigerate the cakes. Could you direct me to the church kitchen?"

The woman lithely slid her arm across the desk to touch Veronica on the arm, "Welcome, dear. I'm Bonnie, the church secretary. I'm afraid I was engrossed in typing the pastor's sermon. Would you repeat your name and your request, please?"

Veronica pulled a card from her pocket and put it in Bonnie's hand. "I'm delivering the cakes for this evening's wedding. I wondered if there was a kitchen with refrigeration."

"Well, there is, but I'm afraid that it's mighty full. We are having a bake sale tomorrow after service."

Bingo.

Bonnie continued, her lips barely moving so that the smile never dissipated, "You know, to celebrate the Widow Braghorn's new windows and to entice other church members to fund summer vacation Bible School. It's never too early or too late to raise money for the Lord."

"Just point me in the right direction, and I'll do the rest. No need to leave the important work of transcribing the pastor's sermon," Veronica said quickly as Bonnie began to round the desk. With luck, the pot cookie snatch would be easily achieved. She went back to her car in the lot and popped the trunk, feeling more relaxed about the mission.

Veronica hefted the first sheet cake, carefully concealing the empty pink cake box precisely beneath. Balancing the box on her hip while she opened the latched door, she walked down the hall with the moves of a thief. Just inside the small galley kitchen she saw baked goods stacked on every surface, almost as many as in the cases at Wal-Mart. Maybe more. Church people were generous with flour, butter, and eggs.

She put the wedding cake on the floor, hoping that ants wouldn't find it before she found the pot cookies, earnestly lifting aluminum foil and reading the names written on masking tape to identify the supplier of the goods.

There it was: Breeden written in boxy letters. She lifted the plate as if it were a Tiffany case, and then nudged the others to mask its absence. She placed the platter of cookies on the island while she assembled the empty cake box, and then lowered the cake plate into its new vault.

Thankfully, her sheet cake fit on a wide empty shelf of the refrigerator. Only a little re-arranging of the few items were needed to make room for the prima donna's bridal cake, which she hurried out to her car to retrieve.

After Veronica shoved the cake in, she stepped toward the box...just as Pastor Rankin appeared at the door.

"Might you be the young woman I can thank for the cookie that I sampled from that box on the central counter?"

Veronica blinked.

"I must say it was flavored with some new spice, but it grew on me. I even stepped to the bathroom mirror to assure that I'd not left any crumbs on my cheeks. I wanted to eat the entire cookie now and not save any for later," Pastor Rankin said.

"Um, I'm the wedding cake maker, and I've got to get to another wedding. Nice to meet you, Reverend Pastor Sir," Veronica said as she grabbed the box and backed out the door.

"Please leave your card with my secretary, so that I can place an order," Pastor called after her after he'd held the door open for her.

Veronica realized glumly that she already had. She could summon no words – good, bad, or indifferent – as she pondered the consequences of his ingest.

All she knew for certain was that she was not going to tell Amy – and for extra assurance, she made certain that she jostled the box, so that there'd be no way to detect the absence of one cookie...but, shit. Amy the banker would count.

Thirty-Six: Taos Time

Steve awakened with enthusiasm, sliding on shorts for the third day in a row. His body aches had dissipated, due to an impressively good mattress, though he knew that another day of driving would refund them. Travel distanced his former life, led in a rut of simple comings and goings. Jackie and he had squared with Amy and Brandon living fully adult lives in their home, assured that all went well with the dairy business by daily calls, refusing to think about the rest, steeped in a 'Let Go, Let God' pattern of peace. Buttressed with the wisdom of age - and wanderlust.

Steve savored every phone call from his son, and Jackie listened in. Brandon's voice was resolute as he shared his checklist of accomplishments. That was half the battle. At least their son wasn't trying to shove ten pounds of shit into a three-pound bag, as Steve's dad used to say.

Today was January 6, Kings Day at Taos Pueblo, the largest, most famous pueblo around Santé Fe.

Today Steve was elated. He'd been a big cowboys and Indians fan when he was a kid, like every boy he knew. Taos was an opportunity to see Indians as stars of the show, unlike old TV plots. At least he'd watched actors – in new living color on a 24-inch TV screen - not the cartoon characters that populated shows nowadays.

He hung a bit of pride on that, needing a boost because Jackie kept correcting him: Indians were now Native Americans. Didn't she know it was hard for an old dog to learn new tricks? Gosh, he missed Sparty, who licked him and didn't pick.

The drive from Santé Fe to Taos was two-lane blacktop, refreshingly slim relative to the Interstates' vast concrete swath, more like back home. They'd left The Alamo at Walt's Wasteland for their exploratory foray. The truck passed few other vehicles on the road winding upward at a discernable grade.

Steve didn't mind. Each driver dipped his hat in signal of passage, just like drivers back home.

Taos was sparse, with buildings lining the S-curved road like football stadium bleachers. One would hardly know it was a town if there hadn't been a sign. Again, tannish soil was pervasive, untouched by grass. Most buildings were built of adobe, and there was little foliage. When they got out of the truck, Steve was struck by the absence of sound. Perhaps all the Native Americans had left, Steve chuckled to himself, looking around for Indians.

He stopped to note their tracks and saw that powdery soil clung to their Midwestern shoes. *Have to stomp it off before we step back into Brandon's prized truck, Apache Red.*

A peeled-paint, two-story saloon attracted Steve, perhaps because its sign was burnished red with black letters. Steve recalled being awarded the cigar band as his dad began his Sunday night smoke. When Steve stepped inside and asked, "Where...?", the bartender pointed down the street, not even pausing from washing bar glasses. He'd obviously been asked the Pueblo location before.

Remnants of nighttime narcissism hung heavy in the dim interior. Steve hustled Jackie back to Apache Red, smiling as he opened the door. The truck reminded him of the cardinals back home, a highlight in the greige of winter. It seemed almost a sin not to be there, but he was acclimating to the grace of good weather, his legs browning to a peanut shell shade. He'd never had the opportunity to tan them at any time of year in Michigan; jeans were the garment of choice.

Steve drove down the street, slowly because one never knew about small town cops, and rounded a bend to see the massed block stacks that was the Taos Pueblo.

"What's that?" Jackie remarked. "It looks like a clay canister set made by Helen Baxter, awaiting its colorful glaze."

Steve smiled. You could always count on a kitchen metaphor from his wife. He thought the place looked like one of Brandon's block complexes, minus the bridges and ramps.

Drum sounds and hoots drifted over the walls, and Steve's heart beat along. Eerie long-toned pipes sounded laments. He was reminded of forced Tonette practice in fourth grade.

There seemed to be no roof. Simple lodge pole ladders were visible to open exterior second story windows without white painted sashes. Steve hoped he didn't have to climb. He didn't have to look at Jackie to know that she was thinking the same.

Steve's enthusiasm was stomped by the ticket window Indian, er, Native American, who demanded a larger sum than anticipated, then cautioned him that no photography was permissible on this sacred Buffalo Dance day. The rites were as reverent as other religions' church rituals, she explained. Since they'd trekked all this way - and Jackie yearned for worship - Steve forked over the money and hurried her into the proceedings already begun.

Inside the austere walls a large crowd of tourists stood, focused on a circular beaten dirt tract where Native American males danced, alternate feet in the air. From here Steve could see that, even when beaten firm, the soil clung to moccasin shoes.

Some headdresses were elaborate and lengthy, extending its wearer's pigtailed braids, and others were headbands with a fistful of colored feathers. Several had buffalo horns mounted on their headdresses. It was mesmerizing, like a flying zoo.

Although the costumes were vibrant, the action was not. The music bleated ennui, too. The tribal dance circled to the hypnotic drumbeat accompanied by haunting chants. No Native American women were in sight.

Steve's mind numbed with the repetitive cadence. His head sunk to his chest, eyes closed. Jackie later told him that she thought he was praying, and he didn't disabuse her of the thought.

When he raised his head from the tidy nap, Steve rolled his head to unkink his neck and looked past the pueblo to the horizon and saw...snow! Perhaps God knew that he missed Michigan's snow, so his partner, Mother Nature, brought it near. When the interminable dance ended and the applause filtered away, Steve whispered in Jackie's ear, "Apache Red wants to play in snow."

Jackie grinned and grabbed his hand, leading the way. They exited the Pueblo without a wave or a deposit in the tip basket, diverted on a new quest.

Steve gripped the wheel assertively as the truck climbed, spiraling around and up the mountain like the little engine that could. The term Native American was coming easier to mind, but he was sick of their atonal music and landscape. A switch to lively rock and roll drove his determination for snow.

As soon as they arrived at the ski lodge, Jackie and Steve parked and ran in between snowflakes the size of a baby's fist, the perceived size amplified by shivering. It seemed incongruous to shield their eyes from glare as they hustled. It was freezing. Steve realized, as he looked around, there were no large, uncloaked trees to temper the sunshine on the full white landscape.

On the porch, Steve lowered his arm. A skier grabbed it immediately and, pointing at Steve's legs, said, "Man, why are you wearing shorts?", and then back at the truck, "How'd you get here without chains?"

The man's awed yet anxious tone prompted them back to the truck, but not before Steve got hit by a snowball. He looked up from his crouched, hurried run to see Jackie armed with a second one. What – her joints weren't frozen? He didn't stop to return the fight, just motioned her to hurry up, turning the key in the ignition. This adventure was too cold.

Steve eased down the mountain, careful not to allow Apache Red to become a toboggan. By 1:30 p.m., the couple arrived safely at the lower, flatter elevation in Taos. God bless it: the change in weather was welcome. Steve glided into the lone gas station for a high-priced refill.

Jackie's nose was runny. She hoped she hadn't caught cold. Her mother used to chide her about traipsing outside without proper clothing.

As she rummaged into her purse for a tissue, Jackie noticed that she'd missed a call. It was from Bonnie, her partner in church crime and consultation.

"What have you been doing, Jackie? We miss you here at church."

That remark connected with Jackie's ever-present undercurrent of guilt. Involuntarily she angled away from the large truck window. "Hi to you, too, Bonnie. We've been to the mountain top."

"Did you bring down any stone tablets?"

Jackie chuckled and turned to repeat the question to Steve, who leaned closer to the phone to say, "That one's already been done. But, a cute girl pelted me with snowballs. Don't tell my wife, okay?"

"Don't listen to him," Jackie said. "I didn't put any stones in the snowballs, so he's not hurt. Anyways, how's things around town?"

"Jackie, you are not going to believe it when I tell you," Bonnie said, and then paused. Trying to make Jackie ask, like always, but Jackie didn't play the part. She was on vacation.

"Okay, I'll tell you: for the first time since I've worked for that man, Pastor Rankin didn't follow the sermon that he'd penned, and I typed without an error. And, when I asked him about it, he said that he'd had a vision. I watched him put three sheets of yellow paper on the pulpit and preach right off the page. A vision, he said, not even apologizing for wasting my 90 words-a-minute."

"A vision? What was the sermon about?" Jackie met Steve's eye with a shrug of her shoulders. He could detect some alarm in her voice. Things were going so well on the farm, how could there be chinks in the holy armor of church?

"Well, it seems that he expanded upon The Song of Songs in the Old Testament." Jackie's mouth flew open and her hands flew up to cover it, as if to cover their good pastor's gaff.

Steve caught the phone as Jackie released it. "Bonnie, this is Steve, the first deacon. What's going on at the church?" His voice was full of his God-given authority.

"Well, Pastor Rankin preached about sex last Sunday." Steve looked at Jackie as Bonnie continued, "And the congregation's buzzing because Fran Blackstone quit the choir, saying it was because she missed Jackie. Each week she has moved closer to the pulpit, from the next to last row to five rows from the front."

Steve punched the phone off and said, "Holy crap." But before she asked him holy crap what, Jackie redialed to apologize to Bonnie and to hear the news first hand. Soon she was saying "Holy crap" – and contemplating the pair at the Thanksgiving feast. Maybe God blessed more than ashes that day.

Jackie put her phone in her purse, kissed her new ring and her husband, in that order, and said, "Let's get back on the road, Steve. They say that close only works in horseshoes and hand grenades, but I think it works for the heaven bound, too. I'm doubly glad that we are away for a while. Want to go Native again?"

Steve agreed by putting the key in the ignition.

When Jackie saw a road sign to the Nambe Pueblo, Steve agreed to venture to another Native American site. They had earned a big meal, maybe a buffalo burger or some squaw bread, pulled pork, and cowboy beans. Not going back to the dank, inhospitable bar. Not going to discuss Pastor Rankin, Fran, and sex. Not going to contemplate nothing but a plate of grub.

Nambe Pueblo was more compact, not ceremonially festive; there were the few whites. It was kind of a thrill to simultaneously experience the diversity of America and to be diversity itself. It was also kind of nice to feel invisible.

After lunch, Jackie insisted on shopping, which didn't take long because there was little in the store. Steve knew he'd scored points with the ring and the prayer and aimed for a trifecta. With little urging, he sprang for a Nambe bowl, though he groused about nowhere to store it. Signs touted the tribe's specially forged metal that could retain hot or cold, perfect for on-the-road dining. Guaranteed to never be hot enough to mar the Formica counter top.

Steve valued hot rolls while he lingered over a meal, so he savored this purchase. He selected one shaped like the single tear cascading a chief's face in a famous ad about the environment, well recalled from the '70s.

The bowl fit in the cupboard over the stove nicely, though Jackie had to stack the blue ashes container inside. Before she closed the cupboard door she noticed that the container was highlighted by reflective glow from the silvery metal, as God's glory sometimes opened up with a sunny blast between clouds after a rain. It looked like a haloed shrine.

Jackie smiled at the underlying blessing to their trip and made a mental note to check with Pastor Rankin about the church window installation plan as paid for by the grateful Widow Braghorn. She'd work in her friend Fran's name and listen closely to his tone.

Jackie glanced at the stove clock. It was late back home. She decided to defer the call, maybe never make one. She wasn't ready for what she might or might not hear.

Further, she couldn't divulge the date of the widow's requested ashes distribution because she hadn't exactly figured out Steve's plan. He wasn't setting dates on a timetable. Jackie admitted that it felt good to be without a checklist or schedule.

Besides, she'd been to an Indian ceremonial rite, so *church* was fulfilled. Native Americans danced in the dreams that came readily after she left Steve reading Indian lore on the iPad long into the night. Native American women got a turn to dance in her nightscape – and Jackie fervently hoped that none of their faces was Fran's, her mother's or Ma Bree's. At least Amy couldn't appear as apparition: she was blonde, as was Bonnie.

Thirty-Seven: Route 66

Steve was born into a generation of men who romanced the road before they romanced women. Need-for-speed men who relished the hot rod years before muscle cars were eviscerated for gas guzzling. As a child he'd watched *Route 66* on TV and often re-imagined his tractor as a Corvette swooping the famed road while furrowing corn field rows that seemed like they could stretch to the moon and back. When Neil Armstrong landed on the moon, Steve was a teen. He rhapsodized about space travel as he sat in the squeaky seat, unshielded from the sun. Any means to recast the tedium of daylong fieldwork.

He embraced the car culture before Americans traded style and design innovation for Japanese reliability and Swedish safety, one concept being foreign and the other feminist, which might as well be foreign in his book. Subversions that thwarted the masculine prerogative of car culture – until his young son, Brandon, was driving, that is. Then, when Saturday turned into the wee hours of Sunday morning, he prayed that good and safe things did happen after midnight. God bless it; he was relieved to not have a girl child.

To cruise and caress the remnants of Route 66 was his initial quest for the road trip, though he'd never admit it to Jackie, the football fanatic. Their novice RVer status confined travel to the Interstates. The fact that Interstate 40 paralleled, and often intersected Route 66 through New Mexico and Arizona's bland sandscape, salved the bite of convenient, high-speed travel.

In the plush truck cab, Jackie alternated gazes at her new shiny ring with impassive sweeps of the flat sandy land and distant mountains, done with window-shopping. Steve fixated on sightings of Route 66 signs. Her hunt was done; his was on.

It began with Santé Fe at 6:00 a.m., continuing past Algodones, Bernalillo, Albuquerque, all cumbersome tongue-twisting words that he could barely register as they drove by. He knew he could neither spell nor remember them.

Until they got to Grants, New Mexico. Steve was so grateful for the simple English word that he selected its exit for a quick pee-and-stretch-the-legs. Jackie was good with the stop and strolled around the gas station lot, to walk off her disappointment that the station stocked no refrigerator magnets.

Then on to Gallup and soon thereafter the New Mexico state line. Before their road trip, Jackie had only been in one state and soon she'd be entering number eleven, Steve told her, doubly proud. He was king of geography and king of the road.

An hour into Arizona, Mother Nature provided a spectacular lunch site at Painted Desert Inn, looking spunky and suitably southwestern, a building style now fully recognized, though dissimilar to home. Steve wasn't used to buildings with flat roofs and no gables or eaves, like they weren't wearing a hat.

Jackie pulled out a picnic. They ate with sunglasses on, like summertime at a Michigan lake. Steve shared his planned diversion on Route 311 to see the Petrified Forest National Park in between bites of a tuna salad sandwich. Jackie couldn't disagree when she was chewing.

It was a crisp winter day that neither could call cold, yet they noted the tall, slim ranger bundled in a jacket at the trailhead close to their picnic spot at the Park Center. They fetched jackets and joined a group of travelers gathering like sheep.

The folks huddled – not for warmth - because the Ranger talked as slowly and softly as he walked. Steve strode along, swiveling his head, figuring he could see 100 miles of landscape, with lines unbroken by natural foliage or people's cultural habits.

The Ranger's carriage was as vertical as some of the massive stone formations that loomed as Nature's skyscrapers. When the Ranger donned his Smokey Bear

hat, the brim lined perfectly with the flat horizon.
The man was a kindergartener's 't', his posture perhaps
formed by military service. Steve renewed his own
posture, proud to have fought for the ideal of open
space as a part of America's freedom. His freedom.

Eyes scanning beyond the trail, Steve was sure he
saw a deer. When he blinked and it was still there, he
nudged Jackie, who immediately whispered, "Just like
Michigan." Steve admired how its markings blended
with the autumn-like hues of petrified wood and
wondered what it foraged among logs that were almost
solid quartz.

Steve added zoology and geology to his list of
learning mourned. But it was all good. It just made
more topics to research on the iPad after Jackie tucked
herself in.

Further on the trail, he marveled at the petroglyphs,
learning that early man kept a social calendar like the
one that Jackie posted by their kitchen sink back home.
His mind traveled briefly to that home, hoping that all
was well. He hadn't checked in with Brandon lately.

The Ranger rattled on, pointing out this and that.
Jackie tugged at Steve's jacket sleeve and, when he
glanced away from rapt attention to the scenery, she
nonverbally requested a stay-on to see the sun fill the
rock gap at Winter Solstice, like the Ranger suggested.

Steve stared at her a moment, and then shook and
threw invisible dice and mouthed "Las Vegas". Jackie
grinned, back on road trip track with him. Giddy-up!

According to the map, the Petrified Forest had wings
like an eagle on either side of the Interstate, but Jackie
and Steve headed back to the highway just after 2:00
p.m. rather than explore further. Jackie had a
destination in mind for dinner and good night: Black
Bart's Saloon and Musical Revue, where she could sing
Broadway tunes. Black Bart's RV Park, reported to be a
bit run-down but in a good price range, was miles and
miles to the West.

So they kept their cheap sunglasses on as they drove
in pace with the sun.

Because she was driving, Jackie commandeered a stop-n-go in Holbrook, Arizona, where the Rainbow Rock shop had gigantic roadside dinosaurs, adding a dino magnet to the collection on the Alamo's refrigerator.

She also wheeled into Winslow for the obligatory Eagles' corner photo, singing the lyrics at the top of her lungs. Steve chanted along, but stopped at "flatbed Ford" because he thought of Brandon, driving his old truck back home.

Jackie and Steve were about to quibble over who would be in the photo when a man said, "May I take your picture?"

Steve's face spread a grin, and he extended his camera to the driver with whom he'd been playing road tag. He recognized the Detroit Tigers cap with its carefully molded bill, but he'd never have guessed the driver was taller than him – nor that he'd have laugh lines, radiating like sun rays, around his eyes. Very much like Steve's own.

"Thanks," gushed Jackie as she stepped to Steve's side. "It's never too soon for the Christmas card photo."

Steve winced because Christmas was 50 weeks away. When the other man winked, the men bonded and agreed to detour together to see the giant meteor crater, just a few miles at exit 233. After all, they'd been happy trailing each other for many miles; it seemed the neighborly thing to do.

When Steve began to analogize the size of the crater in comparison to his milk vats, the male bonding deepened. The tall baseball fan, Joe Adams, and his wife, Sandy, were a farm couple from Newton, Iowa, and on their own retirement road trip quest. They'd bought their Winnebago from the company headquarters, with the blessings of the line manager, their son, also named Brandon, who had narrowly missed lay-off several times in the past 18 months.

Both couples had six hours of driving behind them and eleven days on the road. Sandy and Joe had meandered a bit more than Jackie and Steve, and Jackie was eager to hear all about their travels, hoping to slow Steve back to the original intent: a Charles Kuralt pace and plan. Since Joe, more the talker of the two, was eager to tell, he cancelled their RV Park reservation in favor of Black Bart's, too, freeway close in Flagstaff as per Internet advertisement.

The 'All Stay's Camp & RV' website was correct in its assessment that Black Bart's could use touch-up. The couples snapped a group selfie in front of the sign. Steve emailed it promptly to Pastor Rankin and the church council members, with a quip that he'd found religion on the road. Let the question hang about where and with whom, add a little mystery to drive the town gossips crazy.

Jackie did not email the photo to Fran. She was still wrestling with the principal/pastor relationship, whatever it could/should/would be. She knew that Bonnie would see the email before the Pastor did - and half the congregation would see the photo when Bonnie forwarded it, with or without Pastor Rankin's permission. Surely Fran would be in the better half.

Soon after check-in and set-up of the RVs, the guys headed to Wal-Mart to get converter plugs. Black Bart's only had 50 amp electricity and couldn't handle curling irons, electric shavers, and coffee pots, neither in that order nor at the same time. It was a tool mission of the highest order; the couples were RVing, not roughing it. Now Steve appreciated civilization and its privileges – among them charge cards.

While the men handled the tool mission, the ladies stayed behind to gab. Two curly-headed brunettes seated in almost matching fold-out lawn chairs, the first among commonalities they found. Jackie had warmed to Sandy instantly: her face was a comprehensive encyclopedia of kindness, and her brain was well-stocked, too. Both women had lifetime enrollment in the personal university of wife, of subjugated self. They discussed their sons Brandon at length, while the men avoided the topic because there was no actionable item.

It was supper show time. To freshen up, Jackie put on a dress. Steve stroked an imaginary mustache curled like the one on the Black Bart's sign and said, "You look good enough to be dangerous, dear wife", earning 1000 husband points and a chance at lucky before Vegas. The couples went to Black Bart's Steakhouse and Saloon, enjoying the walk under the wrap-around sky, black as Bart except for the abundant sprinkles of light. They agreed that it was impossible to not believe in God in moments like this, impossible to feel alone in His universe.

The quiet imploded as Black Bart's front door cracked open. Inside the noise was equal to that of the Alamo game, but compressed within old plank wood walls. Steve instantly wished he had earplugs. Though this bar looked similar to the Taos town saloon (Steve had already forgotten its name), its sound announced itself like bars back home after State won a home game.

Steve was relieved that the waitress escorted them to a 'booth in the back in the corner in the dark' with a wink. She apparently thought the senior citizens were courting.

The two couples sank into the worn leather with the tall clapboard back; cocooned, they could hear each other. Steve watched Jackie's face sour as she looked around the room – at most tables the people were texting, not talking.

But she didn't launch her favorite rant; she just elbowed him in the side and picked up the menu, adhering to her mother's advice: "If you can't say anything nice, don't say anything at all." They were with new people; polemic was not polite. It wasn't even their suppertime habit at home, so why bring it into their relaxation and ease, their eyebrows agreed.

The two couples enjoyed baked potatoes and bad steaks, paired with good Broadway musical singing by local college students. All agreed it was wonderful to eat outside of their motorhomes' confined space – on a date - so they'd take the bad with the good. That a busboy and dishwasher cleaned the table and dishes was sweeter than any dessert on the menu, the women agreed.

Eased by beer, the couples' conversation was as chockfull of adventures as their meals were with calories. When the two guys said, "You're the butter on my biscuit", with a wink at their respective wives, simultaneous with the act of buttering a biscuit, they laughed so loud that folks at nearby tables pulled their gaze away from their phones or plates to stare.

Jackie recalled her trepidation about meeting folks on the road, chiding herself for her lack of confidence. The term *vagabond* began to fit as well as her new ring. Jackie gave herself an invisible pat on the back just like she had taught Brandon; later she'd share this with Sandy, certain that she'd done the same.

The conversation was evolving into friendship: *these were Christmas card list people.* As tour busloads swelled the dining hall, it became increasingly boisterous – as if they were celebrating Oktoberfest sponsored by a coalition of community non-profits in Newton, Joe shouted. Steve laughed as he shared experiences at the annual Oktoberfest in Frankenmuth, Michigan - which was officially affiliated with Munich, Jackie bragged, just a little.

This comment launched into girl-talk about Christmas ornament stores that operated year-round; Frankenmuth was renowned for such, but Sandy seemed to know one in every state in the Union. She was collecting ornaments like Jackie was collecting refrigerator magnets. It was all good.

What was bad was that trucks feasted at Black Bart's truck stop across the street from the RV Park all through the night. You never escaped that law of life, to take the bad with the good, making peace with both. Good life was earned, not entitled.

With a night's rest and an early start, the tandem road warriors made it to Kingman, and to the Route 66 memorabilia mecca, the Quality Inn. The men shared glazed-eyed rapture at the vast collection in the lobby, displayed like righteous war relics, which they sort of were. Route 66 may have lost the battle to interstate commerce on highways that were built to Cold War specifications, but it had not succumbed. Though true believers were sparse, they spent their hearts with their wallets.

The women dallied along for a time, then ventured that late lunch would be good. Jackie was certain that there'd be a Route 66 magnet in the gift shop to purchase for her collection. That could be dessert.

She spied an ATM Machine in the Quality Inn lobby and bee-lined to insert her card, carefully punching keys to request $100.00. When the receipt spit out with the cash, she glanced before stashing it — then looked at it again. She knew that figures were not her forte, so she showed the printout to Steve when she gave him all but one of the $20.00 bills.

The look on his face verified that she wasn't wrong. His lips mouthed a curse that could have been lip-read at fifty feet. As Jackie had reckoned, the cash had come with a transfer from their savings account, set up as overdraft protection. How could this be? As a loyal American tax-paying citizen, she figured that she could count on a government unemployment check going direct-deposit into their checking account each month, with the auto-deduct for the HELOC payment following like Mary's little lamb. Their checking account was endowed from dairy profits and her final paycheck to float road trip expenses. How could they be overdrawn? Already?

Now the curses came aloud when Steve looked at his watch. It was Friday and the bank would soon close in Michigan. Jackie called Amy's cell immediately. As a bank V.P. she could straighten this out.

But Amy didn't answer her phone. Since Jackie was hungry, she shrugged and put her hand in Steve's to walk into the restaurant. Everything would work itself out because surely it was a mere silly mistake. They had plenty of money stashed in savings and Steve's retirement. Besides friendly conversation would better fill their heads while they filled their bellies.

Jackie and Steve ordered light for lunch, parsing the cash to Joe, who paid with Master Card. They'd have popcorn in the Alamo later. Jackie winced when she recalled the amount that she'd charged on their Card for her pretty blue ring, recalling something about pride coming before a fall.

Thirty-Eight: Things Go to Pot

I was a little bruised this morning – *from practice with my own team* - so I Miracle Iced my body and limbs after my shower. Until I couldn't stand the smell of myself, almost like a stick of gum. Then I dressed purposefully for the Milkweed business tasks ahead.

I knew I had a tendency to absently wipe gooey hands on my thighs. I'd seen the evidence too often in the laundry I had to do now that Jackie was gone. While I didn't want to ruin my hundred dollar jeans, I wanted to dress for the success I envisioned for today.

Especially when I'd taken Friday off, something I'd learned to do after Thursday night rumbles. I would have felt badly for the other stiffs at work – if I weren't so stiff myself.

Downstairs I banded an ice pack to a shin before I went to the barn's freezer to retrieve cookies for the Milkweed orders. The business was not growing wildly, not like a weed, but this appealed to the control freak in me. Slow growth was good. That's what I told customers with high dollar CDs, so I adhered to my advice: Slow growth was good; I believed it, honest.

Besides, the local electric company had already made a robo call about a mild spike in our electricity usage. Maybe I should check the grow lights. Weed needed its version of the sun, but our Master Card now had its limits as well as its rewards, with a bankruptcy on our record and lots of zeroes on the sum of our debt.

When I opened the door, after fumbling a bit with the lock combination, I almost fainted. Perhaps I sustained a concussion in my Derby fall last night. I quickly pulled the ice pack off my shin and plied it to my right temple.

No, yes, no… I did see nothing except white walls, glaring at me in nakedness like a clean room for making computer chips. Damn, the dozen pot plants were gone. Along with all of the grow lights and equipment, the only light in the room eerie, leaking in the hastily painted windows and skylights. WTF! Somebody had ripped us off!

I'd so enjoyed the space-age look of the aluminum-swathed piping, like an astronaut had jumped from the moon's low gravity down to be the Man in the Moon. I missed his presence, late of childhood dreams.

I missed my blown-up, pot-laced money scheme! I'd done my best thinking in years in the past few months. Wasted, but not in the meaning fostered by pot.

I grabbed at my phone. Shit, it wasn't in my pocket! Who'd think you'd need a smart phone when you were just getting cookies from a freezer! Damn!

Back in the house, I retrieved another ice pack for my shin from the kitchen freezer. I should have sat in the empty garage freezer when I had a chance. My butt hurt from the big fall, and that leg bruise was going to be a doozy! Where was my phone? DAMN! DAMN! DAMN!

Where was Bran? Where was that turd?

He answered, fortunately on the second ring. I knew that he gamed on his phone, which he shouldn't do when he was driving..."Hi—"

"What happened to the pot?"

"What   happened   to   the--?"

"The weed, our plants, our crop of self-determined destiny, fame, and fortune."

"Say what?"

"Someone or something cleaned out the grow barn, Brandon! We've been robbed, and we can't call the cops!"

Brandon almost ran the truck off the road as he flinched. "I'm almost done with the delivery route, Amy, and I shouldn't be talking on the phone while driving. I'll be home soon. We'll figure this out," Brandon said in his calm Dad imitation.

"Don't you hang up on me, Bran."

"Okay. Saturday phone minutes are free anyway," said Brandon, trying to appeal to the unemotional banker side of his wife. "I'll just set it on the dash, so I don't get a ticket, okay?"

"No, at least put the phone by the radio, so I can hear

something besides the shrieking in my head."

"Amy, turn on the radio in the kitchen. Mom has the good old-fashioned kind on the counter. Now walk over there and do it. Pace if you'd like to. Twirl your thumbs to get you thinking of a plan like you do. I'll be home soon."

Though Amy indicated otherwise, Brandon clicked off his phone. He had some profound cussing and shrieking to do. What had that son-of-a-bitch Travis done? He felt like his fingers could surge through the plastic steering wheel to strangle it and themselves, like he wished he could strangle Travis right now. Better him than me, thought Brandon, for Amy would be all strafe-and-bomb at home. She appreciated people who were savvy enough to leave a space when she was about to throw furniture, but now most of the available furniture was his folks'. He hoped she wouldn't go for the silverware. The knife edges were serrated.

He wished he had a plastic Jesus on the dash to pray to or a Hawaiian dancer to hypnotize his mind into hope again. Instead he had a cell phone on his damn dash, one that didn't even have Travis' phone number.

Thirty-Nine: Las Vegas!

Meanwhile, two time zones away, Jackie and Steve had slept well in the Alamo, risen early, and headed out to the Grand Canyon. There they marveled at the focused force of a river, barely visible far below. What power Mother Nature possessed and man's chutzpah tried to emulate! The Colorado River was their little farm creek on hyper-drive. Jackie clicked her camera as quickly as she had at Brandon's sports events, trying to capture every dominant move.

Jackie's phone rang, a musical interlude indicating a call from Amy. She tried to ignore it, but duty couldn't. A phone ring came with a mandate — and maybe some good news about the bank account.

"Where...you?" said Amy, "And... sit down."

"Well, it's often been called the Grand Can, but it's not exactly something I'd want to sit on," Jackie joked, then continued, "Amy, call you later. I don't think there's good cell coverage here."

"Ser...," said Amy.

"Seriously, Amy," Jackie said. "We're at the Grand Canyon, in the middle of glorious nowhere. We're with friends. I'll call you later." She went back to the rim to hold Steve's hand after stashing the phone.

The duo remained as if at attention, transfixed as in no other place, no other time in their lives. An eagle soared across the vista, the proud symbol of America. He made no sound, as did none of the dozen tourists sharing the scene, including their road partners, Sandy and Joe. It was as quiet as the Alamo Bowl game was loud. America really did have everything.

Despite having no hook-ups, the foursome decided to dawdle here, in their vehicles parked side-by-side in the vast, largely empty visitor lot. Lunch was the cold cereal that they hadn't eaten for breakfast in their hurry to get to Vegas. But beside a waffle cone of a canyon, colored like Michigan's fall leaves, hunger for peace trumped tummies. They had to prolong the moment, feasting on grandeur that mankind had not crafted.

There was no churning, hurly-burly spirit of the road, no noisy tires, or music accompaniment, no crowd noise or songs. The silence was perfect and they all wanted to absorb and embody the Zen.

Vegas would be different. While its glitz and glamour had a well advertised, magnetic force, each of them knew it could not compete with this.

After a brief stop at Hoover Dam for a look over the edge at water falling furiously, then a horizon sweep with the binoculars, Steve sighed and got in the truck cab. How he longed to get a look at the innards of that dam, like Joe and Sandy were doing. But, since he was the one who wanted to be at the Cactus Country RV Park before the traffic on the Vegas strip would be thick as thieves, he acquiesced to his own timetable.

As he started the truck, Steve wished he hadn't evoked robbery since someone or something had apparently looted their checking account. Then he recalled that slot machines were called one-armed bandits. That mental trail was not much better, so he turned up the volume of the radio.

An hour later, in the RV Park's common area he spied his first slot machine – and noticed that it didn't take quarters, but dollars. As his mind tracked back to the problem of their overdrawn account, he called Brandon.

"Don't know nothing, Dad. Amy's Roller Derbying, I suppose; she keeps her own schedule. Dairying's good, 'cept it got below zero two nights in a row. Got a portable heater for the equipment room and delivery truck cab. Got a notice from the electric company about a spike in our electric use, but that's about all here," then hurriedly adding, "Did you find that long lost brother yet?" to sandwich the bad news effectively between good topics.

"Glad you're being responsible, Kid," was all Steve said. To fill the silence, Brandon said, "I'll have Amy call you. I'll leave her a note on the laundry room bulletin board."

Brandon scored nearly 1000 points gaming during the call, 10 times as many words as he said. But what he didn't say spoke volumes to Steve, who decided to talk with Jackie in earnest. About Brandon, but not the brother.

Steve couldn't help whipping his head around to look at the expansive phenomenons - on and on and on - of the Las Vegas Strip. The sky was blackening to showcase its starry splendor, but neon explosions on every conceivable space made the real stars fade in comparison. It was all eye-popping wow, especially from the higher vantage point of the truck that was feeling fully at home amidst the Las Vegas kaleidoscopic carnival. If Mag wheels could strut, Apache Red's were.

At a stoplight, he turned to relish Jackie's wide-eyed wonder. He could always count on her appreciation. He joined her in gazing at a lake the size of the one on their land...when thousands of waterspouts began a leggy dance to the tune, "Singing in the Rain." Wish Mother Nature would provide a soundtrack for rainstorms like that.

Then, a woomph louder than thunder! What a report, timed with the lofted waterspouts, some as high as the Bellagio Resort buildings. Think of it! A 14-acre lake with amiable blasts of water; he could cash-irrigate as well as cash-rent his land!

He was almost sad when the light turned green, though he noticed that all the road vehicles merely crept forward as passengers enjoyed the water ballet explosions. Viva Las Vegas!

The Eiffel Tower was across the street, while behind them the gondolas of Venice had clustered in front of a palatial building, and a volcano spewed hot lava. They'd passed the splendors of Caesar's Palace, lit up like morning. Ahead there was a Sphinx fronting a black glass pyramid.

Steve felt he could check world geography off of his study list. He'd found all the sites he could cope with –

within a few blocks, albeit lengthy blocks, so he was glad not to be walking the Strip. Steve recalled the euphoria when he'd gotten everything he'd desired for one special birthday. This moment was just like that.

"There's a half-price ticket stand. Let's go to a show!" exclaimed Jackie, clapping her hands like a birthday celebrant, too. Steve was always perturbed when she pointed, forgetful that he was driving, his eyes strained by the demands of the very crowded, multi-lane road. Pedestrian throngs lurked on every corner as if to step in the truck's path, primed for lawsuit. Wonder if he could pay in Cracker Barrel cards if he lost?

"Jackie, in my pocket, I have complimentary tickets to Harrah's Auto Museum at the Imperial Palace, just a few blocks back. Diamond Joe at the RV Park gave them to me when I checked in. How about if we start there?"

Jackie placed her hands in her lap, eyes fastened on her new ring. *Of course, why not.* A small-scale casino might have quarter slots.

How appropriate that the RV Park's guy would be named Diamond Joe: he had a diamond earring as large as the one in Amy's ring, *about the size of my new turquoise treasure.*

Jackie remembered unfinished business with Amy, but wouldn't call her now, at a farmer's bedtime in Michigan. The time zones required as much calculating as their road trip expenses, and Jackie wasn't up for that. She wanted to get down, on the town in Las Vegas!

After about a half-hour walk from the parking garage—which was surprisingly free of charge—Jackie plopped at a quarter slot machine, patting the seat and machine beside her to invite Steve to shared respite. He retrieved their two rolls of quarters, handing Jackie hers and said, "Are you sure?"

Jackie teased a small crevice in the wrapping paper,

and then handed her roll of quarters to Steve to complete the task, looking at him quizzically.

"Do you think we ought to save these coins for other expenses, like, for example, food?" Steve said as he twirled the coins loose. "The truck is eating gas like it's been at one of the buffet spreads here. Have you noticed the wall advertisements?"

"No sir," Jackie said as she grabbed a quarter, swishing it in the slot and pulling at the handle while grabbing another. Steve had never seen her ambidextrous.

"Our friends gave us these quarters at our go-away party, so we are obligated to spend them. Let's be frivolous like we promised ourselves. It's our time. The bank stuff will all work out and besides, there's nothing to be done until Monday."

They dined, laughed, went to see Celine Dion after the cars, and generally gaped throughout the night at the glories of Caesar, Fendi, Gucci, and Prada, Italian words that Jackie trilled in Steve's ear to drown out mention of the legend of Nero fiddling away while Rome burned.

Forty: Living on a Prayer

Jackie winced when she shut off her phone alarm and checked the time, date, and day. The small screen was incandescent, bright as Vegas neon in their dark bedroom. Again, praise would not be God's. The thought hit before she had coffee, so it must be the Holy Spirit. *Proof it/he/she is still with us.*

Yes, it was Sunday, the Lord's day of the week. She and Steve should not be slinking past their habitual rites of worship for the Lord who gave all. She lifted the blind to peek at the horizon outside their RV hotel, noting the height to which the Vegas lights projected in the early morning sky, like pink and yellow and red were soaring up to hit the few stars remaining and bat them out of place. Below the lights the hermetically sealed opulence of the casino innards was willful, wanton naughtiness, but oh,

she liked the richness of pleasure, just this once. This was God's, too, she reasoned, though it was be-deviled reasoning, she knew. They'd get back on track once they were beyond these pretty temptations. She was sorry that a sliding scale of their values had emerged...but not sorry enough to abandon a final casino foray.

She and Steve readied, and then drove over in silence, which could pass for meditation, Jackie thought. The drive was short, but so had been their night. They'd commune more after coffee – which reminded her that they had to replenish their nearly empty stash.

As they entered the back of the casino, Jackie wheeled her head around, to search and scan. She'd seen a chapel sign somewhere. However, the all-you-can-eat buffet was calling Steve more powerfully, and there was the need for more coffee. She needed fortification to talk to Amy.

So she slipped into line behind Steve, watched him pay the fee, then merrily bubbled to the task of loading a tray with incredible edibles. She'd only watched Steve play pinball a time or two back when they were dating, but the image compelled. She immediately imagined herself as one of the silver balls pirouetting and banking left, then right as she raced among the stations to load up.

Neither of them spoke for the next twenty minutes, though they managed to inhale dutifully in-between bites. When Steve slid out of the booth to make a second raid, Jackie got her iPhone out of her purse. A call to Amy was necessary. The buffet booth seemed to be the only quiet spot in Las Vegas.

"Sorry I missed your call on Friday afternoon, Jackie. I was driving to a Roller Derby meet."

Jackie noted the apology, so uncharacteristic of Amy, and different from the frustration/fear she'd detected despite the patchiness of their Grand Canyon call. "Well, first let me say that you are so proud of us, Amy. We used the ATM card you gave us."

"Before or after Vegas?" Amy asked. Jackie was impressed that the young woman had kept track of their travel progress.

"Before and only for a meal and some expenses." Jackie realized her hasty move to defensiveness and re-asserted herself with a mild, uncharacteristic brag: "We're eating in Vegas now on a hundred dollars that I won in the slots."

Jackie had something important to pose to Amy, so she reset her spine, though it was difficult to sit tall in the cushy, ribbed leather banquette. She wasn't used to speaking direct, but this was long distance. She couldn't reach out and touch Amy – or knock her block off, whichever needed done.

"Well, I was hoping that luck would have something to do with it because we could use some here," Amy continued glumly.

Jackie glanced around, inhaled deep, then ventured, "What's up, Amy? Brandon okay?"

Amy began: "Well, Brandon is okay, but our crop is not…" her voice becoming quiet and slow, without a hint of her customary bravado. She went on in this same modulated voice to tell her mother-in-law about the stolen crop and equipment. Everything, she said, was gone. The grow barn was bare as Wal-Mart shelves after a sale.

But wait, there was more...

Jackie sank into the news and the cushy banquette seat simultaneously, thinking that surely her ears would burn off. She had never witnessed the fiery beacon that forecast her anger, but Steve had, sharing that her face flamed like the Olympic torch.

Miss Priss-I've-Got-To-Have-It-All had doubled the amount of their HELOC to fund the dubious cookie business. *Okay, a business that I helped to establish and banked on.* A business whose prospects were gone, because its basis was stolen. *How was this going to work?*

Jackie stared down at her new ring, wiggling her fingers to re-engage its promise for her life.

After Amy finished regurgitating bad facts, Jackie felt sunburned. She was certain that her hair was afire just as her brain was, melting and spilling out of her ear into the phone that spouted impossible news. The toxicity flowed to her heart, which almost stopped when the full calamity of their situation was downloaded from her central Michigan home to the middle of a desert. Neon gastric reflux surged up her throat and sparked vocal cords to produce, "Holy shit!" as she snapped the phone off and looked at Steve, who'd just returned with a huge piece of devil's food cake for her, stacked in layers to high heaven. *Holy crap, I put the devil and heaven in the same phrase. I am truly losing my way.*

Steve removed her favorite dessert from the front corner of his tray, and placed it before her with a Cheshire cat grin. "Yes, it is great lookin' cake, but it's not manure, Jackie! You gotta get up and roust about. The desserts counter is gorgeous. It has a luscious treat for every day of the year on display. Seriously, this is food heaven."

Jackie mustered a grin that she hoped flushed angry

embarrassment from her face and thanked Steve for the cake, shoveling a bite fast to keep herself from speaking: *If you can't say anything nice, don't say anything at all. Eat, eat, we love you.* Her mother's voice echoed in her head, reciting every platitude of motherese.

Jackie's head and heart were engulfed at this point, but the bad news had not circulated throughout her body. Her hunger was unaffected, just like always. *Starve a fever, feed a cold...* or was it the reverse?

Jackie wanted to gnaw a fingernail, something she hadn't done since newlywed days when Steve chagrined her out of the habit. She thought vaguely of Marie Antoinette: 'let them eat cake' was causally related to 'off with her head'.

There was no way to smile through this: everyone had a piece in letting Steve down, her as well as Brandon and Amy. Finally she put her hands together in silent prayer. She'd need divine intervention to live through the layers of this calamity.

"Oh yeah," said Steve, "we forgot to say grace. Better late than never, Jackie. Thanks."

She smiled as she swallowed and reached across the table to clasp Steve's hands. She looked him in the eye – and then closed hers, bowed her head, and recited their fallback mealtime prayer aloud with him, while silently saying another: *Dear Lord, it is too late, but please help us with all of Your might.*

Telling Mt. Vesuvius, aka Steve, her noble husband, about the double down duplicity of Amy was going to require a thorough think – and a different setting. She couldn't, she just couldn't tell him in a den of gambling iniquity, so publicly apropos of the situation. Though he'd be more peaceable on a full belly, he might leave her here and she'd never get to the happiest place on earth: Disneyland. Or dangle her shoeless feet in the ocean in January, on a sunny California beach.

Her bucket list was short, but, Lord help her, she wanted to dip in that mighty ocean. Her toes tingled with recall of their Mississippi dip. There were many lakes in Michigan but she'd been so busy with life that she had been to few of them. They were for fisherman.

Jackie shook her head: life always compartmentalized into work. Then she grinned as she recalled that several of Jesus' disciples had been fishermen.

Yes, help her He would, she decided. Pastor Rankin often reiterated that everything happened for one of the Lord's good reasons and purposes - and she knew, she just knew that part of His purpose was for her to visit sunny California. After they crossed the border into La-La Land, courage would help her tell Steve all the truths. *'The whole truth and nothing but', including my stake in the marathon marijuana cookie bake and the special brownies before that - as well as the augmented Alamo Bowl experience. 'So help me God'.*

She found herself compulsively stacking the flatware on their half-full plates until a server slid over to remove their meal remains to a tray as big as the altar at their church. Then she jammed her hands firmly in her pockets so that she wouldn't twirl her curls or chew a fingernail. Geesh, this was going to be hard. Holy shit hard! *What are we going to do?*

"Jackie, let's go look for Joe and Sandy. See what they are up to?" said Steve, as he got out his phone to call Joe. She followed him out to the main casino area, allowing the glitz to put their troubles on silent mode.

When they found Joe and Sandy at the blackjack tables, the skillful dealer shuffles, flips, and dispensing of cards flaunted a house of cards metaphor to jolt her again. Steve looked like he wanted to join them, but Jackie begged off to go to the chapel. It was still Sunday, and she had mighty sins to confess. She had to have a chat with Papa God, a name she hadn't thought of since she was seven. The vixen needed fixin', and He would show her the way!

Jackie firmly latched the door of the chapel and stepped into the empty, reverent space. The chapel was cool, quiet in contrast to the claustrophobic commotion of the main casino areas. The filtered light glowed stained glass, like proverbial rose-colored glasses of hope. Thick carpet nourished her feet, and she realized that she'd been stomping them like grapes of wrath. Her ankles hurt and she knew her knees were next, along with her back, big pains suited for the size of her transgressions. *And poverty. Will Brandon be able to collect food stamps as well as unemployment; can we keep the house and farm? Will they take up a collection for us at the church?*

She walked to the altar, folded her hands at her chest, and then expanded them into angel wings to let out the largest, full-bodied scream she could generate.

It felt so good that she whooped again and, before she could think further, she pulled out her iPhone and called Amy, this time with a Bible to bolster her small paper pad. A casino-logo pen hovered to record the details of the debacle, every piece of crap. She figured that the labor of transcribing would curb cussing at Amy, if being in the Lord's house didn't.

"Hello, Amy. Thank you for answering your phone so quickly, dear." Jackie slathered sweetness to cajole Amy's confession. "You know I'm older, and I may not hear well. Please recite the entire tale one more time."

Amy was, of course, pretty detail-oriented and soon the paper was filled with figures, lines, arrows, and Xs...*Excesses, holy crap. All of us wallowing, except Steve, bless his heart.*

Well, bless mine, too, because I have to tell him. Jackie sweated this task most, truth to self. She tried to deep breathe every few pen strokes, but the data from Amy came furiously, and it lined up pretty much as badly as when she'd heard it the first time. The tablet exposed a flow chart of the devil. Their road trip recast as the road to perdition.

She didn't share the holy crap that she and Steve were in the middle of. She didn't want to give Amy ammunition to gloat, though much of the trouble was her fault. Time to get angst out of her system. Two screams had not been enough, but she was halfway there: "Amy, this is just God-awful. Unbelievable. You little twit, with your collegiate California scheming! Ms. 'I've got to go to Jamaica on my honeymoon' like it was a spiritual right. You've lost a house, two vehicles, and now you've jeopardized our home, vehicles, the whole farm, too! I trusted you. It was all good, you said. You plan as tight as your pants, and you couldn't see this coming? What was the basis of your bank loan plan exactly, fooling Steve and me? Was Brandon included in your duplicity?"

Amy's viewpoint cut with a diamond blade saw: "I didn't raise Brandon or it would have all worked out, Jackie. He's the one who made the deal with the devil who stole our plants and equipment! The lazy twerp let us down. He should have been watching over our crop!"

There was that, but dammnit, Jackie did what every parent would do. She fought for her flesh and blood: "Don't you go blame-shifting, Babilicious", using Brandon's pet name for Amy with a twist of derision. "He's been depressed and overwhelmed. You should have stood by your man, like I did with Steve two years ago and, for that matter, 2/3 of his entire life."

"That's right, you are the perfect little wife, a godly example right out of scripture," Amy forged forward in the verbal sword fight. Jackie recognized *Melrose Place* dialogue. Amy would trade barb for barb with the best of them, and she wasn't done.

"Jackie, it's difficult to stand by your man when he's not standing. Remember that Brandon disappeared into his gaming universe; he's mostly couch-slouched since he lost his job. His damn unemployment gets direct-deposited, so he doesn't even have to drive into town, though he does, squandering tanks of gas."

Jackie interjected a huff of disbelief, as if that would retaliate, but Amy drove on, "I've never witnessed, because I have a real job, so who knows if he even hooked the cows to the milking equipment. For all we know, he got Sparty to do it."

"But the heart of the matter is that Steve is a grown-up and Brandon isn't." Amy twisted her sword in Jackie's heart with "I am the wage earner in the family, the only one at the moment, so I have clout."

Jackie took a deep breath. There was no retort to any of it, no benefit. Her internal silence confirmed that she got the message. A trace of synchronicity days fluttered by; albeit brief, she and Amy had a mildly amiable connection, but it was gone to hell and back.

A vision of Amy bolstered to full prowess by her executive chair caused Jackie to straighten her shoulders, hunched by the burden of writing all that crap. On the third try she made it and forced a smile, just as Amy's voice seemed softer and more solid, at the same time.

"Jackie, you and I can agree that the women in the Breeden family are the original thinkers...." And, despite her intention to hang tough, Jackie cracked. That her eyes snapped to the cross over the altar truly shifted her disposition: all sins were forgiven eventually, so perhaps she and Amy could start.

Jackie actually smiled when Amy continued, "Now let's figure out a solution, Jackie. There's plenty of dirt to go around. It's just that none of the dirt is holding up our cash crop just now." Amy paused for effect, "Got any Vegas dirt to share?"

Jackie giggled – out loud. She had seen some obvious movie star types, but she didn't know their names. Deep breathe, think, plan, dream, figure it out – oh, hell, let Amy do that. Jackie was on a road trip vacation.

Besides, Jackie knew that she had the more difficult task: how to break all this to Steve. Holy crap! Soon it might be "Ciao for now" like she'd heard others say in the casino halls - or *"Goodbye for always..."* *Holy crap!*

She wondered if she could get more life insurance with a phone call to their agent back in Michigan. Because Steve would either kill her or she didn't know what, but it would be awful.

Instead she pocketed her phone and did what should be done in a chapel. She fell to her knees in prayer: that was the best life assurance.

Forty-One: Amy, The Bitch is Back

The snowy world outside looked angelic, unlike inside my office, my head. The date on the desktop calendar had a lot of ones: 1/11/10. *Hmmn. I'll assign the numerals in this Breeden family order: me, Steve, Jackie, Sparty, and then Brandon, who will be zero forever more.* *As well as that bald man, Mr. Prince, who is not one.* I smiled as my boss passed my doorway with a cup of coffee in his hand. *And, with my intellect and instincts of luck, I will be number one at this organization.* It was a scenario that I embraced every time the man as gray as his suits trolled my office on his way to the john. He was just so freaking colorless, he would be easy to outclass.

As usual, I had the bump in the road, akin to the potholes that populated the roads, all figured out, and I impatiently waited for my partners in crime to align. I wondered if and when Steve would be brought aboard, sort of willing it because he was an excellent manager and a level head. I'd long since given up on Brandon's inheritance in that department. He was a fallen football hero, looking for respect in the invisible, portable world of gaming. He'd begun to address people with, "Hey, I make milk. What's your super power?" What a fall from grace he'd sustained.

I cringed if my phone rang while he was on dairy delivery, so certain that he'd run off in a ditch. The shallow ones with the broken concrete culverts fairly grabbed at a vehicle's bumper on these icy country roads.

I turned on my computer, and, while it went through its security rituals, I phoned my brother, Andy, in California. It was time to wake him up to my dream. He was a key player.

"Dude," I said to his muffled "Hi."

"Dudess." It was our secret code, acknowledgment that we survived childhood with the queen of emotional roller coasters, our schizophrenic mom. His voice changed so that I could almost see him sit up in bed, so I turned on Skype and beckoned him to join.

And, there he was, with the offset eye gaze peculiar to Skype: "Thanks for waking me. I have class in an hour."

"Confirmation that I paid the tuition. That's the good news. But I have bad news: I can't afford money for living expenses this semester. You're going to have to deal."

"I'd already planned to, Sis. Opportunity's too great not to. Too many people talking like folks off their meds, in classes and out of them," Andy said, his voice warming to the topic. "Besides I'm close to the crops, like you are in that farm town. How's the weather there?"

"Whiter than Carmel's sandy beach," I said. "Shit, you know how it is here – cold and I hate it."

"Well, there has to be a down side to living in a mansion that cost only thousands instead of millions," Andy parried. "Is it true that a nickel bag still costs a nickel in Michigan? I was thinking of coming to the Hash Bash in Ann Arbor and staying with you."

"How do I know what a nickel bag costs? You know I don't smoke and never will!" I almost shrieked because of the next fact I had to assert. "I may have forgotten to tell you that Brandon lost his job and we lost our house and vehicles. We are living in his folks' home, which costs zero."

After a beat, Andy said, "How's that working for you?"

"Fine. They're gone. They are in California, and I'm sending them to see you."

Now my brother's face fell even further than it had when I'd announced my losses: from empathy to flounder with only the split second lag, compliments of our Skype connection. More seconds passed before he continued.

"As if Michigan hadn't frozen over, now you've frozen hell, too? I go from planning to visit you in a few months to having your in-laws in my lap. What, why, how?" he said, now on the edge of his bed.

I gave him a summary, because I couldn't linger on this. There was no fear of eavesdropping, but I did have bank business to do – and other calls to make.

Andy agreed because he had to, simple as that. He'd trusted me to lead the way all of his life. My unerring survival instincts had carried us both this far and he wouldn't/couldn't let go now.

After clicking and keying a few moments of real work, in case anyone asked me any, I stood to walk off a truth told and tension endured. A bio break punctuated with a lengthy Downward Facing Dog yoga stretch got me back on-task. A glance at the clock assured me that Veronica was on the road to work, and I gave her a call.

"Hi, Amy. What could you want while I'm driving to work?"

"How has the Christmas returns and sales season been going?" I asked congenially.

Veronica groaned. "I'd rather talk about the clothes I've gotten. Great deals on heeled boots! Want me to get you a pair?"

"No, I'd rather talk about supplies. Where do you get your product?"

Veronica's voice was circumspect: "I drive to Canada once in a while…"

"While gas is climbing to $3.00?" I said.

"Ms. Penny pincher, the scenery is pretty, the roads are sparsely policed, and my source honors the prescription I don't have, the one written with invisible ink," Veronica said tersely. "Why are you asking anyways? What happened?"

"The crop is gone," I said in a rush. "Don't ask for details. I'm pissed, and I need to move beyond frustration to solution. We have a few orders more than the cookie stash in the freezer, Ronni. You need to bake if we want to maintain the Milkweed Business, let alone expand. The debt mountain just got higher."

"I guess I will buy you a pair of the on-sale Uggs, Amy. They'll keep your feet warm in Canada. But, can this conversation wait until we go to Roller Derby, Hon. I'm in the Wal-Mart parking lot."

Just then the bank president walked by again, craning his neck slightly to look at my legs, which was why he'd agreed to my expensive glass-topped desk. Though I thwarted the perv by wearing slacks, he always looked optimistic - *or was that opportunistic. I get those two confused a lot.* "The answer is yes and good-bye," I said loud enough for Perv the Prince to hear. "Pleasure doing business with you."

After a few clever taps of the keys, I was onto the biggest adventure of the day: tracking down Travis the thief, that soon-to-be-gutted bastard, and grab back my personal crop or its value in trade. Brandon had ratted him out easily, for a slice of pizza and a slice of me.

I'd not even been able to keep track of my own homeless schizo mother, who cycled through the array of Santa Monica, CA shelters, so I didn't know how I'd manage to track Travis down. But, then again, I'd never tried. If I had to, I'd sic Sparty on him. I pondered a private detective whose ad I'd seen somewhere and began my online research.

What I quickly learned – really, in no time at all – was where Travis lived – and where he banked because it was a branch of my bank in a town only forty miles away. *You have got to be kidding. Men were just fucking dumb.*

Within minutes I'd sussed his account, but decided not to loot it. Yet. That would be too obvious - and probably treacherous. There was loads of money in the account, so there was much to win or lose. His account could be raided with a couple of keystrokes, but I wanted to meet this guy. He was a thrill ride, if I didn't let myself get caught in loop of anger. What he'd pulled off – and quickly – was bodacious.

I am bold, too, and curvaceous. *Game on!*

Suddenly I was aware of my thumbs aching from the twitchy twist-around I'd probably been doing for awhile. *At least I don't bite my lip. I am not totally my mother's daughter.*

I sat for a minute to calm my thoughts. I reached for the folded newspaper that I'd brought from the staff lounge, thinking that might be where I'd seen the private dick's ad. When I opened it, my arm almost swept my coffee cup off the desk as I reacted to the headline: *Five at ER on New Years Day.*

As I read on, these patients were middle-agers with symptoms of "nausea, dizziness, and inability to stand unassisted." Expensive testing for such illnesses as polio, influenza (*only newspaper people spelled out that entire word*), and food poisoning had been explored, but the cause was unknown. The news for now was that this was a record number of people who'd arrived with similar symptoms other than two hunters who'd unexpectedly shot each other during the season. I wondered for the first time about the Milkweed cookies because I vaguely recognized the names as people on our customer list.

I needed to get out of the office, move, and do something assertive. Fast. Today *was* the day to confront Travis and take back my crop. To hell with a private dick, I could do this, on my own, as always.

I cursed Brandon all over again. I'd so longed for stability and esteem, yet what I'd developed had been in spite of him. It was almost like he'd betrayed his birthrights. It was time to abandon ship, which in this case was a farm.

I strode out to Jackie's van, thinking suddenly that it was a surveillance vehicle right out of CSI: Miami, NY, LA, and now Michigan. I turned it on with new respect for driving such a non-descript, ill-colored vehicle. It could be a great Milkweed Goods delivery van, once I got the goods back.

I drove with great purpose. The roads weren't as tough to drive with a light snow pack when I got to the gravel, two-lane that Travis' place was located on. This was a TV or movie set location. *Surreal.*

The white one-story home needed a bit of paint, though the snow had powdered the roof to perfection. Or maybe some aluminum siding, so common in this area of Michigan. While there were numerous windows lining a wide plank porch that extended along two sides, white shades were drawn full length. The house looked as if it were in deep winter slumber. Perhaps the three bears were home, awaiting Goldilock's intrusion.

There was no rail on the porch: a sort of invitation to walk up and knock on the door. So, I did, wishing I had Red Riding Hood's basket of goodies to arm me. I felt vulnerable yet fierce, not knowing how to mix the two feelings.

I knocked, waited, knocked and waited more. I was about to turn when the shade on the door's window notched. I stared back at the eye of a thief, forcing a smile on my face.

"We gave money to the lady last week," the male voice said.

"I'm not collecting money. Something else." I used my best coy-toned voice.

The shade went down. A moment passed. The door opened.

I was staring at Ben Affleck or his best look-alike, scruffily bearded as if preparing for the movie I'd read about in People while at Maybelline's beauty shop. It was
a bank heist movie. *Holy shit: this was just all too coincidental.*

"I won't attack you if you don't attack me," the guy said. "What are you selling, lady?"

"I'm not selling, but I drove all this way to meet you. My name is Amy Breeden."

"So," the guy looked me up and down. Apparently he didn't make the connection with Brandon. I moved to sit, but decided against it because, after looking around, there wasn't a place where I wanted to stand or sit. This place was beyond unkempt. I'd thought that Brandon's clothing piles were unsightly, but revised that thinking. Were those really bits of straw strewn around? Had the three bears been here and moved to the back room at my knock?

"We don't need a cleaning lady," the guy said, following my gaze.

"Oh, I work at Home Savings," I said, shifting to business intonation. "I've come to discuss your accounts, Mr. Castro."

That I knew his name caused Travis to blink, and just that quick, the Breeden dots connect. I knew that he knew that I had busted his scheme. I remained cordial, business-like, mild – with a cocked hip and wide smile - and soon enough he was leading me to the basement to tour his grow area, as if I had spread the bread crumb trail myself. I followed him, like Hansel and Gretel to the witch's lair. *Slick, if I do say so myself.*

The stairwell was dark, so that when he offered me shades, I thought he was crazy. He insisted and fitted them on my nose and ears. As I righted them to fit more comfortably, to reassert my will, my body responded in spite of that will, like I'd suddenly gained more pixels.

When he opened the door, after opening its multiple combination locks, I was glad for the shades. The grow lights were blazing in the white-white room and the reflection off the aluminum-wrapped ducting was irritating, even with glasses to shield my light eyes. This was a revelation with a bit of nostalgia. This was my weed, nestled alongside his, only shorter. I was seeing my babies again and I wanted...

But before I could hear the plants calling my name, Travis closed the door.

"You are not moving in, lady."

"My name is Amy. I am no lady and let's talk about our mutual aspirations," as I moved close to wrap both arms and one long leg around him. "Think of me as a flame-'n-go. Got anything to burn?"

Forty-Two: California Dreaming

Jackie and Steve breakfasted with Sandy and Joe in their outfit, one of those behemoth bus-like RVs with the melodious paint job, the better to be a rock star's ride. Jackie tried not to be envious as she looked around the spaciousness, settling into the fact that she didn't have to cook the hash browns, eggs, and Iowa-fresh bacon they were eating this morning. *Envy is one of the seven deadly sins, so I must watch out. My list is already long enough, isn't it, Lord Almighty. Here I am the queen of sloth, not even helping with the food preparation.*

Sandy was so sincere that a person couldn't hate her. She'd give you the shirt off her back. Faced with potential financial ruin with what she and Steve were driving…it was just too sad a comparison. It made Jackie feel desperate. *Let's swallow the topic with some freshly squeezed orange juice before I blurt out and ask her for that shirt, along with $100,000.00 in its cute pocket.*

Jackie shifted her attitude. She smiled with the secret knowledge that she had a weed stash that might be spicing up life when she got to California. She planned to have her own hippie moment, the one she had not had in the 60's, which were really the 70's in small town Michigan. The folk of Woodstock had celebrated its 40th anniversary with a re-issue of the historic event's movie. She and Steve had gone to see it. For not having attended that muddy free-for-all Jackie had no lament, but seeing the movie may have added impetus to desires to be footloose.

With that train of thought Jackie realized that she was circling Amy's suggestion that she and Steve deal the weed to make money for their road trip expenses. Holy crap!

Jackie jerked her attention back to the meal with a hefty forkful of hash browns, chewing with soft "Mmmn's". After so little time, the Adams seemed like kin, while Amy still did not. The two couples were as compatible as mashed potatoes and gravy, which the two men agreed that they could eat for any and every meal, with bowls of salted and buttered popcorn. Each had found a carrot-hating soul mate.

After breakfast, the two couples traded phone numbers, email and home addresses, but stopped at birthdays and anniversary dates. Christmas cards would be exchanged.

Joe and Sandy were not going to California like Steve and Jackie, but looping back through the awesome national parks of Utah before heading back home. Sandy yearned for her grandchildren, and Joe was peeved about his Las Vegas losses.

"I'm ready to replace bad memories with good kids and scenery," Joe said, joking that the unpolished red rocks of Zion and Bryce Parks, the Rockies' granite, and then the winter wheat fields of Nebraska and home, would be welcome counter-point to the Vegas horseshit, especially that damn volcano.

Steve agreed that might be true. He and Jackie would eventually head that way, so the two men kibitzed over the map while the women cooed over photos again.

Jackie was antsy to get going; she could almost see the ocean from here. She was California dreaming to sublimate financial distress, compounded by how to tell Steve about their situation – and Amy's crazy suggestion. Soon, the two men quit kicking the tires, got into their respective vehicles and, with a ball cap salute, switched on the ignition. They were on the road again.

Jackie got out the iPad to research Disneyland, where she'd be in no time, reading aloud its trivia to Steve, the loyal driver. She bubbled on, used to Steve's calm, stare-ahead demeanor, yet trying to entice him with the lure of one of the attractions, perhaps the wild ride of Indiana Jones or, she giggled, of Mr. Toad. Why, California Adventure, the companion park, even had an animated bug show and real corn!

In a couple of hours, they both needed a pit stop. A

thermometer as tall as the water tower back home beckoned. They were in Baker, California and it was 70 degrees, validation of being away from Michigan in January. It was photo stop – and maybe a refrigerator magnet - time.

Jackie smiled, but only for a moment. A sign pointed the way to Death Valley. She began to recite Psalm 23. She didn't need the sign to remind her of impending doom and death.

While Steve gassed up Apache Red, she used the accounting app that Amy had suggested to tally the expenses that they all faced, forcing herself to breathe even, as Amy had coached for finesse and relaxation. In this moment the two helpful actions were the only positive things she recalled Amy having ever done to, for, or with her. How did she get that bad girl as a daughter-in-law anyway? Why, oh why, were they locked in debt together? *I would never have partnered with her on anything if Brandon hadn't.*

When Steve climbed in the cab, he looked at her suspiciously. *Could he read the iPad?* She closed the program and shut the device quickly, shoving it under the seat. She knew the facts, more than she wanted to know – and wasn't ready to share.

Without a word, Steve buckled up and started the vehicle, carefully using his mirrors to guide them back onto the Interstate. As they blended into traffic, she felt his body tense and reached over to touch his forearm softly. The number of vehicles on the road was increasing. It was as if the entire jumble of cars from the Alamo Bowl and the Michigan State stadiums had converged to drive the California Interstate system. Yikes – somebody should be charging money instead of having these roads be free. The national debt could be eliminated in a month; *our debt could be settled in a nano-second.*

They motored along to the tunes of their teens, making time fast toward the 'happiest place on earth.' Steve clenched his jaw against talk of the secret brother, but Jackie wasn't used to keeping secrets. She felt as if she might explode – and not from the scrumptious over-eating she'd done at breakfast. She longed for a conference with Bonnie or Fran.

She intended to tell Steve after they'd gassed up in Baker, with the numbers clear in her head, but her resolve collapsed like a snow cone left to the sun. The telling might have been better when the vehicles weren't moving, when he couldn't open the door and shove her to fall under the wheels. She could see the headline on the paper back home now: ***Local Woman Collapses Under The Alamo.***

Finally, her conscience won the battle, and Jackie asked Steve to stop alongside the road. He looked at her, wondering why she hadn't peed at the gas station or one of the rest stops. Seriously, out here in the open? Jackie nodded yes.

Steve eased the vehicle over and parked on the wide berm of the Interstate. The truck cab swayed with each vehicle that blew past them, but Steve focused on Jackie's face and reached out to hold her free hand. The other was clutching the door handle. She shook her head throughout, gesturing *no* as if to deny the words. Breakfast was still threatening to come up.

She wanted to throttle cock-sure Amy who had sold them down the river, smiling despite herself at the image because here they were in the scrubbiest piece of desert that a devil could imagine. And the sign beside her head, outside the truck cab, pointed to 'The Devil's Playground.' Now that was just right, wasn't it? They had surely taken a detour from the good life and they had arrived.

Because Steve was a just-the-facts-ma'am person, she tried to align the details, hoping against hope that, as she prepared the outline of disaster, perhaps the deck would re-shuffle or Lady Luck would intervene, as she laid all the cards out on the table, so to speak.

Jackie scooped a pencil and paper from the inner pocket of her purse. Steve waited, looking out over the expanse of nothingness. She wrote $50,000.00 twice: it was the amount of their original HELOC, plus the amount of Amy's secretly upped ante. There was more debt, including this devil-red truck with its soft butter seats, but she could not write it. Jackie felt as if the automatic seat warmer was on, looking at the dashboard to be sure. She was past hot flashes, so that couldn't be the cause of her internal heat. *Must be the shame that Pastor Rankin rails about.*

She could tell it was the shame as she gazed at Steve's face. Was he grinding his teeth? He sure was running his hands up and down the steering wheel, as if he could change its shape. *Wish he could change the shape we are in.*

Then she wrote another $10,000.00 because Amy related that this was about the amount of the Milkweed business debt…and drew a dagger through the amount because all of the pot plants and business apparatus were gone, vanished, adios.

And she began to tell Steve…everything, everything including the medical marijuana prescription and the brownies that she regularly fed him. How she and Amy had baked cookies to sell with the micro-dairy milk and wasn't the name Milkweed Goods cute. "How apropos," Steve put in, "Milkweed is poisonous to cows."

All lost, all gone. Her name was surely *Calamity Mary Jane* as she piled dire detail upon dire detail, watching Steve become ashen. They'd traveled through the country where that famous cowgirl used to roam, so perhaps her spirit was aboard. Maybe she could help Jackie if God didn't.

"Holy crap!" Steve shouted. "If we have driven two weeks and we haven't even reached Disneyland, then it'll take us two weeks to drive back. Add time for the blessed burden of distributing Big Braghorn's ashes… We can't be back in Michigan for at least three weeks to fix this mess."

Steve opened the glove box and pulled out the stash of Cracker Barrel gift cards. It was a small deck, something that he might be dealt at a poker table. A darn sight more familiar than dealing the weed in Jackie's stash – which was in their vehicle, holy crap –

as Amy had suggested.

Jackie just hung in there, afraid to move a muscle. She was glad that she'd at least set foot in California.

Then Steve did something unexpected: he smiled crookedly, like Tom Cruise. "What am I going to do now that I've won the shit lottery? I'm going to Disneyland!"

Jackie couldn't believe it. Maybe she'd live after all... She began to hum '*It's a Small World*', the song that a YouTube of Disneyland had already implanted, expectantly, in her mind. She had not anticipated his acquiescence and let's-go-forward attitude. She was used to being the accelerator, while he was the brake. She hoped that the merrily infectious song would cement his positive attitude without second thoughts breaking in, and that his frame of mind would meld with hers. Something was working; it was a miracle.

The next few hours passed easily as both of them got used to the traffic spread across the widest swath of concrete they'd ever seen, six lanes on each side of a concrete sliver. While Jackie and Steve had seen similar masses of vehicles, they were parked stationary like good little sardines. It was if they'd wandered onto a NASCAR track, cars passing them with a noise like an angry cat hiss. The gleam of the sun off the grayish-white surface caused them to bring out the sunglasses. *California, here we come.*

Steve smiled below his Ray-Bans. They were going to be all right. He had a card up his sleeve; he had a secret brother who might have money to lend.

The website for the Anaheim RV park where they'd reserved a space promised that the Matterhorn was visible from every site. Jackie was sure it would look better than the Taos ski resort mountain that she'd barely seen, but it was late in the day and darker at 4:45 than she'd ever experienced in Michigan. Her euphoria went down with the sun.

She glumly thought of Sandy and Joe. They'd see

mountains, too, but theirs could be more viably climbed mountains than the financial ones that the Breeden family faced and were certainly more picturesque.

Forty-Three: Stuck in the Middle

Steve was glad when Jackie went to bed early. Though he had done all the driving and was tired, too, he needed a thorough chat with his son. He didn't like how the scenario played out so far, with Brandon as the scapegoat/buffoon. There were two sides to every story, and Steve wanted to believe Brandon's. In fact, he already did.

He hugged Jackie and tucked her in, then closed the door of the small bedroom. Her fresh Pepsodent breath stayed with him as he strode the short hall to the living area couch. He'd stretched out for several naps there so he knew its restorative strength and purpose.

Midway through smoothing the stadium blanket over his lap, he changed his mind and moved to the truck cab, folding the blanket around his girth. Like an Indian chief, politically correct be damned.

Properly sequestered, he placed his call. Though it was 11:30 p.m. in Michigan, he knew his night owl gamer would be up.

"Hi, Dad." Brandon sounded hurried, a bit brusque. "What's up besides you in sunny California? What time is it there?"

"Brandon, if your game is on pause, you have to close out. This is going to be a serious conversation."

"But my game is near record…"

"Brandon Amos, I'm aware of something serious that went down. We need a discussion. Turn the game off."

"Okay, it'll take a mom…"

"Let it take less. There's a midnight chat we need to have. Remember them, Kid? We had them from the time you were a toddler through the high school years. I missed them when you went to State. Was that when Amy took over?"

But Brandon had apparently put the call on wait, because the phone held dead air, which seemed to spread throughout the cab. Steve was glad he'd brought the blanket. He hadn't expected chill at this time of night, not in sunny California. He idly wondered what the temperature was and wished he had the keys so he could turn on the ignition to read the dashboard indicator. His farm senses told him it was about 50 degrees.

Then he smiled at himself. In Michigan he would have declared that temp worthy of striding around without coat, hat, and gloves when he did his milking chores in the barn. Who knew that thinning of the blood could occur in just two weeks time? *Well, his wallet had certainly thinned, so why not the blood.*

Brandon came on the line just in time to fetch Steve from the path of morose: "So, what's up, Dad?"

"Tell me about the pot, Brandon."

You could almost see Brandon's lips form a silent "Oh, shit" while he hung his head toward his lap. Steve had seen the posture many times, when Brandon was benched after a bad series of downs in a big game, for example. But only in high school; the mannerism was gone after he went to State. Life had handed Brandon another bad series of downs, and Steve wondered how he would handle them this time. Would the family manage their problems together or apart?

"Pot's gone, Dad. It's gone."

"What was the plan, Kid? Tell me about that?"

"Well, you know that Amy and I had a serious need for cash, so we decided to expand the micro dairy business to sell cookies. You know, milk and chocolate chip cookies. The only better pairing is milk and Oreos. Remember how we used to peel them apart and dunk them together?"

"But cookies with pot in them? Without telling people? To my customers, our friends, our community? What if someone got sick?

"What do you mean, did anyone get sick?" countered Brandon. "Mom fed marijuana brownies to you. Did you get sick?"

Steve reflected a moment, hoping that Brandon didn't take his silence as cue to switch back to his game. He realized that he not only had never felt sick, but he hadn't medicated with much Advil, Aleve, or Motrin, sometimes all jumbled together in a tri-color handful, in the past year.

"Okay, but isn't it illegal? What if you got caught?"

"Medical marijuana has been legal since Obama was elected. The very day, Dad," said Brandon, referencing Steve's favorite politician to get his dad on his side.

Steve didn't remember the medical marijuana campaign. His morning paper read was skewed to sports and weather, and when he watched the nightly TV news he was way beyond tired. He didn't listen to talk radio during milking because he and the cows preferred rock-n-roll.

He wondered if Brandon had changed that, so he asked. He needed a pause from stomach-churning topics. And he, for darned sure, didn't want to discuss Ms. Ambitious Amy.

Soon the two were discussing musical themes, the band that Brandon had seen at Darcy's, anything but Amy. There was nothing to say about her or the suspected pot thief. Nothing to do about an emptied-out building or debt stacked to high heaven. Nothing that could be achieved, either locally or from a distance, and by neither man. Steve felt more heaviness than he'd ever experienced in fifty-six years of living.

"Thanks for talking with me, not at me, Dad. A midnight chat like old times."

Yeah, the old times before Amy the brat took off with you and our nice life, thought Steve. "Night, son. I'll bring you a souvenir from Disneyland. Now make sure you are giving Sparty his treats."

Steve woke before Jackie to make breakfast for their adventure in the happiest place on earth, hoping that it was, because they needed it to be. They'd read that the park opened at 8:00 – and they intended to close it down - so he began preparation of bacon and pancakes, the scents sure to awaken her. The menu, to which he'd add eggs, was the one perennially eaten when they needed fortification for a long day, like back in the day when he'd helped his dad harvest.

Steve knew that they also needed fortification to build up the nerve for doing what they had to do to earn money to get home, which wasn't exactly Disney worthy nor was it Christian. At least California had medical marijuana laws – so Brandon said - so Steve wasn't concerned about the weed stashed in their closet. Maybe he'd venture a few questions to his brother when he called him.

Jackie and Steve were striding hand-in-hand down Main Street in Disneyland, nearly $200.00 charged at the entry ticket kiosk outside the gate. Steve expected the day to be priceless, as promised by the Master Card slogan, so he succumbed to the unfelt spending it fostered.

It was interesting to be walking in the middle of a paved street among a hundred other people doing the same, all of them adults. California children were in school, or else these were Amazon kids, stretched tall by constant sunshine.

Steve looked around, scanning faces to determine what a drug dealer might look like. Since he'd heard that there was a lot of dope smoking in California, it was possible that he'd just walked by one. He'd never considered such a look-around at home; then recalled his self-scrutiny in the tiny mirror in the Alamo this morning. *That's what a drug dealer looked like. It was going to be him and not Jees O'Katie.*

Jees O'Katie! That was the term his dad always used when there was deep do-do about, and he hadn't thought it in years! Now seemed the time to evoke that term, so he said it aloud, "Jees O'Katie."

"Steve, I haven't heard anyone say that since your dad, but it sure does apply, doesn't it? I heard the folks back there say the park isn't crowded today and, if this isn't crowded, I don't know what is. How you doing with all these people walking so close, crowding us?"

When Steve just shrugged, not divulging his thoughts, Jackie continued, "I also heard someone say that the Haunted Mansion and the Small World attractions are closed to take down the elaborate holiday decorations that we missed. Isn't that just rich? We paid a small fortune and we don't get to see everything in Disneyland. That does not make me the happiest person in the happiest place on earth."

Steve turned them left into Adventure Land to change the course of the conversation. There they partook of the Tiki Room, which left his head shaking at being such a jerk, glad he hadn't paid extra. He hadn't expected such cornpone humor from talking birds.

The ante was upped with the wiseacre Jungle Cruise operators, but he expected such remarks from humans. The quips sounded like poker table talk. Except for the gunshot, of course.

He got to drive the jeep in Indiana Jones. Gosh, they agreed, it felt like they were inside the movie. Afterward Jackie restrained him from buying a brown fedora, reminding him that he had a horizontal rack of hats back home. Steve wondered if his brother might have one that he could try, with Grover Cleveland bills stashed in the brim. Disneyland was the happiest place on earth when one had a plan. He was definitely going to look up Turlock on one of his apps.

Jackie squealed when Johnny Depp appeared as a Pirate of the Caribbean… and on and on… until Tinker Bell floated across the night sky, followed by a spectacular fireworks display that outplayed any they'd seen in Michigan. Fourth of July at the fairgrounds would never be the same.

It was all like the stories his mother had read to him when he was a kid, one each night from Disney's Surprise Package. It was a treasured book that her Aunt Curtsey had given him before he'd become a reader.

He could see that book in his mind's eye, a cast of kids and characters on the cover, pulling on a pink bow and ribbon to open the book to the surprises packaged inside. There'd been a dog watching the proceedings, and his mother told him to imagine it as his dog, because his father always denied his requests for a canine companion. *I miss my Sparty dog; he'd be watching us open the packages that are each place we visit, each site we see, each person we meet, barking along with my pleasure in each.*

To exit the Park, they walked back down the Main Street. In the last shop, The Emporium, he saw that same book in the window, the vintage re-issue on the 60th anniversary of its publication. What a coincidence! Disney was good at that, forever recycling and polishing its magical presence on earth.

Steve pulled Jackie into the store to buy it for Brandon's future son, leaving Amy out of the family and not unconsciously. Steve could almost feel his grandson in his lap... Hope was easy to come by in Disneyland.

Jackie just watched him, wondering what, but Steve knew it to be the perfect gift, symbolic of the surprise packages that the future would bring. He hoped that some Disney spirit burst forth from the pages, just as it had in his childhood, to transport their Michigan homestead and micro dairy business back into the happiest place on earth.

Forty-Four: Amy, Flame-n-go

Hot sex in the basement, worthy of a romance novel, *as if I'd ever read one.* Surged by the heat of the grow lights that tended my pot plants as well as by the heat of the man who possessed them. Travis asserted himself as *a* real *player* – in the here and wow - not a former, like Bran. Travis Castro was a man of formidable intention for today and the future, not a hopeless replay of the past.

Hair like mayhem, Travis wore a scent of berserk, fly-apart abandon, with a tight black leather vest and jeans. A short sleeve tee to show bravado, white as snow in spite of winter chill, as well as a set of sculpted biceps. Jeans torn artfully in just the right places, as if to beg a girl to rip them open, like a belated Christmas gift. *Santa Baby!* I imagined that he owned a Harley, too, and I wanted to ride.

Our heat felt like heaven. I hadn't realized how lovelorn I'd been until now. Sex-bereft, deprived of more than just intellectual stimulation in the small town climate. This man deserved my competitive drive – and matched it.

I backed Travis up the stairs, delighted to be goal-driven again. Success in kissing and sucking and touching all over, the taste of his fleshy lips, the bump of his nose on mine.

I peeked at my watch. It was 2:00 p.m. Lunch and true bank business were blown, but I was neither hungry nor chagrined. The straw-strewn carpet that led to his bedroom no longer bothered me. I was looking nowhere but at his eyes, trusting myself to their flinty beacon. If he could make his way backwards, I would follow. Hell, if he went sideways, I'd go along. I felt melded to him from birth and I'd just met him. I became dizzy-headed, like every dumb blonde joke, but what the hell?

At 4:30 I looked at my watch, thinking that Brandon was making dairy deliveries. I should return to...no, go to the Homestead and clear out my things. I was moving in on the pot operation and this man. He'd agreed in the manner of all the men I'd had: yes, oh, yes, oh, yes!

Maybe the trash bags I'd thrown my clothes into for the move would still be about; the boxes to unpack sure were, for I could never decide where to stash stuff, not wanting to disturb Jackie's nest. *Nest, that's it. With all of this straw strewn about Travis' place, I can feel nested in a hurry.* Ferocious and fast, Jackie's plain wrap van transported me to match my hurried mental state.

Back at the Homestead I borrowed a broom and dustpan from the pantry, but left the Hoover. I yanked several kitchen towels from a drawer as well as the 20 Mule Team Borax from under the sink. *Wouldn't Jackie be proud that I recalled where that was? Though she wouldn't be proud of where I'm gonna use it.*

Besides my make-up and hair paraphernalia, a small mountain of shoeboxes, clothes and the simple cleaning supplies, I'd need little else. Travis already had Jackie's shears and all of my expensive gear needed for growing. Soon I'd be able to purchase anything I'd ever wanted or needed. Hope and aspirations were again abloom and it wasn't yet Spring, when I'd projected the first fruits of harvest.

Then I remembered the large plastic bags filled with popcorn that were in the pantry and made several trips to lug each one to the van. Travis would be proud of me when he saw these bags, like none other for storing weed. For good measure, I ran to Steve's desk to input the name, address, and number of the small farm's cash renter in my cell. His contact information would be handy when we needed more pot storage bags. In the meantime, Travis and I would have popcorn to eat – as well as the last pre-baked pot cookies from the barn freezer.

As I drove back to Travis' place, I realized that we had conversed very little in our full-on communication. I still didn't know how he'd managed to finagle the product and clear the grow barn. Wasn't Brandon in the nearby milk barn hours on end, tending to the cows and milking?

All the more reason to dump his sorry, wretched ass.

Forty-Five: The License of the Law

Meanwhile, back at the micro-dairy on that mid-afternoon, Brandon was not on milk chores or deliveries. He was gearing up to think and talk fast. Sheriff Daniels and a deputy had shown up and asked for his dad, apparently not aware that Steve and Jackie had left for their road trip, over two weeks ago now. How could that be in this small town?

He invited them inside the house – how could he not – and made coffee, scruffing one hand across his head to ascertain its style, and tugging his jersey down with the other, after shoving his phone into a pocket. He'd been reclining on the football-colored couch, easing out the back muscles bent tight from tending the cows, gaming with one of his online regulars. The guy's non-threatening avatar disguised a malicious strategy that was stalking Brandon's self-esteem. What a challenge he wrought!

But nothing compared to the challenge of meeting and greeting the two stern-faced men in uniform. They looked like statues, frozen in mid-grimace, without a trace of the farm town affability in which Brandon had been immersed. They were not unlike a couple of bulky linemen he'd faced while at State, probably Ohio State men. The world outside of his football career was proving to be more complex than previously encountered, yet not. Brandon began to feel that he could handle this.

He made mental notes, proving some acumen to himself. How different their uniforms are from mine, Brandon thought. Where my clothes have wrinkles, theirs have aligned and tightly-pressed creases. Their pride is different than my lavishly unkempt. Even their hair seems firmly pressed, weighted down with authority. Their personalities could have used some of that grease.

Then he noticed the guns and batons, both black and equally weighted on a black braided belt of precision leather, reminding him of Amy's Mercedes Benz. He stood more erect, as if ready to lead the Pledge at a school assembly. He ran some of his coaches' favorite slogans through his mind, to prime himself, settling on Lou Holtz: "Never tell your problems to anyone…20% don't care and the other 80% are glad you have them".

Brandon answered the beep of the coffee machine, glad for a sound to slice the silence in the kitchen. The two gentlemen looked like they'd swallowed bad news whole – and he felt like he was next. Without food in his stomach, he wondered if he would hiccup. How he wished that his mother were home because there'd be cookies in the jar to offer, to soften the officers' tension. He most certainly couldn't offer the officers the cookies in the garage freezer.

He found three mugs in the cupboards – exactly – all the same size and pattern, manly handled ones that clunked as they hit the counter, the one on his thumb first. He willed himself to count to ten as he filled each mug. He offered sugar and his dairy's fresh cream.

After a few sips of coffee, the bad news spilled out direct and simple, accompanied by some paperwork with an official county seal. The micro-dairy license had lapsed on January 3.

WTF. Why didn't Dad have that covered? thought Brandon. This was not the right time or place to discover that his dad was less than perfect. Not when his dad was thousands of miles away and couldn't defend himself. Not when he wasn't available to fix the gaff. What was happening was not right, and how it was happening was not the right way either. He excused himself to go to the bathroom and retrieved his phone to call Steve, wishing he'd taught his dad to text.

Brandon looked at himself in the mirror and took a deep breath. As his chest filled, he began to feel like a football hero, a man in charge. He envisioned his trophies, lining the shelves of the rec room downstairs, as soldiers ready to muster at his command. Another favorite sports quote came in mind: "I never learn anything talking. I only learn things when I ask questions." Lou Holtz was the man.

He decided to ask some questions. He'd listen to the Sheriff to determine how to solve the problem. He would make his dad proud. He knew from a prior chat that his dad and mom were at Disneyland, the happiest place on earth. Surely they deserved this time; surely he'd figure out something.

For now there was bad news, but there was good news, too. There always was that silver lining to see - if you looked past the shadow the problem cast on your shiny penny self, like his mom said.

The great news was that the pot was gone, Brandon thought, when the two men asked for a tour of the barns. The cattle were lowing, welcoming the sheriffs, though Brandon had to clarify that their call was a "moo", not a "boo". Perhaps it was a quirk of imagination.

Sparty was helpfully playful, yet restrained. He didn't jump and slobber on the men, just tilted the atmosphere from the brink to stable optimism. It was always an icebreaker that he looked like the Budweiser dog.

The men left after a cursory look around, departing as if sheepish for disturbing his day. As they spun down the gravel drive, it popped into Brandon's head who he could call: Coach Uhrig.

"Hello," said the steady timbre voice of Coach Uhrig, the sage of small town football. His image that matched that magic voice rose before Brandon like Obi-Wan Kenobi to the Skywalker father and son.

"Hi, Coach, this is Brandon, Brandon Breeden. Remember me?"

"How could I not, Son?" Coach replied.

Calm coursed through Brandon's body, up and down his spine, at the familiar greeting. Coach had considered each of his boys his son, even the particularly prank-prone ones who endeared themselves with their need of constant rescue. Brandon hadn't been one of those boys in high school, *but I surely am now. This is my turn. Please, Coach.*

"Coach, Mom and Dad are vacationing in California…" Brandon began, but the coach quickly cut in.

"You're welcome at our table anytime, Son. I'll be home soon, but Maybelline's there now, off on Mondays and Tuesdays, you know. There's always room for one of my boys at our table."

Brandon found himself quickly accepting – Coach was just that way. He took a moment to glance at his watch to figure how much time he had before the evening milking. He grabbed his coat and Dad's truck keys, taking a moment to clutch them to heart to mourn his Ford F-150, and headed out the door. He pulled his coat on while striding to the garage where he replenished Sparty's water and dog food, then patted the dog's head a few times for luck.

He needed more totem touching, more luck, so he ran back to the house and tore downstairs to high-five each of his trophies. Then he galloped upstairs to sweep his hand along his line of purple and blue 4-H ribbons. He shrugged off his coat and into his 2003 Alamo Bowl jersey – game on!

He texted his destination, not bothering with a call or note, hoping that she'd acknowledge, affirming interest. But Brandon's doubt was as large as his dread of another humiliating encounter. He was still in the doghouse for the pot loss; she was going to be explosive about this complication.

Forty-Six: How Things are Done

Brandon didn't remain on Coach's front porch long, a good thing because he could hear his heart like a rock drummer's whack and slam: "Born to Run" was winding up, when the door swung wide, oblivious to allowing in waves of chilled air. It was almost as if Maybelline Uhrig had supernatural hearing; she answered the door as his hand raised to knock. She was known around town as a mystic force: eeriness amped his discomfort.

"What's your Tigers hat doing in your hand rather than on your head, Brandon?" the mind reader said. "Are you hat in hand for some help?" Then May smiled and pulled at his arm to urge him in. "Well, Darlin', you're at the right place, you know that. Come in and sit. Let me take your coat."

Brandon had never been to Coach's house- not even with his friend, Phil, Coach's son - and he wasn't sure he was ready now as he looked past Maybelline's well-coiffed head. He hesitated a moment and then stepped into the interior of a home whose owners loved yellow in all of its various shades. The couch was cream, looking like a new stick of oleo plopped on a platter of sunshine. He almost wished that he could leave his sunglasses on. But that wouldn't be polite, and he had to have his polite full on.

"Hello, Maybelline. I hope Coach told you I'd be stopping by. Maybe staying for dinner," Brandon said after she released him from a Mama Earth hug. He removed his coat, stuffing his ball cap in a pocket, and watched it sail down the hall with May. "Of course he did," she tossed back over her shoulder.

The house smelled of pork roasting with cinnamon apple brandy, a home-cooking scent he associated with Christmas. He missed his mom. He went in, following his nose to get closer to the smell of love. Bypassing the buttery couch, he seated himself at the kitchen table. From there he could see out the window, which was shaded by a big oak tree clutching bronze leaves in fisted clumps.

He felt his chest open to breathe deeper. Again.

"There's always room for one more and one more and one more in our home," Maybelline said. "Didn't you know that? Never been here, darlin'? Brandon, isn't it? What do you hear from your folks?"

Brandon took a minute to realize that, while Coach may not know his folks were gone, Maybelline did. She saw the thought cross his face and answered, "I know everything about everything that goes on in this town, most times before folks tip their heads back to the wash bowl."

"But me and Coach made a pact years ago that if I didn't have to listen to game play-by-play, he didn't have to listen to any town gossip." With this pronouncement, she turned back to meal preparations.

Brandon just sat and swallowed. The roasted pork continued to swarm his senses. He salivated like Sparty, and almost teared, his memory of his mother's home cooking refreshed.

"Oh my, I forgot. You're legal now and no longer playing sports. Would you like a beer?" Maybelline said as she swiveled from the slow cooker on the counter, wooden spoon lifted like an orchestra baton.

Within seconds the Mind Reader opened a beer bottle and put it in Brandon's hand. He remembered to be polite: to thank her and to not guzzle the most-welcome suds.

In just a few minutes more, Coach rammed in the door from the garage. Brandon hadn't even heard the garage door open, so loud were his taste buds shouting.

Brandon's mind was also shouting, "No, don't". He was having second thoughts on seeking Coach's counsel. He hadn't recalled that Maybelline, the beauty shop proprietor who owned the town gossip, was Coach's wife. He hadn't planned on the unlawful turn of events being broadcast all over town and Michigan, his known universe.

He hadn't planned on someone who would call Mom and Dad before he did. *Would she or would she not?* He recalled the little girls' recess game: they always kissed him, despite how the petals fell, telling him that he'd won.

While Brandon was often abashed that a catalogue of childhood foolishness cluttered his mind, he was relieved when he knew something besides football. Especially since his people and crop farming skills were suspect.

Coach's coat was off, hung up, and a beer appeared like magic in his hand, too. "Let's move to the living room, Son," he said, as if reading Brandon's mind, well aware of his wife's broadcasting skills.

The two men sat down simultaneously: Coach in his Lazy-Boy and Brandon on the buttery couch. Simultaneously they raised their bottles to their lips after a mock toast. As he took a pull, Coach looked squarely at Brandon, continuing the look as he set the beer down. That was Coach's way, so sternly familiar and fatherly, as if he looked right through you to the bottom of your cleats.

Brandon dug in, rushed to fill in the silent gap, just as he might have in a broken play back in high school. Coach just looked, listened, and pulled on his beer. Only when the bottle was empty and firmly set down, did he talk. The clink on the table resounded like a game whistle, strong and searing, dividing ineptitude from action.

He began as per ritual, "Son, you know where sympathy is in the dictionary, don't you?" He spread his hands about a foot apart, set as close to Brandon's ears as possible, as if to assure that he would not miss the point, and continued, "Between shit and syphilis. At least you came here with a shitload rather than syphilis!" – and Brandon briefly wondered who'd ever done the latter in this small town.

As Coach talked, Brandon visualized a dusty chalkboard filled with Xs and Os and lines with arrows shooting up the middle or going around for an end run.

He felt at ease, at home, with his problems off his chest and onto Coach's broad back. He hoped that the cure for his shitload wasn't as painful as a cure for syphilis might be.

"Let me get this straight, Son. Your Dad, Steve Breeden, one of the elders at the church, the one entrusted to deliver the ashes for Widow Braghorn, the one married to the same incredible woman for thirty-some years, the one who pulled himself up by the bootstraps and walked into the barn to build a micro-dairy business after he got let go by the damned auto company, that sweet little business that he loves only after his wife, son, and dog. That man, Steve Breeden, who never missed one of your games in your career. The one who paid for a tackle dummy when the school athletic funds were lean? That man let his dairy business license lapse?"

"Yes, and the law shut me down. Though, of course, I gotta milk the cows tonight and in the morning. The law couldn't shut down the Nature of the operation," said Brandon, thinking *sure wish it would!*

"Well, I'll be damned and go to hell. Mr. Perfect Propriety made a mistake. That's all. We can fix that." And, without elaboration or permission, Coach went to his phone, giving Brandon a wink as he walked away.

Just then, Maybelline walked into the living room and winked at Brandon, too. Had she been listening around the corner?

Brandon tried to meld with the couch and was glad that she disappeared without a word. His stomach grumbled. What metaphors for problems food had: *in a pickle* came to mind first. But that wasn't enough to describe Brandon's problem. He was feeling like he was in a slow cooker of a screwed-up mess: *Stick a fork in me, I'm done for.*

When Coach came back in the room, his face was unreadable, just as it had been before he began his halftime speech. Whether the team was winning or losing, his face was a blank slate, ready for new plays, new beginnings, going forward, and fighting on, no matter what the score.

Coach motioned Brandon into the kitchen. Brandon saw that another place setting had been added at the table and he lowered himself into the chair, glad to move closer to the sumptuous smelling meal.

Coach went to the refrigerator and got two new beers. He opened them and tossed the caps in the trash, walking purposefully back to the table where he offered one to Brandon, who should have declined, but didn't. He felt that he needed to hold onto something while Coach provided his next play – which Brandon knew was the solution – and a beer bottle offered a good grip.

"Brandon, I just got off the phone with Principal Fran." Brandon blanched at the intimacy of Coach saying the principal's first name, so that she sounded like a regular person, one without authority over detention. He could envision the short brown bob and square-rimmed glasses of a woman whose presence he'd avoided with great purpose during thirteen years of schooling. He knew that she sang with his mom in the church choir, so he'd catch hell for anything he'd done or at school – or home - because they'd share news between songs. He wondered how she fit into the picture. Would she be the one to call his mother or, since she was here and his mother was not, would she nail him to a cross herself? Kids had whispered that that was how she performed punishments in her office.

"As you may know, Judge Coffer is her brother."

No, I didn't know, Brandon gulped, *but go on.*

"She's gonna talk with him. He'll likely put the call in to the county office tomorrow to re-instate the license. There'll likely be a fee, but I'm sure you're good for it. Right, Son?"

Brandon just nodded, thinking that he'd sell blood, if he had to, to cover the fees if this one minor issue was solved.

"And, Son, this here matter will just be between you and me and the County Clerk. Plus the Judge and Fran, but they won't talk. No need to embarrass your mom and dad. Right, Maybelline?" Coach fixed his wife with a stern eye, like Brandon had seen many a time in his household growing up. "Right, Maybelline. We won't go telling this business all around town, will we now?"

Maybelline slowly nodded her head in time stirring the pork roast, then closed the lid, put down the wooden spoon and began to make a salad. She'd been deprived of a juicy bit, but Coach she obeyed. For better or worse. Better would be peace in her home; worse would be word out on the town.

The trio enjoyed a meal together and laughed about the new playground equipment that had been delivered just before the snowstorm last week. What numbskull had pulled that dumb stunt, nobody was saying, Coach related. Brandon felt bad for the kids whose pain of missing recess was doubled by having new slides and swings icily gleaming to taunt them as they played board games at their desks. Life just wasn't fair.

But for others it was doubly fair, and Brandon was feeling blessed. Amy was going to be so proud of him and his big time small town connections. He finally had a way to strut some stuff. His chest ballooned his football jersey, almost like the old days when he wore pads with extra chest protection.

He'd completely forgotten his misplaced trust in Travis, and that the weed was gone. He wondered what time Amy would be home from Roller Derbying, or whatever she was doing. She certainly never came home to make supper, so he knew he was in the right place. He just chewed and swallowed and smiled, in a contented rotation of goodness.

Forty-Seven: Amy, Born to Run

But I was not rolling any wheels at the roller rink. I was ruing my decision to not yank Jackie's Hoover from the closet. I was manually sweeping the floor at Travis' house after toting my bags of clothing and popcorn, while Travis wrangled boxes of boots and make-up. I was singing, ripping the refrain of Jackie's pet song for Brandon. Maybe I'd get a tramp stamp tattoo, since I felt born to run – run things, that is.

When I had arrived at his door, Travis raised his eyebrows, but not for long. You gotta love a girl who has as many bags of popcorn as clothing – and just the right kind of bags for storing weed. This foxy lady – me - came with good baggage.

We tramps recognized our 'born to run' affinity and discussed moving the operation a bit further from this little community. Perhaps North, to Traverse City, which with its Cherry Festival, snow, and summer seasons, its thousands of tourists would be fertile turf for business – and it was closer to Canada, where quick buy-and-sell was feasible when our product grew strong and multiplied its strain. That's what Valerie had mentioned once, and Travis agreed, solidifying the plan. Perhaps she'd like to help us cross the border with product stashed in her boots.

Bring on the champagne! My American dream – to be a millionaire - was going to be realized in one of the few ways available in the middle of the nation's budget crisis: pot growing and dispensing. I recalled from a college Business class that Bill Gates started Microsoft in a recession. Wonder if he wanted to be an investor - or maybe a client?

Forty-Eight: Things Get Beachy

Jackie and Steve awakened early, to the impossible sound of rain shimmying the roof. Steve scrambled into jeans to check outside, while Jackie put on her robe to start the coffee.

She'd showered by the time he returned with info after kibitzing with other RV occupants. Apparently that was the soundtrack of suburban California: millions of busy bees traveling to work by car.

Both drank coffee to get morning sober, and then Steve showered while Jackie dressed, fishing her new Disney shirt out of a bag. She was seated in the kitchen banquette when he emerged, fresh shaven and wearing his Disney duds, too.

But it was a long face that Steve wore with the shirt: "Jackie, it's serious time."

What? Wasn't Disney all happy all the time?

Jackie attempted naivete: "Good, music would mask that traffic. Guess we didn't hear it yesterday when eagerness buzzed in our heads. But, does Sirius pipe into the Alamo?" Jackie said as she retrieved bowls for today's cereal breakfast. She lifted them carefully to not disturb the ashes enshrined in the blue canister, nested in the Nambe bowl, which winked at her as the sun invited itself into their kitchen.

Steve's laughter burst like firecrackers on a summer sidewalk. Jackie flinched, grateful that the bowls were plastic as she grabbed the counter to steady herself and dropped them. She closed the cupboard, picked up the bowls, set them on the Formica, and turned slowly toward Steve, laughing into hands cupped to his face: "Is my underwear showing? It's just us here in a tin can trailer, Steve. What's so dang funny?"

"Sit down and give me your hand, sweet wife," Steve said between giggled tears. As he took her hand, he licked at his cheeks to clear them like windshield wipers cleared rain. He spelled 'serious' in her open palm.

290

Jackie snatched her hand back and shouted, "I'm not Helen Keller. Remember that I got better grades than you, Steve Breeden, and I could whip you at crosswords, if I wanted."

"I don't have cross words for you, darling," Steve said, riffing on her words to calm her down. "Be a good wife and serve breakfast. My knees ache this morning." Then, he added, "Do we have any bananas to slice on the cereal and an Advil chaser with juice?"

Jackie and Steve had closed Disneyland in their new spirit of freedom, after hours of walking and/or standing in lines channeled by chain lengths. They'd overheard among the crowds - and discovered its wisdom after a forty-five minute Jungle Cruise wait - that the popular attractions were more available after the stroller herd went home. *How could a two-year-old be happy, strapped in and strolled at kneecap level? The kids couldn't even see the big balloons tied to stroller handles, but the balloons sure blocked others' view! How did a child deal with a man shooting a gun at a hippo?*

Jackie dumped those thoughts into the cereal bowls, digging in spoons to bury them. "Serious" was the cue to a lecture, so Jackie set her face into its '*I'm listening, dear*' mode. A cereal breakfast was short and sweet, so perhaps Steve's serious talk would be, too. Throughout the road trip he'd warmed to conversation. After late night reads on geology or geography, Steve was as pedantic as he was on dairying, but Jackie didn't mind. She was glad he was talking: she admitted to lonesome times when he'd worked long auto plant shifts, then turned to long hours of dairy farming. *Almost all our lives.*

"Jackie, we are out of cash and gift cards, except for that damn Cracker Barrel stash. I checked on the website; won't be eating until Colorado if we rely upon them."

"Well, we have plenty of cereal," Jackie said, ever the one to be positive. "We've got plenty of our cash-renter's popcorn..." stopping short of mentioning the weed stashed in the fancy cloth hangers. Ingesting it made her hungrier; it wasn't a solution. Besides, Steve's acceptance was fresh.

"I'm tired of kicking myself black and blue for the cash-and-values poor situation we are in," Steve said. His eyebrows rose: "Besides, my knees took over my pain in the butt."

Jackie winced because that was what Steve sometimes called her, but she could tell he wasn't teasing her with the remark.

Steve continued after he chewed and swallowed his last spoonful of cereal, "But we can't fix the farm mess until we get home, and we can't get home until we have cash. I'm going to call my brother..."

"What's his name?" Jackie interjected.

"His name is Carl..." Steve began, but now it was Jackie's turn to giggle.

"Like the wordless picture books that Brandon used to crave. Remember the *Good Dog, Carl* series? You had to make up the story to go along with the pictures, and Brandon would get mad if you didn't recite the same script. Night after night... and your brother's had the same name all this time? Who'd of thunk it?"

"Is it my turn yet?" Steve said.

"Oh, don't complain," Jackie said. "While I said all that, you ate three big spoons of cereal.

"As I was saying, I will call my brother, Carl Edwards. He emailed me again yesterday and sort of insisted," Steve said.

"He has a wife, and he has three kids," Steve added quickly because he knew the details Jackie would request. "Don't know if they have a dog, but you better not say anything about that book, Jackie." Oops, now she was sure to mention the title, seared in memory by warning.

"It's a long way to Turlock," Steve continued, "This state's near triple the length of Michigan. Its shape is an entire arm whereas we always show people where we live on Michigan's mitten shape." Steve held up his open palm, but before Jackie pointed her finger to where they lived, Steve lowered his arm, angling his hand slightly toward him. He pointed out where they presently were in the center of the so-called California 'bite' where the coast curved east and traced a route with his forefinger, stopping where she knew his small pox scar was.

"We may have food, but the truck needs food, too. Do you have any money stashed in the Winnebago, in one of your purses, or," Steve chuckled in mid-inquisition, "in the dirty laundry bag?"

"Let me look," Jackie said, "but please pull up the AAA map to show me where Turlock is, which sounds like an old gun or a Harry Potter character."

Fifteen minutes later, Jackie turned up with 15 rolls of quarters. "If we forego laundering for a few days, I think we can make it with these," she said with a smirk. "Do gas pumps take coins like the slots?"

Steve sat up suddenly, his eyes alert and focused. "Jackie, I read John Steinbeck's book, Travels with Charlie, before we set out. Pastor Rankin loaned it to me, remember?"

"I don't, but go on, get to the point," Jackie said.

"As I recall, Steinbeck rigged a bucket of soapy water in the shower stall and put dirty clothes in it, letting the motion of road serve as a washing machine agitator."

"Did it work?" asked practical homemaker Jackie.

"Well, he didn't elaborate," said Steve.

"Was his book fiction or non-fiction?" Jackie quipped.

"Non-fiction," Steve said. "What's the point?"

"Just checking the veracity of a man's point of view on laundry." Jackie smirked and continued, "Well, Steve, I can't wait to use a famous author's laundry tip."

Steve retrieved the bucket from the vehicle's storage area. As she watched Steve tether the bucket, she ventured a question with a response that she suspected and didn't like: "Does this mean that we are not going to stick our toes in the ocean?"

"I'm afraid not, Jackie. We have almost no money. We have to rush home pronto. Plus we have a sacred mission to accomplish for the church. It's time to forego the pleasures of the flesh," Steve said gently, yet in a mock-serious tone.

Jackie stomped her foot, causing the wash bucket to splash. "We've come too far to not do this one little thing. Get out the iPad to check the mileage, Steve. I know the state is big, but it can't be far."

"It's 15 miles! Why do you think that the street at Disneyland's entrance is named Harbor Boulevard?"

The shout came from the RV nearby... they'd forgotten that neighbors were close in the park. Jackie and Steve held their sides as they laughed all the way to the couch, where the iPad peeked behind one of the pillows.

"I gotta say that news travels as fast here as it does in the telephone gossip at home," Jackie said. "Now, please check the mileage. I want to run in the surf."

Steve took in her attitude and plucked the iPad from its pillowed seclusion. He quickly verified the short route to the ocean on either Harbor or Beach Boulevards. Steve didn't want to join the buzzy bee-sounding traffic on the freeway route suggested. Interesting coincidence that Jackie had retrieved 15 rolls of quarters; she deserved a 15-mile trip to the ocean.

Steve stayed on the iPad while Jackie put on her bathing suit, sorted their laundry by color, figured the laundry detergent dosage, and splish-splashed the first load clean. He calculated the mileage to Turlock, and then browsed the California college system website. Wasn't there a sport in season to watch somewhere? "Hey, isn't Chico State where Amy's brother goes to college? Plays soccer, doesn't he?"

Then Jackie recalled that Amy had suggested a check-in to buy more dope. Wouldn't they be 'dopes' not to do this? Amy's brother was sort of a relative, she rationalized, so she handed Steve her phone where she had stored Andy's address, simply stating "Amy's brother" to his quizzical look, no elaboration. She'd find a way to mention a weed purchase later, perhaps on a family credit line.

After Steve keyed in his brother Carl's address and the address of Amy's brother, Andy, he perused the state map. This state was vast, requiring several pages on the
iPad.

Then, he spied Yosemite Park, a place famous in imagination, and a large patch of green on the California map, unlike the cities' dots. *Just a tiny detour for so much glory to witness of Mother Nature.* It was America's first park, so Steve felt honor bound to visit.

His mental calculator switched on: mileage to the brothers' cities was 500 miles totaled. It'd take about 50 gallons of fuel at $3.00…Jackie's stash of quarters would suffice. He rifled through various pants and jackets pockets and placed $14.00 more on the table. With the money from their respective wallets to add to the clump of cash, they could even buy food for themselves, maybe splurge on a Yosemite magnet for Jackie's souvenir stash.

Master Card was a good rescuer, but Steve was more used to cash than plastic relationships. Then he realized that he'd lived like this his entire life: hanging onto a budget like it was a physical cliff, with full solvency an unreachable mountain peak.

His mind returned to the iconic visual of Yosemite: Half Dome, and he thought the vision apropos of their situation: was the mountain half-empty or half-full?

Go for it! The devil shouted louder than the practical angel that held Steve fast, lock-stepping him through life as if he'd never left the Marines. The cartoon character Yosemite Sam joined the devil in his urging: *Roll the dice, run in the surf, go for it, Steve. It's your turn!*

So, go, they did. *Splish, splash, their toes took a bath!* They took photo upon photo, even snagging a guy walking his dog along the surf edge to take a couple of them. The dog offered a driftwood stick to Steve, to play a game of fetch. That drove a stake of homesickness into Steve's heart, so they moved onto the trek again.

They navigated the concrete freeway that snarled north through Los Angeles, a stupendous contrast to the sputtering Autopia attraction at Disneyland. Apache Red lumbered a lengthy incline called the Grapevine, among more truck brethren than since the flatlands of the Southwest. Here the trucks looked bolder, more sinewy, as they tackled the incline; more like panthers than desert snakes. Perhaps it was the Hollywood touch: Steve noticed that all vehicles were spruced clean as they traveled here, as if it was always Sunday best, and he wondered why Michigan, the land of automakers, didn't share that pride.

They were *mercied* - the truck made it to a town called Merced before it needed fuel. Here Steve was unabashed to use quarters – the man who took his money had no teeth. As he returned to the cab, large road signs pointed arrows toward Yosemite. Impulse born of freedom's lust prevailed to set their course: Steve turned.

The long-lost brother in Turlock was only a half-hour further on the Interstate, but he was forgotten. Now that the quarters were spent, Jackie chose to tell Steve about selling dope. With his hands on the wheel, he couldn't throttle her.

The highway reduced to two narrow lanes, a wigwagged trail to the mountains. Their tree line contrasted so strongly with their snow that it looked like dark hair splaying out from white knitted caps; craggy mountain sides formed into faces as deliberately carved as Mount Rushmore. Steve shut the Nav Nazi off so as not to disturb the peace.

Once inside the park, it took another slow hour to get to the main lodge and lot, in a place called Yosemite

Village, that didn't look like any village in Michigan. A massive wall of stone extended upward behind the lodge, as if it were the backstop of God. Steve parked Apache Red and the Alamo carefully. He and Jackie got out and shrugged into their jackets. They looked up and around, almost falling flat on their backs as they swirled about to take in the splendor.

This kind of scenery sat on speech, smashed it back down your gullet into your Adam's apple, which triggered an image of Adam and Eve. Steve thought of their original sin, and how he was about to embark on one. He looked around the parking lot, sizing up the few other tourists that were winter-viewing Half Dome.

As if by magnetic force, a guy with pants dragging the ground hitch-stepped his way over to Steve. His parka made him bulky as a snowman, though snowmen seldom wore stringy hair and a threadbare mustache.

After he'd returned from Vietnam, Steve had let off haircuts for a year as personal protest, so he felt as if he was looking at a younger version of himself. Under the bulky parka, pants billowed like a banquet table skirt. Steve considered whether he'd once looked as strange as this young man did.

Suddenly arms, apparenty hugging the body for warmth, unwound from the parka. The 'stache quivered as a raggedly voice spoke: "Yo, you got something to smoke?"

That's how it's done? Simple as that? Steve couldn't believe this might be happening, so he remained stoically circumspect. "We're from Michigan. We're on a US road trip vacation. What brings you here?"

"I'm a rock climber. Just finished Half Dome. Quite an achievement, but not many people to celebrate with."

"Well, I'd be glad to shake your hand and pat you on the back. Wouldn't you, too, Jackie?" he said as he turned to include her in the conversation. "We got coffee. We could pop some corn."

"I was hoping to have a little toke for the triumph," said the scraggly-faced dude, who seemed disinclined to give his name. He stashed his hands into pockets, after miming slowly inhaling on a cigarette.

Steve had seen that action in movies and 'Nam. He looked quickly at Jackie. Without a word, Jackie grabbed Steve's keys and ran back to unlock and climb into the Alamo.

She dumped the dresses from the padded hangers and hurried back to the kitchen, where she opened the stovetop drawer to fetch a sandwich bag. She worked the weed out of one hanger niche into a large wooden spoon whose measure she knew to be half of a fluid ounce. She enjoyed the pop-pop-pop as the bag sealed.

Amy didn't answer her phone, so Jackie got on the iPad to web-search a price for a half-ounce of weed. *What was up with the little bitch and her phone?* Jackie didn't know what quality the weed was, but decided to go with medium, and then almost choked when the charts showed that they'd get $50.00, whereas they'd have gotten triple that in Grand Rapids, Michigan. *Holy crap, there is no place like home.*

She tapped on the window to get Steve's attention, mildly surprised to see that he and the climber dude were still talking. *It hadn't been a mirage.*

When Steve came to the door, she handed him the bag inside a glove, feeling like a spy engaged in a secret information swap. She whispered, "Get $50.00 cash, no checks." *Did I really do that: give drug sale advice to my husband?"*

A few moments later, with little gesture or movement, Steve whipped into the Alamo, locked the latch, and wheeled around while he pulled folded bills from his pocket. He fanned them over his forearm to present them like a magician's paper flowers. He grinned as he bowed as far as he could toward the floor, which was about counter height.

Jackie successfully clicked her heels, then hugged him, but said, "You better have my glove, Steve. I need a pair in these snowy, cold mountains."

Steve retrieved her glove from his pocket and said, "I've proven that I have a pair, don't you think?" She cuffed him good after she grabbed her glove and ran to their bedroom. She had to re-stitch the silk hanger that she'd tossed hastily on the bed – and not let him see her laugh so hard. Steve had definitely loosened his image.

Jackie and Steve might have lingered to notice more of Nature's miracles, but, having garnered a miracle of their own – and by illicit means, they scooted themselves out of the Park and on to Oroville, where they parked in the outer portions of Wal-Mart Store #1575 - after they spent the entire $50.00 to refill the gas tank.

They had gotten away with a sale, made road trip pro-*grass,* and were about a half-hour from a possible meet-up with Amy's brother tomorrow. They popped some corn and watched 'Annie,' one of Jackie's favorite movies. She sang the title song at the top of her lungs.

Later Jackie dreamed of the Avon Lady selling pot in lipstick tubes back home in Michigan. She bought one in every color, using quarter rolls as payment.

And, in the middle of the night, Steve thought of his brother, Carl. He picked up the iPad, clicked to the AAA map, and saw that he'd been 25 miles away from his never known brother just before the adventure in Yosemite. He hoped that they hadn't made a wrong turn.

He also learned that Half Dome was closed to climbers in winter.

Forty-Nine: Church Gossip

Back home, Pastor Rankin was getting hot above the collar. Bonnie could see it as he talked on the phone with Fran. The slow burn of what? Fran Blackstone wasn't the trouble type. But she'd been calling more often than the problem children of the parish. Sure wish that Jackie was here to talk this over with...and dialed her number pronto, hoping no parishioners would call for few moments' consult.

"Jackie, how are you? Where are you, dear friend?"

"In central California," Jackie said. "Are you checking in about the ashes? You know we're not due to be in Colorado for some time."

"No, just miss you. How's the weather there?" Bonnie said.

Jackie's stall was uncharacteristic as she said, "It's an overcast 55 degrees."

"Overcast or not, the Pastor would rush to the golf course in shorts if we possessed that temperature here. Send some east," Bonnie quipped, noting that the Pastor's line was clear.

"Done, friend," Jackie said. "None of the silly folks here appreciate it. We parked overnight at Wal-Mart, and I'm watching people swaddled in jackets and scarves walk in to shop."

"Well, I'll be," Bonnie said.

"I will be, too," Jackie said. "Toast if Steve doesn't get breakfast. You know how he is about his meals."

Bonnie knew, and she rung off, wondering if she had the nerve to make a hair appointment with Maybelline. No, she treasured her job and her pastor more than that. She'd call Jackie again tomorrow.

Just then, Pastor Rankin stepped to her desk. He had his coat and muffler on, reaching in his pocket for gloves. "Do I have any appointments, Bonnie?" he asked, looking down at the desk blotter where she wrote everything, coded in several colors of ink. "No, I see that I don't. I'm going to the Koffee Kup for lunch."

"Could you have a dozen roses sent to Fran Blackstone's office? It's her birthday today, and she's apparently decided to retire at the end of the school year."

Did he actually whistle as he pulled on the gloves and walked? That did it. Bonnie needed a body to talk with about this. She called Maybelline to make an appointment.

But that wasn't until 4:00. Before she had time to stew, Avonelle swished into the office.

This was a woman with serious fingernails, always painted perfectly in pearlized coral. Bonnie wondered how she could hit the correct organ key, and in the right sequence without spiking herself. Or how she could follow all the black notes traipsing across the sheet music – which must be difficult to see from under the tangle of lengthy red curls that flounced around her head like a Flying Swing carnival ride in full furl.

Avonelle's spirited organ playing could be a distraction during church – the choir director angled the choir members' seats away from the organ so their eyes would stay on the hymnal pages – but the pastor insisted the music boosted parishioner benevolence as she played when the collection plates were passed and scintillated them in the interludes between liturgies.

Bonnie agreed with the latter, but would have put it another way: to keep them awake. Bonnie felt that Avonelle's attraction was due in large part to her artsy clothing, which she hoped were replicas of the tie-dyed marvels of the '60s and not the originals. Size certainly didn't matter; the clothing all draped from shoulders like the choir's robes, though it was multi-color, like Bonnie imagined a wizard's to be. The Sunday School children had cast Avonelle as one of the Hogwart's teachers when the Harry Potter series was popular.

"How may I serve you today?" Bonnie recited what Pastor had taught her to greet each parishioner. You never knew who and how God called people to serve – or who had a donation check to deliver to a church that needed funds. The Braghorn windows were ordered and would be put in as soon as the land emerged from the snow – wouldn't want them to be dropped from the frozen fingers of window installers. For now, the Pastor had had the windows shrink wrapped by the local boat dealer, since the caulking around the current windows that lined the lengthy sanctuary had gaps bigger than the one between his two front teeth.

"The organ seemed a bit wretched today," Avonelle said, taking the seat beside the desk. "I think we need to have it serviced."

"I'll most certainly put it on the list," said Bonnie.

"I sorely miss accompanying Jackie Breeden during her sweet contralto solos," Avonelle said, as she smoothed her skirts under, over, and around her ample body. "Have you heard anything from her and her husband? I miss him, too, always sitting at the end of the fourth aisle, so that he'd face his wife. He used to wink at her a lot, in case you didn't notice. Cute couple. Made you have faith in marriage to see how they held hands, looked each other in the eye and smiled, almost as if they were still in love."

"In fact, I just spoke with Jackie," Bonnie began.

"Well, what did she say? When are they coming back?" Avonelle said. "Though, if it were me, I wouldn't come back until the trees bud and the flowers grow. Love them perky daffodils and blue bonnets."

"Jackie couldn't talk long. I hadn't thought about the three hours time difference, so they're eating breakfast. Which reminds me that Pastor Rankin should be back from lunch soon. I'll be sure to tell him about the organ problem."

Some might have taken that as a signal of dismissal; Bonnie was a busy church secretary who had church bulletins to type, copy, and fold. Avonelle, however, remained firmly seated. She was systematically massaging the knuckles of both her hands. "Arthritis," she said when she looked up into Bonnie's stare. She continued a few moments, and, just as Bonnie had turned to her keyboard, she said, "Do you notice who was sitting in Steve Breeden's usual seat last Sunday?

Someone who had moon eyes, who should have been singing in the choir, especially with Jackie Breeden gone."

Bonnie didn't have to wait for Maybelline's gossip palace; she spilled, knowing that Avonelle was a loner who cut her own curly locks, so the chat about Principal Fran and Pastor Rankin was safely 'just-you-and-me.'

After Avonelle left, Bonnie whisked a benevolence envelope from her desk and put the $40.00 she would have spent on her hair appointment inside. She sealed the envelope and put it in the Suggestion Box on the wall. Pastor Rankin would be pleased to find money in there for once, rather than just parishioner complaints. Maybelline wouldn't mind if she cancelled her appointment – and Bonnie would sleep more soundly tonight, having paid her gossip indulgence.

When Pastor Rankin returned, he was whistling like a harbinger of spring. When he praised Bonnie for being at her desk after a quick lunch, she realized that she hadn't eaten a bite. Thank goodness she had a stash of Snickers in her bottom drawer.

Fifty: Oh Brother, Where Art Thou?

The breakfast of champions arrived at the table with only a splash of milk. Jackie joked that there'd be gallons of milk when they got back home, but Steve did not appreciate the irony. He was mortified that he'd let a little weed – which he hadn't imbibed – cause him to forget his long-lost brother. He wasn't one to let another person down, let alone himself. He was not used to working without a fixed routine, a list. He stared at his napkin as if he wanted to chew it, then lifted his spoon with an air of resignation and began to eat breakfast. But he did not lift his head.

"You're saying a mighty long prayer this morning," Jackie ventured between crunches. She had no milk in her bowl, Steve could tell by the sound. He was reminded that sacrificing was part of the good wife charter, and he felt compelled to share.

"We bypassed my brother in Turlock," Steve said.

"Bypassed? Isn't it close?" Jackie said. She hadn't bothered to check the map; Steve didn't like his wife looking over his shoulder anymore than he liked the Nav Nazi's nagging. He had turned the system off, just when he'd needed it most. Jackie inhaled a spoonful; she didn't need her imaginary mouth guard with cereal in her mouth.

"Turlock's a couple of hours back, down state. It was just beyond that gas station where I paid for the gas with quarters."

"I hope that guy without teeth wasn't your brother," Jackie said, and then put her hand on Steve's forearm to soften her sarcastic insight.

Steve didn't say a word as they prepared for the day, not even when Jackie hung wet laundry all over the interior of the Alamo, using every window treatment bar. Their damp garments hung like shrouds of their trip, whose only purpose remained the delivery and distribution of Big Braghorn's ashes since the long-lost brother ideal was abandoned. Perhaps it was for the best; Steve felt chagrined for even considering hitting up the man for cash.

They were about 2500 miles from home, feeling like the Grinch stole their after-Christmas vacation. They had seen one of Nature's best wonders, but maybe missed a better prize: a sincere family relationship. They were only twenty-five miles from meeting Amy's brother, Andy, who couldn't be better than she was, though he had potential to replace the weed that they'd sold. While Steve may have not been up to task, it was his by default, penance for not meeting his own relative.

Who knew what a long-lost brother would be like, if they backtracked to his place? Was it worth the risk when they had no funds and little food? One would think that, as a farmer, Steve was used to unknowns; however, as a union man, he'd come to know and adhere to expectations. He'd managed just fine all these years without this brother while distancing the one he had, so he couldn't wrap his mind around what would be gained by meeting Carl Edwards. God had acres of grace to disperse. Why had He flung some of the family's seed out here? A life of integrity earned didn't jive much with surprise in Steve's view. As with many acts of nature and crime, Steve wondered what God was thinking.

The half-hour to Chico passed swiftly. The atmosphere and architecture shifted markedly as they drove into the college town, but not like the one they were used to in Michigan. A briskly righteousness anarchy hung about, with banners over businesses and cafes that proclaimed their devotion to sustainability – and green. Steve powered down the window and inhaled, to get the scent of this new scene, familiar in its small town antiquity, yet shiny penny new like the entire of California seemed. It even boasted an art deco movie theater with a gold halo-like marquee.

Jackie got wistful and said," Steve, we could pop some corn and go on a movie date?" Steve just stared at the streets and gripped the wheel more determinedly.

Apache Red pulled up easily to Andy's address, courtesy of the Nav Nazi. Jackie looked at Steve and he looked at her, re-affirming that she'd remain in their vehicle. No doubt the inhabitants knew they were here, since the truck color was arrest-me red. The presence of the vehicle was decidedly strange, based on the look of the people they passed on the sidewalks. Jackie expected a constable to pull up behind the Alamo at any second, so she began preparing a cover.

Steve opened the truck door and stepped out, looking back at Jackie as he inhaled the clear, semi-rural air of late January in northern California. *Look, Ma, no jacket!*

He forced his shoulders down and his chest up before he strode to the door of 133 Pomona Street and knocked.

As he waited for somebody to acknowledge his knock, he became aware of knocking inside the single story home, as if a gigantic woodpecker was the occupant. The rhythmic cadence became a pound, like the Michigan State drum line whacking their snare rims in unison, or the most unbelievable migraine on the planet. He looked back at the truck, saw that Jackie was safe – and pounded on the outer door some more, trying to syncopate his knocks with the blows, so that the creature within could hear.

And he waited. Then, as abruptly as Christmas came after a lengthy period of anticipation, the door opened wide – to reveal a Chinese guy wielding a meat cleaver. He was wearing a blood-spattered butcher's apron over jeans and a Chico State hoodie. Steve's mind flashed on the 'Texas Chain Saw Massacre', a movie he'd never seen – and then to Vietnam.

Curses came to Steve's mind from nowhere, maybe surfacing from the period when Brandon was learning the dairy business. Holy shit! Could Amy's brother be an Oriental serial killer?

"Hi, my name is Steve Breeden," Steve said, though he didn't extend his hand, keeping both in his jeans pockets, where they were glued with sweat.

The man didn't move a muscle, not a smile, grimace, or twitch. He could have been a statue or a freshly killed stiff.

"I've come here from Michigan to meet Andy..." and then his mind faltered...he didn't even know Andy's last name!

The man bowed deeply and swept his arm to invite Steve into the home. Steve looked over his shoulder and cocked his head to Jackie. She was out of the truck and by his side in a flash. They entered the den of whatever together; they were partners in life, so they might as well be in death, too.

Once inside Steve did what came to mind: he flashed his driver's license, with its unflattering picture, elbowing Jackie to do the same.

The Oriental man looked, but didn't flicker a smile, calling over his shoulder for someone to come. *As back-up?* Steve had heard of the Chinese Mafia. They figured in TV crime shows, but had always dressed in black with Ninja sunglasses and brilliantly jeweled watches on their wrists. What was going down here was not scripted like that.

Chop! Chop! A younger Oriental man appeared in an arched doorway that led to another room, probably the setting of the extreme chopping. He grinned affably as soon as he saw Steve and Jackie, and the other man stood down. Steve felt his Vietnam-tinged tension recede, a return of normal breathing. Jackie let go of his arm, and he felt the blood pressure cuff release.

Both resolutely avoided looking at the bloodied butcher apron shrouding the man's normal clothing.

"Hello, my name is Chong. I understand that you are looking for Andy. He is my roommate, but he is gone. He was arrested yesterday. How do you know him?"

Well, how do you like them apples – not very much.

Jackie looked at Steve with her 'no-say-em' look and Steve mumbled something about Amy, who was a Californian, and possible mistaken identity as they backed as graciously and rapidly as they could – out of there, back to the safety of their shiny red truck. They didn't want more details given on either side. They wanted to be gone.

Steve hoped that the Chinese guy didn't have Mafia connections – or a photographic memory of their driver's license information. Hoped he wasn't running the trailer and truck plates to discover who they were… Jackie's look said it all: stop hoping and drive really fast.

Only when the Nav Nazi – bless her heart – had gotten them back on the road to Oroville, and onto Interstate 80 did Jackie and Steve breathe, truly breathe, not knowing what to do next. Andy was busted, but they were, too. Flat busted, with a need to be home, longing more than Dorothy ever could.

Steve called Brandon, a sort of reverse justice, he guessed. Anyone but Pastor Rankin. He felt heavily frantic, like back in 'Nam or when he got the pink slip from GM. He needed help to figure out what to do. He knew no one out here except Jackie, who depended on his solutions. He may have a new brother, but he'd be pissed off. They had little money and no prospects, something with which his son had a wealth of experience.

Brandon, connected as always to his phone, answered at one ring: "Hi, Dad".

Steve wondered when he would stop reeling when Brandon immediately addressed him before he said a word. It felt like a small version of identity theft. But, after a little banter and explanation, his wonder bloomed into relieved admiration when his plugged-in son had a fresh idea: the tickets to the annual Burning Man Festival, which wasn't that far from them, were going on sale. They should buy a couple of tickets and scalp them; an ironic term to Steve since he'd survived Indian country just a few days back.

Steve asked Brandon to hold on while he chatted with Jackie, whose eyes widened, incredulous at this turn, and said, "So, we ducked a major drug buy, only to buy and sell tickets illegally? Instead of being dealers, we'd be scalpers? It all sounds insane. Why do good people get together to burn a man?" she said.

"Dad, I can hear Mom's shrieking all the way in Michigan, so just put your phone on speaker," Brandon said. "But, really, it's a no-brainer. You're near the holdover hippies your own age and the neo-hipsters of Google. Super freaks who let it all hang out in an experiment of self-reliance in art's name. Didn't the 'let it all hang out' phrase come from your generation? The credo is to burn everything that is beautiful, so it will make itself anew, if you can believe that. I've never seen new trees rise out of the leaves Mom burned after raking, so I think it's all nuts."

"What gets burned is a gigantic wooden man, not a real person, Dad, after a week of frenzied partying. I'm online now. It looks like an oil derrick with a face, like a stick man on steroids. Loads of moneyed Californians do it. You know, the Internet geeks. The festival has been famously described as a "physical manifestation of the Internet."

As Brandon narrated from the website, Steve imagined thousands and thousands of Brandons at the world's largest pep rally. He could relate to that.

"And, if you don't sell the tickets, Amy and I will come out to Burning Man over Labor Day or whenever it is. Just her kind of wild hair adventure, I think. Heck, she might know a few of the attendees. You can't lose."

"You can't lose. I think I heard that a lot in Vegas," Steve said, "and Reno is just ahead. Maybe we should play the slots again. Your mom was pretty lucky."

But Jackie's look told him that she didn't want to re-cast herself as Lady Luck. 'Quit while you are ahead' was a tenable premise for this moment, as it had been in Vegas. They'd find another way to eat – and feed the vehicle beasts, too. The Lord would provide.

They drove a bit to think, then pulled into the next rest stop to check several sites and articles devoted to Burning Man via Google, a veritable speed dial information system and purported home of many of the revelers. Though Brandon tried to brush them off to get back to his video games, he patiently repeated the directions of how to accomplish mobile ticketing on Jackie's iPhone, pausing the task to call him four times before they accomplished it.

Soon they had two Burning Man Festival tickets, which Brandon assured them could transfer to another smart phone easily. Jackie thought, for the first time, that it was good that phones were smarter than she was. And she found new appreciation for her son's wits and wisdom.

They had raised Brandon, so they had to believe in him, just as they had through football and 4-H years. For the present he was the winner while they were the sinners. He was home, like they longed to be. When they were desperate, he had a plot; wholesome or not, it was accomplished. He was a blessing.

Then Jackie smiled as her oft-repeated phrase went through her mind: *God help me endure my blessings.*

She diverted her attention back to Internet search of Chico, the place they had fled. *We are definitely not doing the Charles Kuralt tour, so web-surfing must suffice.*

"Oh no," Jackie said. She'd looked up Chico State University. "Chico State has a huge College of Agriculture. The department has an 800-acre University Farm, with organic milk production. Their herd of Jersey-X cows was due to calve now through March. I'm so sorry that you missed out."

"I'm sorry, too," Steve said. "Unbelievable, isn't it? We've come so close and yet so far from our roots twice in the past twenty-four hours. I'm wondering what's to become of us?"

"Well," Jackie said. "We are going to be consoled that a $25.00 payment satisfies Master Card this month, dispense Big Braghorn's ashes somewhere honorable, and drive 'til we get home. Then, I'll probably click my heels twice, saying 'there's no place like home' while you shovel the walk, so we can go to church."

They drove past Reno, plowing on to Winnemucca, an Indian name no doubt. The AAA map showed that their route was angling north, but they hadn't a choice. They were fortunate that President Eisenhower had planned an Interstate system when they were toddlers, expediting their trek across this arid wasteland.

The weirdest day of their mutual existence ended in the parking lot of Wal-Mart #2617, a Super Wal-Mart on Potato Road. There was a Potato Road near their home in Michigan with large potato farms along each side, though the soil color was decidedly darker.

Jackie wondered if she was more broke or homesick, not wanting God to answer that question, any more than He'd answered her childhood query about the chicken and the egg. Back then she'd stuck by her grandpa's answer: the egg came first because that was what you ate for breakfast, while you always ate chicken for supper.

Fifty-One: On the Road Again

But early the next morning, the earth didn't move and neither did Jackie and Steve. There were several flat tires on the Alamo. Had the man with the bloody meat cleaver slashed them? *Oh my, how was this going to work?* Jackie couldn't even imagine Steve using a jack to lift the Fifth Wheel, even if they had one; and they only had one spare.

When Steve came in from his kick around the vehicle, he didn't look concerned, so Jackie waited for his word – which came as soon as she'd put his cereal in front of him.

"I've already got it handled, Jackie. Not to worry. This here is a Super Store, open 24/7, and Mr. Ritalin Jones says he can fix it pronto."

"Ritalin Jones! You have got to be kidding! That is a real person's name? You'd trust Brandon's truck and our road home to a man that is on medication?" Jackie was incredulous. She remembered Fran's complaints that dispensing the drug was one of her main school occupations and there ought to be a law against it. Fran was certain the teacher's association was behind the proliferation of Ritalin in schools, to keep behavior problems contained. While she ought to have been happy with less paddling, pill pushing wasn't a good use of her administrative degree – and it didn't square with her ideals of parenting and personal responsibility.

Jackie didn't think about the drug she dispensed *and sold,* when she continued, "So, Mr. Jones seems to be a responsible adult with purposeful mechanical training."

"Yup, he did, he does, and he insisted that I call him Ritalin," Steve said, his hands squared on his hips. "His brother owns a bar nearby, and he'll unhitch the truck so we can drive over while he works on our rig. Shouldn't take more time than lunch, he says."

What could Jackie say to that? They had no more milk, bottled water, or pop, so perhaps a beer would taste good. Jackie hadn't had one since they drained their Silver Bullet stash; she was just parched.

"A Fat Tire and a Blue Moon, please." Steve ordered off the menu posted above the liquor bottles aligned on dusty glass shelves, without looking at Jackie, who sat like collapsed balloon. Though he'd never heard of the beers, the names seemed appropriate to the situation. They had $6.00 between them, so it was zero sum.

The bartender didn't look at either of them before he pulled two bottles from the fridge and popped the caps in a motion so fluid that he likely performed it in his dreams, his thumb stuck up, approving his customers' choice.

Only after the guy thumped the bottles on the bar top did he pause to retrieve two napkins and place them beside the bottles. He didn't ask if they wanted a glass. As the frost began to drip, the bottles looked bearded like Santa.

Jackie flashed back to their departure just after Christmas – was that really only three weeks ago? - from their farmhouse in the palm of Michigan's hand. Their gift to each other was a road trip in a new Winnebago/Off-We-Wanna-Go. It hadn't worked out like they'd dreamed, starting with the Alamo Bowl loss.

Naming their transportation home, Alamo, hadn't compensated for the loss, but it had added to the fun, so Jackie mentally named the stone-faced bartender. Mr. Ambidextrous stabbed at the cash register, an honest to God cash register fit for Antique Alley, and then placed a bill beside the Santa tableau.

Steve ignored it and took a forceful swig. It was before noon, but he was fuming about their road trip misadventures, too, Jackie could tell. Today's disaster added to the stew, which was boiling over. She could only hope that his attitude would chill with the beer.

Flat tires were more of the unforeseeable crap that plagued their trip, what happened to them when Jackie and Steve had other plans. She'd read somewhere that dreamers were planners, not enactors, but hadn't they sought the blessing of God through Pastor Rankin and the ashes stash quest? What was up with God's apparent lack of reciprocity?

Have a drink. As during other adversities of their marriage, Jackie felt fortunate that her husband loved her, and that Steve was a silent, forbearing man.

Jackie settled onto the bar stool and slowly sipped her Blue Moon beer, forgetting to remove the little orange slice that was installed like a flag atop the bottle: it fell and hit her napkin, like an Olympic diver seeking gold.

She picked it up and squeezed it into the drink. *At least I'll be Vitamin C rich.* Steve ordered another beer within two minutes, but that probably wasn't a record in here.

To better dispel fuming energy, Steve began to chat up the bartender, whose name turned out to be Steve as well. The conversation focused upon Burning Man when Mr. Ambidextrous told Steve that Ritalin did a lot of work on motorcycles that returned from the event, all gummed up with gray dust from the playa. The Super Wal-Mart where they were beached – a doubly apropos term because they were surrounded by sandy soil - was apparently well-known as the last stop for provisions before heading out on the notorious Jungo Road "short cut." The name of this nearby bar was 'The Last Place before Burning Man'.

Mr. Ambidextrous said he was especially bummed because he had to work last year when the Man was burned, so he'd never witnessed the spectacle. The Saturday night revelry was legendary, but his work schedule prevented. He got to slide by during the week to help build a little of the brave new world and described some of the ludicrous, gerry-rigged art. Jackie and Steve just listened, rapt and slack-jawed. The bartender, whose look Jackie thought fit well into the hippy freak scenario he described, claimed to know some of the creators.

He wanted to show pictures of the semi-nude women that he had on his phone, but Steve declined.

Jackie could feel Steve's demeanor shift, and she surfaced from her visions of Burning Man art to hear good news. It seemed that the tickets were resalable, like Brandon said, and the price could go as high as double.

Steve Two offered to broker a deal, and Jackie's Steve brought up his hand to shake so quickly that Jackie almost twirled on her stool as his arm brushed by.

Jackie knew better than to interject unnecessary comments. The guys' pantomime assured her that the deed was done. She handed over her phone. Out of the corner of her eye, she watched a guy catch the bartender's nod and walk out the door. It seemed like a good time for her to use the restroom.

Steve almost sprinted, apparently to the truck, and returned in minutes with a spring in his step. It was the most effortlessly athletic that he'd moved in quite awhile. He smiled for the first time all day, sharing that he sold the two tickets for $300.00, then bent into Jackie's ear to whisper, "And he wants to buy some weed. Should I charge $50.00 again?"

Jackie raised her eyebrows as she stared in Steve's laughing eyes...he was no longer her straight arrow man. And it all transpired, right under her nose, while she relished the scent of orange and beer. *New Age cheers! They had money to get home!*

Steve commented that it felt weird to drive Apache Red without the Alamo attached as they left the bar to drive back to the Wal-Mart Auto Store. The two vehicles were a couple, like he and Jackie, and hadn't been disassembled in a week, since they were in Sante Fe.

Jackie looked down at her turquoise ring. The big sky here seemed a different color, but she still loved her ring. They wouldn't have to hock it after all, like they'd discussed when they drove past Reno. When she reminded Steve that the Pawn Stars, his only non-sports TV heroes, were in Vegas and not Reno, that had been nixed. *Thanks for taking my side of this, Lord.*

Meeting Ritalin Jones – "Call me the Horse Power Whisperer" – was like being in the middle of a tornado,

Jackie guessed. His limbs moved at a speed that was almost not visible, so she surmised that he wasn't on his meds, perhaps the secret to his success. Steve seemed pleased, however, so what was she going to say? Jackie just wanted all of her dishes to be intact on the shelves, as well as their stashes.

Simultaneous to that thought, Steve looked at Jackie and walked over to where she was standing just outside of the Auto Store bay, holding the bill in his hand.

"Jackie, the bill is $50.00." Steve said, more serious than the situation called for. She spent that on groceries each week back home.

"I'm figuring that it'll take all of the $350.00 for get home gas. Maybe more. It's well over a thousand miles. While we are nearing Cracker Barrel country, so that we can use the gift cards to eat, I'd like some milk with my cereal." He just looked in her eyes. Obviously there was more.

"And…" Jackie said to help him spit it out.

"Ritalin says he'll trade a half-ounce of weed for the bill."

How had weed come up? Jackie admired her husband's horse-trading and she wanted to get home something fierce. Their bud, Advil, could corral body aches until she went to the Michigan pot pharmacy for a new supply.

"You do what you gotta do," Jackie said. "Let's get the ashes distributed and get me home."

It was about 350 miles to Salt Lake City, where the Wal-Mart app declared that there were three stores, one of them a Super. That was six hours away because Apache Red and Alamo didn't dare go 80 m.p.h. like the cars that whizzed by them on the Interstate.

Jackie thanked the Lord for their cash influx – and for His plan to relieve them of the weed before they arrived in prime Mormon country. Now her voice could resonate with a clear conscience, as she sang along with the famous choir on the radio.

316

As if to add benediction to her prayer, her phone rang.

"Jackie, is that you? Where are you? I've been calling you for several days?"

"Who is this?" Jackie said. Steve caught the tone in her voice and looked over, ready to defend her as needed.

"Howard Prince." Steve shook his head when Jackie mouthed the name to him.

"I go to your church, but you may not know me, because, unfortunately I'm seldom in the pew. I'm the First Bank President, Amy's boss."

Jackie put the phone down against her leg and told Steve who it was. She could tell that he was checking the Rolodex in his mind, but came up blank, as she had.

"I'm sure there's a reason you are calling, Howard, but I can't imagine what it is. Perhaps you know that we financed an RV with a Home Equity Line of Credit. We are traveling out West," Jackie said, hoping that she sounded sweet and accommodating. After all, Steve was still a church deacon - and she was an integral church lady who was embarrassed in this moment that this was someone she'd missed. Perhaps Mr. Prince had been on Pastor Rankin's tithe call list.

She was also embarrassed because she knew their bank account was overdrawn.

"I'm trying to get in touch with your daughter-in-law, Amy. I can't reach her by phone, and I've left several messages at the house where I know she and Brandon moved after they lost their home. Sorry about that, by the way. There was nothing I could do, Mrs. Breeden." The man paused to let that sink in, to appear more cordial, and then continued, "Do you know where Amy is, Mrs. Breeden? She hasn't been to work in a week."

Well, I'll be... Jackie swallowed her shock and assured Mr. Prince, in what she hoped was a level tone, that, since she was five or six states away, she could have no idea of her daughter-in-law's whereabouts. Then she pushed END and cried.

In response Steve pressed the accelerator to 75 m.p.h.

Fifty-Two: It's a Small World

"Well, I'm bored and stressed already. Forgive me if I got the order wrong. Feelings are hard to sort while I'm driving," Jackie said. "I trust Red Apache and the Alamo's new tires, but I'm restless. I am over the shock and awe of mountains. The ring of them around Salt Lake City was nice, though. It looked like a crown set on earth, didn't it?"

When Steve didn't respond, so she continued, "I need to avoid thinking. It's a list: our bank loan mess, Amy's absence, and poor Brandon's noble hurting, none of which can be helped from here. Read some stuff on the iPad, Steve, like I did for you."

"How can I read if I am taking a nap?" teased Steve as he reached under the passenger seat for the device. "What do you want to hear about?"

"How about Native Americans, since we are heading to Cheyenne? How about Mount Rushmore, since we aren't going to see it? How about the Rocky Mountains since our view is clogged in the clouds?" Jackie said. "Look up Wyoming's state website and see what it has to say for itself."

After several minutes of stabbing at the screen, Steve spoke: "Did you know that we are going to cross the Continental Divide halfway through this day's travel?"

"Seriously, what's that all about?" she asked, then wanted to swallow her question because she realized she'd just served herself a science lecture. Now she was going to be put to sleep. "What kind of Native Americans roamed the plains, Steve? Tell me that first. Tell me about the Pony Express Riders while you are at it. Remember those cute cowboy pajamas that Brandon cherished? I finally had to cut them off at the knees when he wore through them, playing with his trucks and tractors when he was supposed to be tucked in bed."

She'd talked long enough to sidetrack Steve from the Continental Divide lecture, she could see, wondering what he would come up with to tell her about. They'd planned between 400 – 500 miles on this leg of this trip.

"Jackie!" Steve suddenly shouted. "There's a Cracker Barrel restaurant in Loveland, just above Denver. We are going to eat real food tonight!"

"So popcorn for lunch?" Jackie said.

"Well, I'm thinking that we could pop a big batch and baggie snacks."

"Okay. We can eat in the truck. It's ours officially, and I don't mind the mess like fussy Brandon would have," Jackie observed.

"Let me tell you about the railroad tracks beside us and how that all came about. I know that the Golden Spike was driven near Salt Lake City where the eastern and western halves of the transcontinental railroad came together. Wish we coulda seen that!"

"Next time, Steve. Our list grows. We'll have more adventures in the Alamo after we get all this sorted out, though I think we ought to re-name the RV for the next trip. Our freedom died like everybody at the Alamo."

That comment zapped the happy air of adventure inside the truck cab. Steve looked like a helium balloon the day after the birthday party, so Jackie spoke fast, "Why don't you call Brandon?"

"No bars on the phone, Jackie," Steve reported. And just then the iPad went dark. "Must be really spotty coverage out here, what with the mountains all around us."

"Home, Home on the Range," Jackie began. Soon they were singing every cowboy song they remembered, from the TV shows of their very young years.

It was dark, damn dark, and Jackie was glad that Steve was driving. Even where they lived in rural Michigan, there was the occasional farm lot security light to welcome you down the road or twinkle on the next one, miles over. Out here clouds sealed off heaven, and mountains shouldered out any lights of civilization.

Jackie supposed the mountain goats, Bighorn sheep, and miscellaneous deer didn't carry flashlights, and were likely asleep. Jackie recalled the Interstate lookout stop at dusk, catching sight of the animals drinking from the river far below. She and Steve sipped their sodas in silence, though the popcorn crunching seemed loud to inner ears.

They'd driven past Laramie and Cheyenne of Wild West legend. Steve reminisced aloud about his cowboy aspirations and Jackie listened, not interrupting to mention Brandon again. She cherished their marriage and prayed that Brandon and Amy would have some semblance of one by the time the road trip ended, all of them re-united.

Homecoming was a couple of days, and she hadn't heard from Amy, not even when Jackie left a message about her brother's arrest. Now the bank president had called them to report her AWOL. It was a worrisome thing to ponder, so Jackie clipped it as quick as a hangnail. She could only fix what she could fix, and Amy had more than once declared a boundary at in-law meddling. Weird how she and Amy had briefly merged with popcorn balls, pot cookies, and potato casserole when lithe Amy seldom ate carbs.

Jackie and Steve agreed that next time they'd traverse the country as tourists and tarry a bit in the areas of their lengthening list. No more quests like the football game and the ashes distribution, just pure freedom. *Next time, another day; what I've predicated my life on. My oft-stated wish was that, in my next life, I'll have thick hair and a tan.*

For now their quest was the righteous home cooking of Cracker Barrel, with its rocking chair greeting. Though Jackie and Steve had triple popped mid-day - pop, popcorn, and Advil - rocking chairs were Mecca for achey knees and semi-locked hips.

The parking lot was full and a little precarious for their tandem vehicles. Steve drove slowly on the perimeter where the lanes were larger. He had paused at the entrance of the lot, captivated by the familiarity of the Cracker Barrel sign. Who knew that this would be one of the high points of their trip?

Then Jackie let out a yelp, "Look, Steve, there's Sandy and Joe's rig." There was space nearby it to park.

It was a blustery, chilly night. No one was sitting on the porch, rocking in one of the chairs that they were surprised to see in place. Jackie and Steve were barely able to stand up straight, so huddled into their own bodies they were, to fend off wind blown straight from the Arctic. Jackie wished for her puffy parka, with hat and gloves to match, that she'd given to Goodwill last month. Brandon had teased her about looking like the purple dinosaur, Barney; but, oh, it was warm and toasty inside. She hoped its recipient felt as blessed as she wished she were now, cocooned inside its cushy warmth.

The hostess was pert and ready for their appetites, turned on high by the homespun odors and interior.

Jackie spoke first, "May we look around? We believe we saw our friends' vehicle parked outside."

"Be my guest," said the slim young lass whose nametag indicated that her name was Janice. Darned if she didn't sweep a Vanna White arm.

Steve led the way, with Jackie following after. They wound around the restaurant, looking left and right, but Sandy spied them first. She banged her thighs on the booth in her haste to greet them, so Joe, who was more careful and calculated anyway, got the first hug.

"Gosh, your coat is chilly. Is it really that cold outside?" Joe said.

"Colder than a witch's tit," said Steve, winking at Jackie so she wouldn't be offended. She elbowed him anyway, just because.

"Surprised to see you here," said Joe. "What happened to the grand adventure?"

The men always get first dibs at talking, at anything if they want. This time I'm glad. I cannot wait to hear how Steve handles this.

"Have serious business to attend to here in the Rockies," Steve said, "and I'm really glad to see you. It's as if God placed us in each other's path." His pause had the desired effect, because everyone moved in for the rest, barely breathing. "We have to develop a ceremony and distribute a deceased church member's ashes. Would you like to help?"

"But we're not Lutheran," said Sandy. "Wouldn't that be against your religion?"

"He must not mind because He brought us together once and once again," Steve said. "He's got His will to be done. Our church is getting new windows in exchange for our good deed. It's a bit of a responsibility. We'd appreciate your input. Though our Pastor gave us some cue cards, we've never done this before."

Jackie smiled. She had to admit he was speaking silver-tongued. She wished she had a collection plate to pass around the booth just now. They needed money to find their way home, and who would one ask if not a friend?

"Why don't you order first?" suggested Sandy.

"Amen to that." said Jackie, "I'm so hungry I could eat collard greens."

"What are those?" Steve asked.

"I don't know, but our trip was about "off with the old; on with the new", so I'm going to order 'em."

"Have at it, woman," Steve said. "I'm having chicken-fried steak, mashed potatoes with gravy, followed by some pecan pie. Our California drive-by featured acres of orchard trees, and some of the fence post signs indicated pecans. I've been tasting pecan pie every since."

"Well, to get into the spirit of the occasion, I'll have a slice of pie with you," Joe said with a wink.

After their food arrived, which came just as the busboy was clattering Sandy and Joe's plates, knives, and forks away, Jackie and Steve were invited to share what they'd been up to – or not. In response to the query, Jackie eased back, just a bit, in the seat, so that Steve was in fore. She switched on her best dutiful wife smile and tilted her head to tune in fully, so that she could memorize his version of the truth. They'd have to tell it over and over again to their family and friends in Michigan, especially since they would be arriving home earlier than anticipated.

His version-lite sounded squeaky clean and emphasized Yosemite and Disneyland, to which, Joe quipped, "Why didn't you distribute the ashes at Disneyland? Someone named Braghorn would justify a big venue, and Disney created one of the biggest. I heard that Walt Disney's ashes were strewn from the Mark Twain boat that circles Davy Crockett's island. Don't they have a Haunted Mansion on the premises? Seems perfect for sprinkling someone's ashes."

With that, Steve was happy to let Joe take over the conversation and guide them through the red rock lands of Utah and through the mountain pass town of Durango because the meals had come. Jackie and Steve happily re-affirmed their status as carnivores, while Joe helped himself to one buttered biscuit from the basket. Just one as fuel for his ode to America the Beautiful, he said with a side-glance at his wife.

As Steve and Joe leaned into eating their pecan pie, Jackie got out the small tablet from her purse to take notes while they planned a suitable ceremony to honor Big.

The 23rd Psalm would be read from the Bible downloaded to their iPad. They all agreed that the perennial favorite, "Rock of Ages" would set the tone. Joe suggested a YouTube of someone singing the song, and Sandy offered her iPad.

In addition to Pastor Rankin's religious cue cards, Widow Braghorn had given them a map of Big's former ranch. Now the problem might be to find where these vital pieces had been stashed; Jackie knew where Big's ashes were enshrined.

Joe picked up the check 'for the privilege of being in your company again' and they all walked to the Alamo for some coffee with data searches.

It didn't take long for Steve to fetch the directions given by the Widow at Thanksgiving dinner – there were only a few hidey holes in the tightly packed space. He got out the iPad with its Google Earth, AAA, and assorted other map systems, tinkering in the corner while the others idly sipped decaf and gabbed.

Steve looked up, electrified, and said, "You are not going to believe it. Just not!"

"I always believe you, dear, but what?" Jackie said.

"The Cracker Barrel was built on a part of Big Braghorn's former ranch. We are there - here, here now."

The four of them sat a moment, unable to discover their tongues. Unbelievable. God's path could be the easy path sometimes.

"Forever more," Sandy said.

"Let's do it now," said Steve.

"But it's nearly 10:00," said Jackie.

"Well, that'll be midnight in Michigan," said Steve. "We can proclaim it as New Year's, a new year of worship windows for our church."

"We're on the outer edge of the parking lot. No one will be able to see what we are doing and Big won't care," Joe reasoned, nodding his head at Steve. "Let's do this."

Everyone scattered to put on suitable clothing for the deep, dark cold of the night.

They reconvened on the far side of their vehicles. Jackie was holding the canister of ashes, while Steve held Pastor Rankin's remarks and a small flashlight. Joe held the iPad with the Bible verse because he'd offered to read it in his baritone voice. Sandy was ready to cue the YouTube on the Adams' iPad at Steve's signal. Jackie was poised to sing along. The quartet was proud of the honor vested upon them, though nonplussed that they couldn't hold hands for a quick silent prayer to bless the service.

Because it was cold, they made the ceremony fast and serviceable, like the weddings that they'd glimpsed at a drive-up window in Vegas. Last, but not least, Jackie released the ashes along the snow-covered berm on the perimeter of the Cracker Barrel parking lot, wondering what euphemism Steve would figure out to describe Big's final resting place to his widow. Sandy clicked the You-tube arrow.

The white powder sifted into the wind, settling on the new snow – to the tune of the 2009 Tony Award 'Rock of Ages' production number. Jackie's jaw just hung open: *Thank goodness I didn't dial up the Widow Braghorn to include her in the service via speaker. She'd probably personally yank out the new windows of the church!*

Jackie looked around the small group gathered for the service, hoping that the white ashes didn't settle on their respectfully black and wholesomely warm clothing, complete with gloves, scarves, and hats, like funeral Ninja. As she widened her field of vision, she noticed that the wind seemed to be carrying snow with it – the flakes melted as they hit each coat. She recognized that the wind was building up to some serious weather, so they'd better get home. Amen.

Fifty-Three: Rock of Ages

Steve awoke and peeked out the window: no ticket on the windshield for the overnight stay at the back of the Cracker Barrel lot. Since the rest of the lot was barren, it was unimaginable that they'd blended into the scenery... Apparently God divined this place of rest for them as well as for Big Braghorn.

He dressed quickly and walked just as quickly to rap on the Adams' family's coach to roust them for a bite of breakfast. He and Jackie had six remaining gift cards, and he wanted to reciprocate Joe's kindness. Besides, all of their breakfast provisions were gone.

He shivered all the way back to the Alamo and found Jackie getting dressed. She refused to hug him in greeting: he was cold, cold, cold. "Steve, why didn't you just call them on the phone, like Brandon?" she said.

In response Steve searched out his phone and dialed Brandon. "Morning milking done?" Steve said as a greeting.

"Sure, Dad – and the dairy license renewed."

"What's that?" Steve said, catching Jackie's eye when she walked into the living area. Laundry – shirts and pants this round - was hung on every available surface, looking for all the world like Steve had a gallery listening in on his conversation.

Jackie settled on the couch and picked invisible lint off her slacks while she stared at Steve, for a hint at what was going on inside the phone. He looked bleak, a sentiment she hadn't often seen on her awesomely competent man. *He is my rock of ages* and, with that thought, she brought the nearby shirt's cuffs together for applause, beaming at Steve. But this did not alter his solemn expression. Uh-oh. *Whew, he smiled. All's well.*

Jackie waited. Steve put the phone down and just looked at her. He looked and looked, then sat down on the couch and held his head studious to the carpet.

"Is Sparty okay?" Jackie asked.

"He wasn't even mentioned," said Steve as he lifted his head to look at her.

Jackie just held his look, already absently taking down and folding their clean clothes as if she'd done it all her life, which, by the way, she had. The air was too still in the Alamo; her movement seemed to bring in fresh air for both to breathe.

"I forgot to renew the dairy license, Jackie. Brandon handled the situation. On his own. How does one mix pride with humble pie? I'm so glad we are going home. I miss every inch of that land, its products, and its people."

Jackie walked into his arms, and every inch of him welcomed her hug. Together they hastily scooped the clean clothes stacks and stashed them in drawers, navigating the tight space as nimbly as Brandon had navigated an opposing team's tackles and traps. They were hungry and had much to celebrate. They were on fire to get home.

They scooped up their coats, still draped on the bench seats, to don and dash out the door for the short walk to the Cracker Barrel. The Adams were just ahead of them, so there was no detour to knock – straight to a booth they all went, waved in by another skinny hostess girl.

The group ordered pecan pancakes pronto, speaking little until coffee was downed. When the mounded plates arrived, the pancakes were powdered with sugar, with a generous scoop of butter in the middle. Each looked at the others, recalling the ashes sprinkled last night. As they slurried the pancakes with real maple syrup, all agreed that the surreal 'Rock of Ages' YouTube was going to be with them for a long time.

"Better to dig into pancakes than frozen soil for a grave," Joe Adams quipped. Nobody choked on the macabre remark. They were too hungry.

After the gooey plates were cleared, Steve and Joe spread the table with a map and agreed that a caravan was in order. Steve was squeamish about flat tires, so it felt good to have a cohort – one with tools and mechanical inclination. Both men figured that they'd save a little on gas, because they could coast off the mountains into the plains of Nebraska and Iowa. The game played across the Southwest had been tag; now the game was slide.

Can't wait to see cornfields again, Steve and Jackie agreed. Further, they agreed to mingle some Michigan popcorn with the Sandy's 'Pride of Iowa' brand.

As she sat in the passenger seat Jackie practiced clicking her heels, liking Dorothy's ignition switch to return from Oz to Kansas. She had something to fete: after an overnight on the Adams' family farm in Newtown, Iowa, Jackie and Steve would only be a day away from their home without the wheels.

There's no place like home. There's no place like home.

When they all arrived at the Adams' family farm, children streamed out of the house to greet them all, as if the old woman who lived in a shoe had taken up residence. Jackie could almost greet each one by name, because she had seen their pictures multiple times. She and Steve were getting hugged, too, because each child seemed to need berth on someone's legs. The hug fest made its way inside – Jackie was reminded of the rugby scrum they'd shared with friends at their farewell party. The kids had hot cocoa and cookies waiting, like the snack prepared for Santa in homes around the country, less than a month ago.

Jackie ran back to the Alamo to fetch popcorn, pausing when she spotted the empty Nambe bowl. The tear-shaped bowl looked abject, so she brought it to hold some freshly popped Michigan corn to be fingered out by little Iowans.

Why am I empathizing with a bowl, even if it does look like Oscar night jewelry? I think that I have been away from home too long. I need country farm rehab and some small town stabilization. I need to reconnect with Michigan pride and content.

The next morning, Jackie and Steve freshened up in a flurry of homesick fever. Being with family increased their longing. While they'd put in a twelve-hour day of driving yesterday, today's hours would be more like union and the pay would be great.

Steve drove steady, but he hadn't figured that fatigue compounded like interest on a loan. He and Jackie were mutually road weary, so they left thoughts unvoiced.

Steve was scared about their debt crisis though assured of dairy business success by Brandon. They had some CDs, as needed to rescue them from the shithole that Amy had dug for them. There was always that pension, but he didn't want to tap it yet, wishing that the bank would trade debt for a stash of music CDs.

Eight hours until he spied Sparty wagging his tail and jumping up and down. He knew that Brandon would be there, anchoring Sparty's leash, but what about Amy? The mystery portended good or bad, but not indifference.

Jackie remained concerned about different kinds of dirt: niggling curiosity of Fran and Pastor's romance and their home's condition braided into her weary, worried happiness. Amy never tangoed into the mix.

Jackie decided that it was time to call Pastor Rankin. He'd want to hear that they'd distributed Big Braghorn's ashes, though he might not have expected it to be this soon. Widow Braghorn had mentioned something about Big's favorite season being Spring with its wild flowers, lovely for him to fertilize.

She wanted to tell the good pastor over the phone, so that she wouldn't have to worry about keeping a straight face. She'd edit the truth about 'The Rock of Ages' that accompanied the ceremony – and the precise location. She was very sure that the widow wouldn't approve of the Cracker Barrel nor would the pastor, who often said he was neither a fan of irony nor of wrinkly.

At least they had accomplished his quest, as good servants of the Lord. Besides, the congregation would enjoy the wildflower colors of the new church windows and always think of Big - and wasn't that for the best? She patted herself on the back as the phone rang, mentally rehearsing her speech.

"Hello, Jackie Breeden. To what do I owe the pleasure of this call?"

Jackie could see the Pastor as if his head loomed out of the visor in front of her: famous pie-eating grin and all. She was glad for the visual, still uncomfortable with her phone's FaceTime feature, and began to enthuse: "We just had some of the best pecan pie on the planet."

"Okay, what Cracker Barrel restaurant did you visit?" the pastor said.

Jackie should have known that she'd served up a huge clue to a pie expert: "The one in Colorado Springs; it was our last supper before distributing Big Braghorn's ashes. Are the windows in?"

"God rest Big's soul," the Pastor said. Jackie would have fallen out of her seat if she wasn't belted in when he continued, "Fran's here with me. Can you put me on speaker so that we can join in prayer?"

Fran entered Jackie's visual of Pastor Rankin on the visor – my heavens, they were cozy. She began to hum "Rock of Ages" – the authentic churchy version – and Fran joined in, following the prayer. Poof went the visual, praise God, as all rang off .

Jackie needn't have worried about the details of the ashes distribution; Pastor Rankin always blessed deeds done with benevolent hearts and, besides she had more present contemplations. Jackie was too dumbfounded to speak, so she didn't. Too much God-incidence for a suspicious mind, too much to process for a woman who'd been away from the thick of things for a little over three weeks. Besides, Steve was not a fan of idle gossip – and idle she was as he drove. If she opened her mouth, he might make her switch seats. It was imaginary mouth guard time.

Fifty-Four: Safe and Sound

After the long and exhausting drive home, Jackie felt like she was walking through water, imagining how a salmon must feel at the last lock. Emotion compounded her fatigue. Steve slipped the key in the back door of their house...only to discover that it wasn't locked.

"What's wrong," said Jackie as she bumped into him with her arms full of bags that she'd already packed from the Winnebago.

"I'm going out to the barn and get Sparty," Steve said.

"But it's cold out here. Should I go on in or what?" Jackie said.

"Go back to the Winnebago until I come get you," Steve said. Jackie was startled by the command, and grumbled that the contents of the bag were perishable. Oh well, it was frigid outside, so she placed the bags on the small concrete patch outside the door and obeyed.

Steve re-pocketed the key. The farmhouse door had been locked since the hobo days of the Great Depression at his grandfather's order. Though he groused, Gramps reportedly allowed his wife to feed the rag-tag men when they came to the door, while he was in the next room with a rifle. "Restless men with empty stomachs and little ambition to do good", he warned. Steve's father repeated that phrase as he locked the door each night, to remind himself of the good of his father, Steve thought.

"I've done my best to keep up farm traditions. I wonder what Brandon's done in our absence. I wonder if Amy's home or haywire," Steve muttered as he walked out to the barn, encouraged by their security light.

Brandon wasn't in the barn, but Sparty was. He jumped and almost squealed, delightedly barking when he saw Steve. Steve noted the empty water bowl and filled it, watching Sparty alternate between huge laps of water and lunges at him. Something was going on, but at least Sparty made him feel welcomed home, and he unleashed the dog who pranced and danced over the snow-covered turf on the way to the farmhouse.

Steve sent Sparty into the dark house, turning on the lights as he entered rooms, one-by-one, behind the dog by several paces. Sparty circled round impatiently, sniffing and nosing furnishings as if he hadn't been inside since Jackie and Steve left home.

After Steve toured the entire upstairs, he retrieved Jackie from the Winnebago, carrying several more bags that she'd packed while waiting. Jackie fetched the foodstuff.

Jackie wasn't as inquisitive as she usually was. For that, Steve was glad. She was tired and could become cranky if frightened and/or overwhelmed. They toured their home to see a few furniture arrangement changes, notably their proudly plaid winged back couch pushed up against the wall as if it were in time-out. Taped cardboard boxes stacked along several walls.

Steve and Jackie moved in tandem to the family room window when they heard truck tires rumble on the gravel. Brandon parked, not even garaging the family truck, which seemed to reach out to hug its red brother.

As Brandon loped to the house, he rifled his fingers through his hair that was without a cap despite the chill air. He still wore a Spartan jersey, visible in the gap of his unbuttoned coat. Steve knew he ran the heater full blast in the truck.

Jackie ran to hug that shirt to hide the fact that tears were welling in her eyes. He hugged back and extended his arm to shake his dad's hand. Nobody said, "Welcome home" or anything. After all, the parents were the prodigals.

Why it didn't even look like he'd gotten a haircut, though he'd need one soon, thought Jackie. Perhaps she'd get out the shears that she'd used to buzz his hair when he was a kid, hidden way back under the downstairs bathroom sink. She hoped.

Jackie returned to the RV for their hanging clothes, including the slumped satin clothes hangers, and tread lightly upstairs. She took a deep breath and entered the master bedroom.

She expelled the air with a "What?" The bed was pristine, the curtains closed as if someone had died. Jackie dumped the clothes on the bedspread, re-envisioning it smothered with sorted clothing pre-trip.

She was almost afraid to enter the master bathroom, but she stepped in quickly to fetch the trashcan, in case she felt a need to vomit in reaction to a mess.

Before Jackie could bend – gingerly to buffer her knees – she noticed that Brandon's brush and hair products were scattered about the bathroom counter. An electric razor was inexplicably stacked with several high tech toys in a multiple dock charging station. A well-stocked library of game cartridges filled a wire basket she'd used to hold extra rolls of toilet paper. There were no cosmetics for Amy, she of the leggy eyelashes and shimmery, expensive eye shadow of every color on the wheel.

The towel racks were empty. Hmmn.

Jackie replaced the trashcan, deciding to avoid the closet for now. She'd seen enough, too much. She turned after relieving herself and stalked into Brandon's room.

The present housekeeper definitely had different standards than she did. She resisted collecting the multiple plops of Brandon's clothing; he'd always told her to leave them because he had a system. Rumpled sheets on beds drawn close gave her mixed signals about her son's affairs and his wife's whereabouts.

There were more male products in the bathroom across the hall. While there was no platoon of female cosmetics, it seemed that all of the household's towels had been marshaled into haystacks on the floor.

She trotted downstairs, puzzled yet content to be home. *Diddle-diddle dumpling, my son, Bran; one bed tousled and the other's occupant gone.*

She sent the men to bring in the linens and Steve's clothing while she made some supper, not surprised that there was little in the pantry. Guess they'd be eating popcorn again. She and Steve would be swallowing Advil with beer, because the fridge was stocked only with Pabst.

As Steve dropped his armload of bed sheets and towels into the washer, he looked at the map on the wall with its multi-color pushpins blooming like dandelions in his yard in June. He walked over and pulled out the ones in places unseen and dumped them in the drawer, perhaps more aggressively than he intended because one seemed to purposefully bounce out.

As he bent carefully to retrieve the errant pin, he shook his head. There were dust bunnies everywhere – Jackie was going to be pissed.

Steve reflected on the dust of errant dreams and then shrugged off regrets because he knew they'd go out on a road trip again. There was always next time. He'd get a fresh paper US map from AAA tomorrow and push pins in it anew, perhaps adding the Grand Canyon's North Rim along with a tour of Hoover Dam, more time for California beach runs with Sparty, and the grand National Parks. They'd had their trial-run shakedown trip – they'd even collected the name of a good mechanic whose brother owned a nearby bar. Perhaps he and Jackie would go see about that Burning Man thing. Perhaps not.

What shouted the loudest in Steve's reflections was his brother in Turlock, California. He'd seek Pastor Rankin's counsel on this one, though the psychology of the lapse was easy enough to determine. Steve prayed that Brandon wouldn't bring up the topic before his pastoral session.

Steve was glad that Jackie was as good at sucking up chagrin as she was at cooking and cleaning, among the many noble lessons of farm life. They'd lead each other back into the fold, as they had forever and ever. Amen.

Besides, he had something new to tease her about: while she'd always said that she could only be good in one room at a time, she had now proven that she was good in two homes. The laundry tale was going to star in the road trip stories.

Steve smiled as he exited the laundry area: he smelled popcorn. Jackie was already mounting the road trip magnets from her memento stash on the refrigerator.

His memento was a sore butt from a 500-mile day, but no locked knees or hips, having maintained his regimen of muscle stretches for three weeks. His physical therapist would be proud.

Steve joined Brandon in the night milking chores while Jackie began to clean house, ruminating. Chores always came first in farm life. This was how the family related to the earth and to each other. There'd be time for talking, complaining, and explaining later.

To which was added dumping the tanks and cleaning the Alamo inside and out. More chores: action to displace emotional reaction.

January was half gone. Jackie winced at how little she had to show for their wild ride road trip as she returned to the kitchen to take her evening pills. Only a few trip photos were taken and they hadn't yet printed them, so the magnets held Brandon's football photos. Amy photos were stashed, with kitchen towels to pin them on the bottom of the drawer. Her ring winked on her finger, catching a bit of the fluorescent light. The Nambe bowl waited patiently on the kitchen island until Jackie found display space. It was good conversation, not to be stashed.

Quests sidelined by money problems. *Who'd have thunk it from a frugal farm duo like us.* Well, at least she hadn't gained that much weight and didn't saddle sores on her rump.

She'd seen Steve usher the map pushpins into the desk drawer. *Anything to defer discussing resolution of the financial mess.* Jackie assumed Amy, the perpetrator of the debt and other crime, was gone forever, but refused to be the one to bring up her name. She was finished with the little twit, well the tall twit, so she didn't mind if Amy was finished with her. But there was Brandon to worry about.

Brandon seemed forlorn, yet not, as buoyant as new shoes had always made him on the first day of school. He'd gained pride in responsibility, in solving the problem of the dairy license lapse without his parents' intervention. It was easy to see even under rumpled, sloppy-fit jerseys.

Fifty-Five: There's No Place like Home

Throughout the first day together the Breedens skipped chat. Unpacking, washing, and grocery chores mixed with dairying consumed all physicality while mixed emotions scratched at their hearts. Jackie stood back, way back, to watch the uncommon tango of two men in charge of a close-quartered dairy operation. Besides there was a small mountain of mail along with a river of email to interact with.

There was a chasm of uncomfortability between them that rivaled the 'Grand Can', what Brandon famously called the canyon he built with blocks, so his Evel Knievel doll could jump with his motorcycle. Jackie smiled ruefully as she thought of Brandon at play. Who knew he'd grow up and fall as far from his target as Evel had? Well, if Evel Knievel had lived and surmounted the public collapse of his dream, she was certain that Brandon could. Her boy had fixed a huge problem, and she was as proud of him as for any award he'd earned. Maybe since he'd survived nearly a month without her doing his laundry, she'd just let the smother go. Fran had teased her enough, Jackie thought.

Within twenty-four hours Amy's name was mentioned aloud, and then it was at beauty shop, where Jackie went for a haircut. While Saturday was usually the shop's busiest day, Maybeline made time for Jackie, the town celebrity.

She'd barely settled into the shampoo bowl, with her head under the running faucet so that she could barely hear, when Maybelline mentioned something about Amy's new hair color. Jackie was relieved to be near drowned and unable to communicate, like when the dentist asked you a question while his probe was in your mouth. Maybelline didn't mention the blush that Jackie could feel, almost as if she were under one of the old-fashioned hair dryers that lined one wall of the shop like aliens.

Apparently the hair color was electric red with shocks of hot pink. Jackie didn't have to feign exhaustion so as not to speak. The appointment couldn't be over soon enough for Jackie, who promised to bring pictures of their trip next time.

Steve had announced in their driveway that the Alamo odometer registered nearly 6000 miles driven in a month. Holy crap! Jackie knew that she previously amassed mileage like that in a *year* of farm country life: to the store, church, school, and back, like a sprint car oval track. From the mileage aspect of the road trip, she could surmise little benefit. Their free-form idea of adventure had morphed into a race around the western two-thirds of the US with mere glimpses of scenery and fun. Even State had let them down at the Alamo Bowl. It was going to take more than rose-colored glasses to think positive about the trip.

If Jackie had learned anything on the road, it was that a home on terra firma had foundation – unlike an RV on wheels. Terra firma had heart, and hers was here. Thank goodness farmers were next year's people – always looking forward to a better crop, not backward at the failed ones given by Nature and God, because next year they'd vagabond again.

Jackie wondered if Brandon would mind a Native American name of his beloved truck, and how soon he'd scrutinize the F-150 odometer, gauges, check the undercoating and paint, and kick the tires. It was to be parked beside the other farm truck in the garage as soon as the Winnebago was unattached. The van was gone. She went further to contemplate if the two trucks would get along as well as Brandon and Steve did, always had. Watching the truck key two-step would add spark to their interwoven lives, now that Amy appeared to be gone for good and good riddance.

The answer came Sunday, when Steve selected his old trucks keys from the mudroom rack, and he and Jackie went to church as per their ritual. The truck seats were firm, preparing them for the unpadded pews at church.

The rose-colored re-casting of their trip began as soon as they entered church. When Jackie's eyes swept the sanctuary, she saw Pastor Rankin perk over to the altar table to make notes. Spying Fran Blackstone, Jackie guided Steve to join her in her prominent pew. The two women clasped hands and smiled, and then pulled apart for the opening prayer, in which Pastor mentioned Jackie and Steve by name. The Lord praised, they all opened the hymnals, Jackie thinking it odd to sing on this side of the prayer rail.

Jackie and Fran wrote notes to each other on the church bulletin, rather than sermon notes, gleefully agreeing with exclamations that, yes, they'd meet for lunch at the Koffee Kup the next day. It was a fortuitous school holiday. While the nation honored Martin Luther King, they'd be honoring their longtime friendship.

Steve nodded off – Pastor Rankin's sermonizing skills had slacked off in the deacon's absence.

Settled into the faded upholstery booth of the Koffee Kup Kafe, Jackie looked around the open room. Nothing had changed, not even Fran, whose face had not become more creased with concerns like Jackie was certain hers had. Stability led to serenity, she recalled her mother saying as mantra for life on a farm. Fran surely looked serene.

"Are you ready to talk about your trip?" Fran was ever the gentle topic opener. Jackie was ready or not. It was a moment-by-moment stance. She began by showing Fran her turquoise ring.

Is it a Native American original?" Fran asked.

"Yes, it is. It was pricey, but it's color near-matched the sky in Santé Fe, New Mexico, a town that had a central square like ours, but looked about as different as could be. That was what we discovered often, Fran; that there was so much the same and different from here, all at once, every place, that it was difficult to assimilate.

Don't know if I'll ever succeed with that. Makes me wonder why I ever left."

"Jackie, you are as flexible as people come. Don't doubt that," said Fran, taking a sip of her tea. She replaced the cup in the saucer, working it a bit to align its pattern of small shamrocks just so.

Jackie smiled at the action. Fran did everything with precision. Even the way she'd set her purse and coat on the seat next to her, neat and compact.

Fran set her elbows on the table. Jackie recognized that posture. It was as if Fran needed to brace her body before she actively engaged her brain, as always at her desk in the school office.

Then Fran's shoulders dropped, like a flag sagging as the breeze died. It was Martin Luther King Day. With the day off from school, she had all the time in the world to listen to her friend, a much more pleasant duty.

"Jackie, dear friend," she said as she silenced her phone and stuffed it deep in her purse, "I like you better than any travel commentator, including Rick Steves."

And so it began. Jackie talked and talked. Fran waved the waitress away if they were in a tight spot in the monologue, and then waved her forward as needed for more scones, coffee, or tea.

When Jackie wound down from the telling of the tale, the version for mature adults only, Fran consulted her committee of one and proffered her best financial aid: she offered Jackie her old job back at the start of the second semester, which was only a week away. By then Jackie would be done with double housecleaning, so that the cafeteria job would be a getaway.

Jackie gaped, speechless, then reached across the booth in a spontaneous, but vain attempt to hug Fran. Gosh, it was great to be back in the bosom of community and a dear friend.

Could it really be possible? So little time had passed, while the Breedens traveled so far around the American West. *We really hauled ass*, Steve would have said, back in the days before being a church deacon revised his vocabulary. Jackie said she'd think about the job offer, though both knew that the answer was yes. The Master Card bill was due any day.

She had to talk it over with Steve. They had to become truly comfortable in their home with Brandon in it, mess and all, as well as winterize the Winnebago before they stored behind the garage. New chores added to the daily drills to the farm, and worries worked out along with them. *The absolution of routine.*

The waitress filled their cups during the silence after the momentous offer. After refueling with caffeine, Jackie resumed. She may have wound down from telling about the trip, but now she wound out the changes to her home. Can you believe it? The broom was gone – that little witch flew away on it, she was certain. It was the oddest thing, but a comfort of sorts, that the kids elected to sleep in Brandon's room, shoving the twin beds together. Relieved, she washed the sheets on their double bed twice anyway, just in case; cleansing to reclaim her home.

Round and round and round, a Tilt-a-Whirl of topics as if Jackie hadn't talked to a friendly woman in a month, Fran remarked. That gave Jackie pause. She had, and she had not, not in one whole piece, a few steps back from events. She looked inside her heart, and then she looked at Fran: "The best thing about the entire near-month trip was that Steve talked to me, fair and square. He got beyond that stoic manly frame of mind. He paid true attention – I got to skip in the ocean!"

"It's nice to know that water can perform without a washer agitator pushing it, isn't it," Fran said wryly. Jackie had only mentioned the ocean twenty times in her narrative...

"So, Fran, tell me about Pastor Rankin," Jackie said. "Perhaps you can tell me his first name, which I've never thought to ask."

Fran raised her hand to signal the waitress for more tea, and then she began. Round two of the old friends' lengthy chat was just as interesting as the first.

Fifty-Six: Amy's Next

So, you heard about the hair on an AWOL babe, intended to shock the Breedens and their traditions. But, I'm not AWOL – I'm underground. I am a farmer, and I like it. It matters not what my hair color is in a basement, tending rows of pot plants under hot lights. I smile when I use Jackie's sewing shears to trim, with time outs to use them as a microphone. I imagine myself as Katie Perry on a stage – soon I am going to be as rich as she is. Screw Taylor – I am swifter.

I feel as famous as a rock star – I'm getting lots of calls and texts. I ignore the ones from Bran and Mr. Howard Prince, but I've taken Ronni's. She is a weed friend. She can know 'wassup'.

We agreed to meet in that chicken restaurant, which was situated between my humble abode and her gingerbread house. While I wondered why we couldn't feast on her awesome food, I didn't protest. I ate alone most often, making meals of popcorn because Travis was out: on home deliveries at all hours, on-call like the house doctor that he was. We met in bed and, as I soon discovered when I called him, our phone sex was bang-on-the-money grand.

"So, Chicka, how is Tobin?" I asked to lead her away from Travis' scent. It was probable that Veronica didn't know that I'd left Brandon – and the bank. I wanted to have a little girl talk before she got around to clucking her tongue.

"Dude dumped me," Veronica practically shouted. Her eyebrow jewelry lifted with the blast of hot air. "I am so pissed. Where have you been, girl? Been trying to call you for a couple of days. Want to go to Canada now? I need a dharmic strain of dope."

I smiled; I couldn't have scripted this better if I'd tried. What an entrée to: "You can buy from me, Ronni."

"Really?" Ronni said, putting her hands on her hips. "You sure went to the head of the class fast. Wassup?"

"I left the bank for fulltime pot operation."

Veronica's jewelry popped its Band-Aid as her eyebrows raised.

"And, I left Brandon," I said, reaching across the table to grab Veronica's hands. "Let's just call it girlfriend payback for Tobin dumping you."

Veronica didn't speak. I was used to having that effect on bank customers, so I pressed on. "He was a dweed, bad in the sack. Bad at everything on earth, broken as his shoulder on our honeymoon. I should have left him then, seen the disaster coming." I allowed myself a second of self-blame and continued: "I thought that I'd find middle class life sublime, feeling safe and content, not realizing that that was the same as bor-ing. I was not made to live life in a fifty-mile square around nowhere."

"What about Roller Derby?" Veronica asked. "Do you still live nearby? Are we still going to see each other?"

Ronni got answers to those questions, but I segued easily back into ranting. I had much to get off my chest. I felt cheated by the flimsy Breeden dreams, so I was making my own good life, my way with Travis. He made Brandon look like Mr. Potato Head.

Veronica began to call our sessions "Groundhog Day Redux". I never saw the movie, so I didn't get her intent. I was too busy talking trash and hash. I had to make a lot of money fast to pay for Andy's lawyer, then mine for a divorce.

Fifty-Seven: Copacetic

The Breeden routine was re-established in a seamless rhythm of work ethic. The family was good at marshaling massive effort to move forward and beyond. There was still no word from Amy, though even Steve joined in calls and texts, which must have totaled into the tens. Brandon trotted out a sports quote to recite at breakfast each day. Put to a vote, the favorite was Vince Lombardi's "It's not whether you get knocked down; it's whether you get back up."

On Tuesday, Howard Prince, the Farmers and Merchants bank president, called to invite Jackie and Steve to lunch, affirming that word got around fast about their return. A date was set for Friday, but they weren't meeting at the Koffee Kup. Jackie rolled her eyes at Steve when she told him: they were meeting at Lake Look About's Yacht Club.

Jackie wondered what one wore to a yacht club. She only had one winter dress, but it had been resting its shoulders on a weed-padded hanger in a tiny closet for a month and had a distinct odor. Jackie wished that she'd taken it to the drycleaners when she grocery-shopped after her hair appointment on Saturday. Guess she'd be wearing her pleated front gabardine slacks.

Jackie panorama-viewed as she stepped into the yacht club on Steve's arm, relieved to see that her slacks and blazer fit in. The hostess, dressed similar to a Cracker Barrel gal, guided them to a round table overlooking the lake, which was near frozen. Jackie noted numerous boats, mounted on gigantic racks, wrapped in shiny plastic film. They reminded her of the multi-car transport trucks that they'd seen in California just ten days before. She plopped in the chair that the hostess slid back, lest she fall from the dizzying impact of the time and culture warps.

Howard Prince, the Home Savings bank president, was as bald as the lake surface looked. His suit was brown striped with a tie to match the yellow silk handkerchief puffing out of the chest pocket. Jackie thought he looked like a bee, and half-expected his handshake to sting when he extended his arm across the table. She wondered why he hadn't stood in greeting, as Pastor Rankin always did.

"I understand that you've just returned from California," he said after they settled into their chairs. "Shall we order some wine?"

"Well, we really didn't have much time there," Steve replied. "If you don't mind, we'll have beer."

Mr. Prince raised a hand, and a waitress appeared as if she were a genie from a bottle.

"My wife and I will have beer," Steve said.

"Which one would please you, sir?" the tiny feminine voice said. She rattled off a list, staring at the lake throughout. She held her pencil like a child and sounded like one, too.

When she got to Blue Moon, Steve interjected, "We'll take two of those." This lunch was on somebody else's tab.

Howard was direct. "I am sorry to have troubled your vacation and now your homecoming, but I must ask if you have heard from Amy?"

"Can that question wait until we've had a drink?" Steve asked with a look at Jackie, who nodded assent.

"Well, I must say I am chagrined beyond words. Our records show a Home Equity Line of Credit that was opened last October at a rate that was well below market. Our bank had frozen existing HELOCs at that time and wasn't in the mode to grant new ones. Did Amy secure that for you?"

The beers arrived. Jackie and Steve squished their orange slices through the bottlenecks, surprising the waitress in her mid-arm stretch to accomplish the task, but then allowed her to slush beer slowly into a tilted, frosty glass for each. The practiced pour of a professional felt respectful - rather than amateur splash or the straight drink from the bottle they did at home.

Steve replied, "Yes," – and only yes. He'd seen Court TV.

"What was the amount of the loan?" Howard pressed. Steve really did feel like a witness on trial, so he deliberately took a drink. A long satisfying one, with closed eyes, so he could not see his inquisitor.

Steve placed the bottle firmly on the table top, intending it to sound like a gavel. "It was money to buy the Winnebago for our trip. Amy assured us that it was copacetic because our farm house was long paid off and there was a 300 acre farm surrounding it." Steve realized he was defensive, but the man's tone made him feel backed against a wall. "We only borrowed $50,000."

Howard Prince smiled. He clasped his hands together in the middle of the table, advancing into Steve and Jackie's territory, "I have good news, and I have bad news. Which do you want first?"

Jackie interjected, "We've had a lot of bad news, Mr. Prince, so we could use some good."

"The Board has decided to forgive your entire loan."

Steve was glad that he didn't have a swig in his mouth because Howard's yellow tie would have looked like it just rained. It was Jackie, the church lady who said, "Well, thank you, Sir", with her most grateful smile affixed firmly in place. *Whatever for? was* her unspoken question.

"The loan amount was $100,000.00 dollars," Howard continued, looking back and forth between their faces.

Because Jackie and Steve remained silent, saying prayers to echo Jackie's statement as well as silent question, he continued, "I believe you both are acquainted with the Widow Braghorn. She is the largest shareholder of our bank." Howard Prince paused for effect, but Jackie and Steve remained dumbstruck with the unearned, unaccountable blessing.

Howard took a sip of his water with lemon wedge and continued, "Widow Braghorn informed me of your good deed on her behalf, that you distributed her dear departed's ashes out west to help her carry out his wishes. She stated that your nobility of character came only after that of Jesus. If you were Catholic, I think she'd be putting your name in for canonization."

Howard put his hands together after straightening his tie to cover-up a gulp before he continued: "I am more than embarrassed and must admit that the Widow questioned my bank management closely." Steve and Jackie looked at him empathetically, thinking that the bad news was that Mr. Prince was fired. "Because none of us at this table was aware of the amount of the loan, and you, yourselves, did nothing unlawful, you shouldn't have to pay. Forgiving it is the least we can do."

The waitress arrived at the table, so Howard added, "And you won't have to pay for lunch today, so order whatever you want. Have you ever had Maine Lobster?"

Jackie and Steve ordered lobster and didn't question much. They'd worked hard, paid the bills all-or-none their entire lives. Earn is what they did, and what they'd hoped to teach to Brandon, starting this week. *Yet, how will we explain getting a Winnebago practically free? Hope Brandon employed a 'don't ask/don't tell' policy.*

Brandon and Steve worked side by side pretty well, acknowledging each other's expertise with more eye contact and conversation. Steve approved of the new Detroit Lions posters on the milk barn walls. In 2009 the logo had been overhauled, and new coaching staff hired. The team had a future to invest in and so did Brandon; Brandon had moved on from Michigan State.

That was the only change to the milking area that Brandon had made. The operation represented robust health in the milk and bristling energy in its stainless steel equipment. Steve was relieved each day by its welcome chores, with his equilibrium returning to full force.

The men split the milking shifts: Steve took the mornings most days while Brandon took the nights. He couldn't carouse since he was still officially married, to Amy, though no one knew where she was. Steve joked about putting her picture on their milk bottles, like the Lost Children Network, but Jackie failed to see the humor. Who cared where she was. Good riddance, she was gone.

In fact, Amy gave notice to the bank on Valentine's Day, with divorce papers served to Brandon the next. Steve chuckled that Brandon would be a free man by the next football season, but Brandon didn't laugh. He was morose, feeling like he'd been bullied by fake romance. He buried himself in Tiger baseball, memorizing stats like he had his coaches' playbooks. His World of Warcraft world lived on, though his avatar was noticed to sulk if it lost.

When Spring melted the snow pack so the grass perked back to green, the Breeden's dairy business grew along with the grass. At first, a few customers attempted to order those dreamy cookies, but then they backed off. Once they realized that Amy had left Brandon and taken her business with her, they were embarrassed to have even mentioned the cookies. These customers apologized by ordering more milk, so it was all good. Brandon suggested that the dairy buy more cows, but Jackie insisted that she needed a new vehicle. She was tired of truck tango.

After all, she had her own paycheck, her own needs.

Thankfully no one ever connected the chocolate chip dots with the few people who'd sought emergency room treatment for the possible pot-related symptoms. Everyone had always obeyed Jackie's rule of 'just one', so neither the Breedens nor their friends had had ill effects.

Life chugged on, like the motors of the dairy delivery truck and its truck compadres.

Jackie deferred visits to the pot dispensary. Now that she and Steve were following their home exercise program religiously, there didn't seem to be a need. She confessed to herself – but not to the pastor - that she was embarrassed at what she'd done behind Steve's back.

The motor home nestled behind the garage throughout the spring, and when Summer landed firmly in their laps, Brandon moved into his own suite – out there. Jackie re-named it 'Winnebago Heaven', inspired by the fancy names for the high roller suites in the Vegas casinos. She knew that her kitchen appliances would remain pristine because Brandon came in for every meal. His hunger timing was perfected just like his dad's. She rarely needed to ring his cell as call to chow.

Life moseyed along with the easy momentum of a contented cow swishing its tail to counter the inevitable flies. And, on April 15, coincident with tax-filing day, Brandon's divorce decree arrived in the mail. Steve recognized the county seal right away when Willard Partin, the mailman, handed him the legal-sized envelope. Willard didn't look surprised when there was no male gossip that day.

Steve unfolded the morning paper quickly, eager to get to the Sports page to find out what time the Tigers were playing, but bold black letter caught his eye: **FROM BANK TO DRUG BUST.** Could it be – well, better Amy than them. He read hastily, and then put the paper down to call Jackie.

"I'm in the middle of putting a big pot of water on to boil, do you mind?" Jackie said. Steve pictured a huge cauldron over a fire, but suppressed the emerging image of a witch to replace it with an image of Amy, ready to be boiled in oil. He chuckled because he knew that Jackie was just the woman to do it.

"Sorry, call me back," he said, but he heard the dial tone before he finished the sentence.

In the time before she called back, he had read and digested the entire article. It was light on details, but Amy was named. She'd been the one on the premises during the daylight marijuana bust. There apparently was an active marijuana farm in the basement of a ramshackle house north of their farm… a house that looked similar to a Cracker Barrel Restaurant. Holy crap!

"What's up on the farm?" Jackie asked without preamble when she called back. "Time is short when you have to feed 400 men, women, and children. I have potatoes to peel."

"You are not going to believe where dear Amy is living these days, Jackie."

"Wherever it is, it had better be far from here," Jackie said, tucking her curls behind her ears. "Do tell."

"County jail," said Steve.

"Come again," Jackie said, "I think my phone is breaking up in the heat of the kitchen."

"J-ai-l." Steve emphasized every sound, as if he was talking to a deaf or foreign-born person.

"Holy shit!" Jackie said. Then her voice was muffled by the gesture that Steve could see in his mind's eye: she'd covered her mouth with her hand because she'd cussed in the proximity of children. "Jail? 'Splain, Lucy," she continued in her best imitation of Desi Arnaz.

"Well, near as I can tell, she set up shop north of here with some guy named Travis. How many marijuana plants did you say she had?"

"As I recall, twelve was all that she could order under the law. Who knows if she skirted that, like she did everything else?"

Then, before Steve could go all Christian family on her, she said, "No, I will not consider paying for an attorney for her. Do not answer the phone when the reporter calls."

Reporters not only called, they encamped until they got a photo of each beleaguered Breeden family member. So Steve made certain that Sparty was in pictures with them.

With Principal Fran, Pastor Rankin, and, best of all, Maybelline's apt assist, the Breeden story played to gain great sympathy for the family. How they suffered in the hands of that warped California woman.

Everybody knew that the sun fried the brains of those people on the left coast and, if that didn't work to make them brain dead, then the earthquakes shook all common sense out of them.

Milk orders went through the roof.

Only Veronica mourned Amy's transgressions and loss to the community. For awhile. After visiting Amy once in the Gray Bar Hotel to get her permission, Veronica began to call on Brandon.

She felt she'd earned the right; she was entitled.

352

ACKNOWLEDGEMENTS

Thanks be to

- God for gifts of literacy, empathy, character, and a tape recorder memory
- Larry Colando, 'the best man alive', who supports me and my writing pastime beyond words
- To mentors, critique groups, and writers who famously shared: Katherine Louise Jackson, Tom McCranie, Barbara DeMarco-Barrett, Teresa Cullen, Ari Jochai, Marla Noel, Ellen Bell, Ben Peters, Travis, Lonnie Painter, Gary Thompson, Polly and Ron Riley, Jessica and Dan Kiesling, Gail Breslin, Jim Hale, Diana and Bob Slane, Sandy and Joe Uhrig, Susan and Denny Grotrian, MaryAnn Easley, Melissa Sokol, Louella Nelson, Veronica, Al, Janice Maxson, Anne Durham, Meredith Resnick, Amy Wallen, Alice Vernoux, Dirk Sayers, Bill Young, Greg Hanour, David Jackson, Cheryl Hall, Robert G. Quinn, Mike Foley, and Peggy Glenn
- Art Plotnik, who explained 'Voice', of which I have plenty
- Jess Walter, who subvocalized at a book signing: "You can look anything up on the Internet. What you write about is Emotion."
- Fanny Flagg, who shared her writing secret: that she'd been raised a Southern woman, one who never speaks ill of others, bless their hearts. She mined her covert commentary to create spritely prose and plot - and I aspired.